VISUAL
COMMUNICATION
INSIGHTS AND STRATEGIES

VISUAL COMMUNICATION
INSIGHTS AND STRATEGIES

JANIS TERUGGI PAGE

University of Illinois at Chicago
Chicago, IL

MARGARET DUFFY

University of Missouri
Columbia, MO

WILEY Blackwell

The right of Janis Teruggi Page and Margaret Duffy to be identified as the authors of this work has been asserted in accordance with law.

Registered Office
John Wiley & Sons, Inc., 111 River Street, Hoboken, NJ 07030, USA

Editorial Office
111 River Street, Hoboken, NJ 07030, USA

For details of our global editorial offices, customer services, and more information about Wiley products visit us at www.wiley.com.

Wiley also publishes its books in a variety of electronic formats and by print-on-demand. Some content that appears in standard print versions of this book may not be available in other formats.

Library of Congress Cataloging-in-Publication Data
Names: Page, Janis Teruggi, author.| Duffy, Margaret, author.
Title: Visual communication: insights and strategies / Janis Teruggi Page,
    University of Illinois, Chicago. Margaret Duffy,
    University of Missouri, Columbia, USA
Description: First edition. | Hoboken, NJ : Wiley Blackwell, 2022. |
    Includes bibliographical references and index.
Identifiers: LCCN 2020043378 (print) | LCCN 2020043379 (ebook) | ISBN
    9781119226475 (paperback) | ISBN 9781119227298 (adobe pdf) | ISBN
    9781119227304 (epub)
Subjects: LCSH: Visual communication. | Visual analytics.
Classification: LCC P93.5 .D86 2021 (print) | LCC P93.5 (ebook) | DDC
    302.2/26–dc23
LC record available at https://lccn.loc.gov/2020043378
LC ebook record available at https://lccn.loc.gov/2020043379

Cover Design: Wiley
Cover Images: © Janet Trierweiler

Set in 10/12pt Ubuntu by Straive, Pondicherry, India

10 9 8 7 6 5 4 3 2 1

Contents

Preface

How can we make sense of the myriad visual images surrounding us today? How can we strategically use images with a clear understanding of their function and impact?

This book answers these questions by providing new "ways of seeing" visual representations through different lenses and in different contexts. It then provides practical guidance for creating purposeful and ethical visual communication.

The authors recognize the accelerating dominion of images in communication, society, and culture. We human beings process images and video effortlessly and automatically. Visuals carry an emotional and visceral punch that text can rarely, if ever, match. As multinational marketers, social media influencers, and teenagers on TikTok know, visuals create their own language, accessible to all, regardless of traditional textual barriers of understanding such as education or language.

We've watched as entertainment and information have morphed into largely image-based communication including advertising and brand messaging, organizational communication, and individual creation and uploading of images, memes, and videos of all kinds. As of this writing in early 2021, people are watching 5 billion YouTube vides every day and Instagram has over one billion users worldwide. U.S. digital advertising expenditures are projected to grow to 22.18 billion U.S. dollars in 2021 (https://www.statista.com/statistics/256272/digital-video-advertising-spending-in-the-us/).

Most of us take the sphere of images for granted: it's just the way the world is. Of course, human beings have always created symbolic structures of meaning that shape how we interpret and participate in social life. However, we also tend to treat these image systems as natural phenomena. We conveniently forget that we ourselves invented these structures of meaning and it's important we understand their significance and meaning in more thoughtful and nuanced ways.

For some years, we've been conducting research on images, moving and still, and their various roles in society. We've studied and written about digital visual folklore in emails about President Obama, the widespread sharing of memes of football star Richard Sherman, comedy television's performance of vice presidential debates, presidential candidates' online visual storytelling, images of morality in political TV ads and news coverage, sexual imagery in advertising, issues in visual persuasion ethics, photographic coverage of the Pope's 2015 visit to Cuba, ethical implications of VR, AR, and 360° technologies, and satiric images of Trump as spectacle in global magazines, among other visual topics.

Inspired by our previous work, we wrote this book for students and scholars with the intent of providing insights into the role of visuals in our dynamic social environment. Ralph Waldo Emerson said, "We are symbols and we inhabit symbols" (*The Poet*, 1844). We hope this book connects with a broad range of scholars and practitioners in the arts, humanities, social sciences, engineering, technology, and neuroscience and serves as an invitation to future study.

Acknowledgments

Both authors made generous contributions in the research and writing of this book. As this project has evolved through its various phases, there are many people to whom we owe special thanks.

We would like to begin by thanking our academic colleagues in visual communication for inspiring and challenging us to create this book and extend our theoretical, applied approach to visual communication education to students in all preprofessional fields that encounter visual phenomena.

Many thanks to the anonymous reviewers who offered clear critique, advice, and suggestions based on their own teaching experiences in visual communication. We also benefited greatly from our students who, through classroom engagement, provided helpful feedback on lessons and exercises.

We want to acknowledge our colleagues and administrators at the University of Illinois at Chicago, Department of Communication, and the Novak Leadership Institute at Missouri School of Journalism for their support during the research and writing of this book.

We also deeply appreciate the contributions from the professionals and academics who shared insightful profiles in our chapters and who offered their suggestions and ideas as we developed the outline of the book.

Drawing from years of study and practice in fine art, Janis is especially grateful for the long-term mentoring in visual metaphors by Sr. Alyce Van Acker, O.P., of the Fine Line Creative Arts Center, St. Charles, IL.

Finally, we would like to thank our spouses William Page and Daryl Moen for their constant encouragement throughout our long process of shaping and perfecting each chapter, resulting in a work we are truly proud of.

About the Authors

Janis Teruggi Page is a faculty member in the Department of Communication, University of Illinois at Chicago, and has been affiliated with the Strategic Public Relations Master's Program, George Washington University, for more than a decade. She has taught visual communication courses throughout her academic career. As a Fulbright distinguished chair, in 2018 she researched intercultural visual communication and taught visual literacy at Masaryk University, Brno, Czech Republic. An award-winning author, her research includes "Images with Messages: A Semiotic Approach to Identifying and Decoding Strategic Visual Communication," published in the *Routledge Handbook of Strategic Communication* (2015), and "Trump as Global Spectacle: The Visual Rhetoric of Magazine Covers," published in the *Handbook of Visual Communication* (2020). She is also coauthor of the textbook *Introduction to Public Relations: Strategic, Digital, and Socially Responsible Communication* (2019, 2021) with Lawrence J. Parnell. Prior to joining academia, she had a 20-year career as creative and marketing director for various US media companies. A former student at the School of the Art Institute, Chicago, she holds a PhD from the Missouri School of Journalism with a secondary emphasis in art history.

Margaret Duffy is Professor of Strategic Communication and cofounder and executive director of the Novak Leadership Institute. She led the effort to obtain a $21.6 million gift to endow the Institute from David Novak, alumnus of the Missouri School of Journalism advertising program. Mr. Novak is the retired CEO of YUM! Brands (Pizza Hut, Taco Bell, and KFC) and credits his education in advertising as the catalyst for his leadership success. Until 2016, Dr. Duffy chaired the Strategic Communication Faculty at the Missouri School of Journalism. She also served as associate dean for graduate studies. Dr. Duffy directed the Missouri School of Journalism's Online Master's Program from 2001 to 2016. An award-winning scholar, her research focuses on leadership, organizational communication, visual communication, and persuasion ethics. She coedited the book *Persuasion Ethics Today* (2016) and cowrote *Advertising Age: The Principles of Advertising and Marketing Communication at Work* (2011), Dr. Duffy is a founding board member of the Institute for Advertising Ethics and an inaugural fellow at the Donald W. Reynolds Journalism Institute. In 2019, she received the University of Missouri Distinguished Faculty Award. She is a former marketing executive and earned her PhD from the University of Iowa. An author and consultant, Dr. Duffy conducts research and advises media companies and brands around the world with clients as varied as Estée Lauder and the US Army.

PART ONE

Understanding Visual Communication

Chapter 1
Making Sense of Visual Culture
1000 Words or One Simple Picture?

"Pics or it didn't happen."

By 2015, this phrase had morphed from a meme to a catchphrase that seemed to be everywhere. If a friend tweeted that she'd been cliff diving in Acapulco, you might respond with that phrase suggesting that perhaps she was being boastful without any evidence to back it up (Whitehead, 2015).

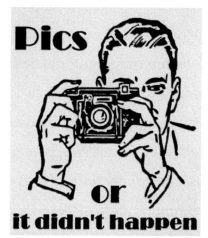

Source: http://www.dpreview.com/forums/post/58791114. Reproduced with permission of RetroClipArt/Shutterstock.com.

Visual Communication: Insights and Strategies, First Edition. Janis Teruggi Page and Margaret Duffy.
© 2022 John Wiley & Sons, Inc. Published 2022 by John Wiley & Sons, Inc.

If your gamer pal claimed to have reached level 60 in World of Warcraft, you might demand some proof.

Other phrases call on our desire to tap into what Whitehead and others have called "visual authority." You've all heard that "seeing is believing" and heard people say, "I'll believe it when I see it with my own eyes." And consider the famous Chinese proverb, "a picture is worth a thousand words." Here's the thing: it's not Chinese, and it's not a proverb. In fact, it was likely the creation of ad man Fred Barnard[1] in the 1920s. As William Safire (1996) writes, Barnard, trying to increase his agency's business selling ads on railway cars, came up with the phrase. He had it translated into Chinese characters with the caption "Chinese Proverb: One Picture is Worth Ten Thousand Words" and it passed into popular culture as "one thousand words." Whether it is one thousand or ten, Barnard tapped into the notion that most people find visual evidence more credible and interesting than verbal or textual expression (Graber, 1990).

In entertainment, politics, interpersonal interactions, and at work and at play, we're all consuming, evaluating, and creating visuals. Our culture is increasingly suffused with images aimed at selling us something, persuading us, informing us, entertaining us, and connecting us with others. Your skills and capabilities in communicating effectively and critically evaluating what's around you are crucial to your personal and professional success and that is what this book is about. In the following chapters, we'll provide you with the tools to become an ethical and effective communicator in an era increasingly suffused with images of all kinds.

Key Learning Objectives

1. Understand visual culture and its transformation in the digital age.
2. Explore the fluidity of visual meaning.
3. Identify ways to research and analyze visuals.

Chapter Overview

In this introductory chapter, you'll explore five important issues relating to visuals in contemporary society. First, you'll be introduced to how visuals work and how we interpret them. Second, we'll review the astounding growth of visuals and video in recent years and how this trend is on a steep upward trajectory. Third, we examine the concept of visual culture and how changing technology relates to that culture. Fourth, you'll delve into how individuals can draw different meanings from the same visuals or video artifacts and how that process relates to social life and the meanings we take from our environment. Fifth, we preview ways to analyze visuals. At the close of the chapter we offer two vignettes illustrating how visuals work and provide an overview of the book as a whole.

HOW VISUALS WORK

LO1 Understand visual culture and its transformation in the digital age

Today almost every part of our lives is visual and visualized. We routinely use devices to see, to capture experiences, and to communicate. As suggested by Tavin (2009), visual culture is "a condition in which human experience is profoundly affected by images, new technologies for looking, and various practices of seeing, showing, and picturing" (p. 3, 4). We are now at a place of unlimited visual culture and thus how we understand media and visual literacy has changed.

Photographic Truth?

Among the things that strike us about images and photographs in particular is how they *feel* as if they are presenting us with a truth about reality. Sturken and Cartwright (2009) call this the "myth of photographic truth" (p. 24) because it obscures the roles of human beings who are creating the image. Those acts of creation include many factors such as the choices the photographer makes about the scene, lighting, and composition. Indeed, the photographer decides what subjects are worthy of their time or attention.

Even with technologies that make it easy and inexpensive to capture images of all kinds, the picture-taker must choose those subjects, whether they are powerful images of war or funny pictures of grumpy cats. All of these will affect the tone of a photo and thus the interpretations people take away from it. Even though we may know intellectually that the photographer has chosen a certain subject at a certain time and framed it a certain way, a photo still carries a sense of legitimacy. Put differently, it involves the "legacy of objectivity that clings to the cameras and machines that produce images today" (Sturken and Cartwright, 2009, p. 18).

FOCUS: A Historical Perspective on Visual Culture

Another way to understand visual culture is to look at it historically. This example illustrates the role of perspective. When we compare medieval paintings (1300–1500) to contemporary paintings, we see remarkable differences. People in today's societies are used to seeing two-dimensional (flat surfaces) that depict three-dimensional spaces such as a road receding into the distance. In medieval times, Christianity was the primary organizing principle of society and artists presented religious and historical images based on the importance of those portrayed rather than more realistic representations (Willard n.d.). The world depicted in the paintings was the domain of God, not the lived experience of people, as shown in this two-dimensional artwork from 1295 depicting the Twelve Apostles receiving inspiration from the Holy Spirit:

Source: Art Collection 2/Alamy Stock Photo.

In fact, it's thought that the highly religious yet illiterate people in medieval times would have found 3D representations to be puzzling and even heretical. The Renaissance in the late fifteenth century led to the emergence of interest in science, intellectual pursuits, and the more realistic depictions of the world. With this societal change, artists began achieving three-dimensional effects using a whole range of techniques including linear perspectives, in which the "illusion that objects appear to grow smaller and converge toward a 'vanishing point' at the horizon line" (Jirousek, 1995). This is illustrated in Rembrandt's 1632 painting, *The Abduction of Europa*:

Source: GL Archive/Alamy Stock Photo.

Growing Importance of Visuals

Increasingly, visuals dominate how we communicate and how we understand other people, our society, and the culture in which we live. The line between the media we consume and what we used to consider "real life" is largely erased. Media *are* our environment as much as the physical spaces we inhabit. Old ways of belief are challenged even more in a world built of visual communication. According to Anderson (1990), this is resulting in an "unregulated marketplace of realities in which all manner of belief systems are offered for public consumption" (p. 6).

Groundbreaking journalist and social critic Walter Lippmann (1922) was likely the first to apply the term "**stereotype**" referring to attitudes people acquire without specific knowledge of an event or individual. People tend to quickly process visuals along the lines of what they already believe or think and interpret them in terms of familiar categories (Graber, 1988). This may lead people to reflect less on the credibility and accuracy of visual claims than those made in type.

Our Precarious Visual Culture

Today, something that looks like a photo may be an image that's digitally produced, altered, or enhanced. Many images are essentially fictions deliberately created to amuse, to deceive, or to offer an artistic perspective. Many of these are shared and even go viral. They range from silly fictions and jokes, such as fried chicken Oreos and a man presumably holding an 87-pound cat, to manipulated photos attempting character assassination, such as President Obama shown smoking and President George W. Bush shown reading a book upside down (Hoaxes, 2015).

Some are **memes** shared by like-minded people. These images with text make fun of public figures or celebrities and often call on well-known popular culture references and icons. For example, during the Obama presidency, many forwarded email memes pictured Obama through the lens of racial stereotyping portraying him as a witch doctor, an animal, and even a pimp (Duffy et al., 2012).

For some people, such images are plausible and shareable and even if they don't literally believe the message, they nonetheless appear to believe that the visual joke carries an element of truth. The same message put into type likely would be patently offensive. However, in a cartoon-like meme, senders and receivers of the image can claim that "it's just a joke." For others, the images offer the opportunity to further manipulate or mashup visuals and videos to create entirely new messages and meanings. People can take photos and add stickers, filters, doodles, and text overlays. They can edit and crop images, create collages and mashups. And, of course, they can and do share them.

Political Persuasion

Images created to intentionally mislead are increasingly part of the promotional strategies for political candidates and their supporters. In pre-Internet times, visuals and video, usually on television, played a major role in positioning candidates and their opponents. Political consultants have frequently harnessed the power of the visual because human beings are able to quickly interpret and process those messages. Early on, researchers found that in news coverage and advertisements, visual elements overwhelmed verbal elements. In 1988, an ABC news correspondent, Richard Threlkeld, voiced a spot that was aimed at discounting the claims of a George H.W. Bush presidential ad called "Tank Ride." The piece showed the visuals of the ad as the reporter's voiceover detailed the false claims it made. However, research revealed that people who saw it tended to ignore the verbal statements and internalize the message of the original ad. An intentional alteration of images in an ad from President George W. Bush's 2004 campaign was digitally enhanced to add images of soldiers into a crowd he was addressing. After criticism, the campaign withdrew the ad.

Another questionable use of images is found in a web video by the Democratic National Campaign that used a dramatization of a man in a business suit pushing an elderly woman in a wheelchair off a cliff as a way to attack Republican Congressman Paul Ryan's proposed plan for health care reform (Raposa, 2012). While no one was likely to believe that Ryan's plan would literally involve throwing old people from high places, the powerful visuals coupled with a soundtrack of "America the Beautiful" nevertheless sent a deceptive message about the possible effects of Ryan's plan. As we examine many media artifacts, we can see the power of visual metaphors – in this case, a policy change – equated to a violent act against a helpless and vulnerable person.

Political persuasion has always drawn on popular culture and the conventions of films and other audiovisual devices. You've probably noticed that negative political ads (NPAs) tend to present opponents using dramatic conventions drawn from horror movies or crime dramas because viewers find it easy to understand and connect with those conventions. For example, often opponents will be portrayed accompanied by dark atmospheric visual effects, unflattering images, and scary or ominous music. YouTube, Facebook, and scores of other social networks provide low cost ways to distribute content beyond television programming.

Digital Transformation of Visual Culture

Much research on digital visual content in the twenty-first century points to a tsunami of images washing over words. WebDAM, a digital brand consulting firm and data science company, reported that verbal intelligence is dropping while visual intelligence is increasing (Morrison, 2015). Scores in the SAT reading exam hit an all-time low in 2016 (Kranse Institute, 2017) and three years later, with an increased number of student test-takers in 2019, SAT reading scores again fell nationally. Research surfacing in many parts of the world now cautions that essential "deep reading" processes may be under threat as we move into digital-based modes of reading (Wolf, 2018): essentially "skimming" with low engagement and retention.

But we're incredible at remembering pictures, writes biologist John Medina (n.d.) in his multimedia project Brain Rules. Three days after hearing information we may remember 10% of it but add a picture and memory increases to 65%. Thanks to the digital revolution, visuals have become a universal language. A whopping 82% of all Internet traffic globally will be video by 2022, estimates Cisco (2019), up from 75% in 2017 – and **virtual reality** (VR) and **augmented reality** (AR) will increase 12-fold globally between 2017 and 2022.

Instagram had one billion monthly active users in 2018 according to TechCrunch (Constine, 2018). That same year, the total number of photos shared in the platform's history was recorded at more than 50 billion. Dating apps like Tinder and Friendsy make it easy (some say *too* easy) to exchange photos with others and find romance. When it comes to the essential organizational website, research suggests that well-designed and highly visual sites are more trustworthy than poorly designed sites (Harley, 2016).

Members of Generation Z, those born in 1996 and later, are even more visually oriented than the much-discussed Millennials, those born between 1980 and 1985 (Williams, 2015). Research on Gen Z finds that 44% play video games daily and 72% visit YouTube daily (Claveria, 2019). Advertisers and media companies are responding to shifts toward the visual by redesigning their communication on big and small screens. On the so-called "visual web," brands and news organizations have moved to image-based content creation. The massive use of mobile is a major driver of these changes as smaller screens are friendlier to visual content than textual.

Smartphones and Visual Culture

Smartphones have become so central to social life in many countries that the prospect of losing one's phone is more distressing than losing one's car. Owning a certain type of phone or wearable technology also communicates aspects of your interests, beliefs, and priorities. Today, most people in most countries are swimming in media images or being monitored by cameras in most public and private places. Signage and outdoor advertising are everywhere.

People are sending and receiving messages on screens of all types, large and small. Smartphones and tablets capture both the mundane and extraordinary in digital photography and video. Individuals are creating their own reality shows in real time, broadcasting their activities to users who can favorite or save the videos for later viewing or redistribution. Some people post funny animal videos (Figure 1.1), others create videos aimed at inspiring and motivating, and still others vlog with beauty advice. Some of the myriad of postings are more instructional such as how to install a garbage disposal, how to build and fly a homemade drone, and even how to give an opossum a pedicure.

All these technologies and their diverse applications affect how we see others and our environments, how we are seen and see ourselves. Some suggest that the visual web is a phenomenon largely fueled by social media, smart phones with sophisticated cameras, and apps that make it easy to create and share visual media (eMarketer, 2015). Hubspot lists the 10 best user-generated content campaigns on Instagram, for example, the UPS Store showcases a behind-the-scenes look at small business owners; online furniture store Wayfair lets customers showcase the results of their online shopping sprees; and Netflix lets fans promote their favorite shows and movies (Bernazzani, n.d.).

Figure 1.1 Smartphones and visual culture. *Source:* Supparsorn Wantarnagon/ Alamy Stock Photo.

MULTIPLE MEANINGS

LO2 Explore the fluidity of visual meaning.

For most of us, everyday communication seems effortless. We chat, text, and share photos with our friends with an expectation of how the receivers of our message will react. However, as you know, communication can easily go wrong. A friend's mom, acting very concerned, recently asked her son what "LOL" meant on emails. He replied, "laughing out loud. Why?" She said, "that explains a lot. I thought it was 'lots of love' and I sent it in a message to someone whose pet had died."

Similarly, that photo you shared thinking it was hilarious may or may not get the reaction you expect. Intentionally or not, images and text point us to certain interpretations of their meanings while downplaying other interpretations.

Polysemy

Different images, words, and even different fonts carry cultural meanings that may resonate or puzzle, anger or offend. These differences in meaning and interpretations are called "**polysemy**," quite literally "multiple meanings." These multiple and shared meanings shape our culture and how we understand our world. When most people hear the word "culture" they tend to think of fine arts, opera, or esoteric French films. In this book, when we refer to **visual culture**, we're talking about "the total way of life of a people . . . the social legacy the individual acquires from his group" and "a way of thinking, feeling, and believing" (Kluckhorn, 1973, in Geertz, p. 3).

Along the same lines, renowned scholar Raymond Williams (1958/1993) suggested in his foundational essay that culture is ordinary. By that he meant that we should not think of culture as simply artifacts or materials that people in a society make, whether they're smartphone photos, paintings, or Photoshopped memes. While these are part of culture creation, cultures are also created in our actions and practices in everyday life, as we individually and collectively assign meaning and morality to what we do, say, and communicate. Similarly, Clifford Geertz argued:

> Believing, with Max Weber, that man [sic] is an animal suspended in webs of significance he himself has spun, I take culture to be those webs, and the analysis of it to be therefore not an experimental science in search of law but an interpretive one in search of meaning.
>
> *(Geertz, 1973)*

This helps us think of our world not as something fixed, static, and "out there," but as something we are actively creating as we interact with each other, with media, and face-to-face. The expectations and strictures of our cultures establish our identities and our places in society and lead us to judge what is valued and what is deplored, and make us evaluate what is worthy and unworthy. This doesn't mean that there's no "real" reality out there, but it does mean that in social life and our interactions, we socially construct the meanings of that reality.

In pre-Internet 1990, Walter Anderson wrote that in society, the "mass media make it easy to create and disseminate new structures of reality" (p. 9). We as individuals now don't need special tools and training to alter and edit videos, photos, and images of all kinds. Those with more skills can create entire worlds peopled by highly realistic images of individuals and environments as seen in games like the Grand Theft Auto series and Madden NFL. Some wearable technologies put the user "into" realistic 3D environments where they can "walk" through rooms, "drive" on simulated roads, and "shop" virtual products.

Semioticians, people who study the science of signs and their meanings, argue that all of the things human beings construct or create are "containers of meaning" (Anderson, 1990, p. 21). Thus, everything we use and wear from the shoes we choose to the ways we decorate our homes carries meaning both to the wearer/user and to those around us. Anderson suggests, "all the T-shirts and jeans and sneakers . . . are not only things but ideas" (p. 21) and they all may be studied as cultural facts and activities (Eco, 1978). For example, someone wearing a T-shirt with the message "I hate T-shirts" may be sending a message meant to be ironic or jokey. A man wearing a blue blazer and khakis may be sending a message that "I'm a guy who knows what's appropriate to wear to work." Or a small boy donning a straw hat, bandana, and strung-up tube toys may be sending the message, "I'm a cowboy today" (Figure 1.2). In addition, memes, Photoshopped photos, social media photos, nine-second videos, and emojis carry, in their form and content, ideas and values.

Because we're immersed in a world of many messages or representations, many of them visual, we can see that our social worlds are constantly under construction through our interactions with images. Rose (2012) uses the term "scopic regime" and defines it as "the ways in which both what is seen and how it is seen are culturally constructed" (p. 2). Visual culture is often criticized as turning society and human life into a spectacle and that the move from analog to digital culture not only allows for endless replication, but itself is different and worse than, say, traditional photography. Thus, Rose concludes, "The modern connection between seeing and true knowing has been broken" (p. 4).

Figure 1.2 Everything we use and wear carries meaning.

FOCUS: Trump's Hand Gestures

Some scholars attribute the success of Trump's candidacy in the 2016 Republican primary in part due to its value as comedic entertainment. One study, "The hands of Donald Trump: Entertainment, gesture, spectacle" (Hall et al., 2016), analyzed the populist candidate's comedic performances during the Republican primaries. The study proposed that in an era when style attracts more attention than content, Trump took this characteristic to new heights. The authors concluded that Trump's unconventional political style, particularly his use of gesture to critique the political system and caricature his opponents, created a visual spectacle. Through his exaggerated depictions of the world crafted with his hands, he succeeded in ignoring political correctness and disarming his adversaries – elemental to bringing momentum to his campaign. Among Trump's many hand gestures, the study notes Trump's use of the pistol hand, his signature gesture used on *The Apprentice* with his catchphrase "You're fired!" to fire unworthy contestants. When Trump used the pistol hand, it conveyed arrogance, sovereign power, and commanding force – as seen in the photo below:

Source: AP Images/Stuart Ramson.

The gesture is understood through its gun shape and its associated swiftness and precision of striking down an unworthy opponent. Yet the gesture is also playful: when Trump thrusts his hand forward to mimic the firing of a gun, he brings a child's pantomime of shooting to the firing of an adult in an entrepreneurial battle or the dismissing of an opponent in a political arena.

Media critic Stuart Hall (1997) writes that "culture is about shared meanings" and "primarily, culture is concerned with the production and the exchange of meanings . . . between the members of a culture or group" (p. 2). He suggests that people who are in the same culture will tend to interpret the world in generally similar ways while warning that things or actions cannot have stable meanings. Hall tells us that meanings are produced in multiple ways: through personal interactions, through our use of media and technology, and in what we create and how we share those creations:

> Meaning is also produced whenever we express ourselves in, make use of, consume or appropriate cultural "things;" that is, when we incorporate them in different ways into the everyday rituals and practices of daily life and in this way give them value or significance. (p. 3, 4)

Human beings have always created and responded to shared and differing interpretations of reality. All societies have systems of belief that carry values and seem natural to those who are part of that society. Like all cultural products, visuals are created within "the dynamics of social power and ideology" (Sturken and Cartwright, 2009, p. 22). Those with greater material wealth or socioeconomic status generally have more resources and abilities to use and influence the creation and dissemination of images and video. Thus, their worldviews are likely to have more prominence and influence than those from people with fewer resources. This means that we experience images within changing social contexts that can change rapidly and that the meanings we assign to them aren't neutral. Instead, they carry values and privilege certain interpretations over others.

Form and Content

READ THIS BOOK! That statement in all caps and in boldface, communicates something different from "read this book." How is it different from read *this* book? And why include it here? We include it because it reveals, in an unexpected way, how the form and not just the content of a simple sentence can communicate and conform to or violate cultural norms.

You probably don't think of letters and words as visuals, but even the choice of a font can make a big difference in the meanings people take away from the message. Imagine a condolence card that says "With Heartfelt Sympathy! ☺ " It feels strange because it violates our cultural expectations about what's appropriate for such a message. Because type and text are so much part of our environments, we may not think of them as visual. But each typeface, each font, has a different personality and may convey different emotions and meanings. Perhaps without even being aware of it, you have certain expectations of the "rightness" of using a certain font to communicate a particular message.

Apple's "Get a Mac" video campaign offers another example of how content can be differentiated by its form (Figure 1.3). Actors and humorists John Hodgman and Justin Long posed as human interpretations of a PC and a Mac. Against a white background, Long, dressed in casual clothes, introduced himself, "Hello, I'm a Mac." Hodgman, dressed in a more formal suit and tie, adds, "And I'm a PC." Even before the characters act out attributes of each brand (a laid-back Mac and an uptight PC), we can deduce these attributes from their form: two men standing in a blank void, staring directly at us, but one with rigid posture and business attire, and the other posed and dressed casually, hands in jeans' pockets.

Figure 1.3 *Source:* YouTube.

DECODING VISUAL MESSAGES

LO3 Identify ways to analyze visuals and conduct visual communication research.

As you can see from this discussion, images we consume and create don't have fixed meanings. Instead, people go through a process of coding and decoding messages and images that they send and receive (Hall, 1997). For instance, when we see a forwarded meme, we "**decode**" the meaning of the image and text. How we decode will have to do with our individual experiences, our skills in interpreting messages, our values and beliefs, and the cultures and subcultures we are part of. In addition, the source of the message or visual affects how much interest and credibility we assign to a phenomenon.

Semiotics: Signs and Symbols

A useful way to understand and analyze communication involves semiotics, the science of signs, an approach we will cover in detail in Chapter 4. Semiotics begins with two important concepts: the **denotative** and **connotative** meanings of signs. Think of denotation as the dictionary definition or a description. For instance, the denotative description of the American flag might be "13 equal horizontal stripes of red (top and bottom) alternating with white; there is a blue rectangle in the upper hoist-side corner bearing 50 small, white, five-pointed stars arranged in nine offset horizontal rows of six stars (top and bottom) alternating with rows of five stars" (Central Intelligence Agency n.d.).

However, connotative meaning has to do with the associations, emotions, and cultural expectations of individuals that are evoked by a symbol. It would seem that burning a piece of white, blue, and red cloth shouldn't be controversial. But for many Americans, the act of burning the flag is an act of treason. For others, it's a symbol of free speech and First Amendment rights. For those with negative views of the United States, it is a symbol of oppression deserving of desecration. Semiotics is a way to understand signs and their interpretation in a more systematic way.

Consider how advertisers communicate with audiences and the denotative and connotative aspects of ads. The image in Figure 1.4 was part of an advertorial (also called a native advertisement) for Toyota Tacoma trucks. Most people effortlessly interpret that this is an image of a truck and know that the advertiser wants viewers to consider purchasing it. Advertisers expect their target audience not only to see the literal or denotative aspects of the image (this is a big, shiny, new truck), but also to assign connotative meanings, presumably positive ones.

In this advertisement, the outdoor setting is rugged and framed by a beautiful cloudless sky. The connotation the advertiser likely intended may be a sense of manliness, power, and virility. For other viewers, the ad may suggest freedom, a statement of success, or the opportunity for adventure. And for others who assign oppositional

Figure 1.4 This image communicates that it is possible and desirable to own such a machine. It tells us that this product, if purchased, will fill important functional and psychological needs. The ad suggests that buying this truck will make the purchasers happy and provide them with freedom and independence. *Source:* Zach Joing/Alamy Stock Photo.

meanings, it may be a symbol of irresponsibility, squandering the earth's resources, and contributing to climate change. Beyond the feelings that the advertiser hopes audiences will decode, the ad, like all ads, tells us something about our culture once we metaphorically look under the hood of the ad. What could this tell us about our culture and values?

Visual Rhetoric

The photograph in Figure 1.5 became an Internet sensation. Taken at the premiere of the film, *Black Mass*, almost everyone pictured clutches a smart phone and is excitedly trying to find an angle in order to take a photo of a celebrity. Only one individual stands out – an older woman who is serenely observing the event – without a camera.

Why did the image resonate with so many? Tweets and shares often commented that the woman was the only individual living in the moment and truly having a genuine, unmediated experience. And of course, the image resonated because it was unusual – the woman's behavior was unexpected and outside the bounds of today's culture. This can be explained through understanding the cognitive perception of selectivity – our brains draw conclusions from stimuli that are significant within a complicated visual experience. Whether the woman was, indeed, living in the present or she didn't own or use a smartphone is unanswered. Nevertheless, by showing something outside the norm, the image communicated aspects of culture to many people.

In the following "What's Ahead" section, you will see a preview of the book's chapters and the many methods of visual analysis that you will learn – including **semiotics**, **visual rhetoric**, **narrative analysis** (how visual compositions tell stories), **metaphor analysis** (how visual images propose comparisons), and **fantasy theme analysis** (how visual messages converge in groups to develop cohesive understanding).

Figure 1.5 *Source:* John Blanding/The Boston Globe/Getty Images.

FOCUS: Saving Big Bird

"I'm sorry, Jim. I'm gonna stop the subsidy to PBS . . . I like PBS. I love Big Bird. I actually like you, too. But I'm not gonna keep on spending money on things to borrow money from China to pay for it." With those words in the first presidential debate of 2012, moderated by Jim Lehrer of Public Broadcasting System (PBS), candidate Mitt Romney made Big Bird the star of the debate and launched a tidal wave of social media messages. Most of those messages were highly visual. A @firebigbird Twitter account popped up almost immediately and social and traditional media exploded with memes, jokes, parodies, and videos.

In a frequently shared image, a child holds a sign while standing in front of an American flag. The sign, written in childlike printing, reads "My American dream is to save Big Bird's job so kids can learn."

A close reading of the image leads the viewer to several interpretations. First, it draws attention to PBS and its programming aimed at educating diverse young people and dependent, in part, on the financial support of the US government. Second, the image alludes to Romney's proposed funding cut. And through the image of the child (of indeterminate ethnicity and sex) against a background of the US flag, it suggests that all of America's children are threatened by the potential loss of PBS programming and their "American dream" of educational opportunities. Thus, the viewer is invited to fill in the blanks and complete the meaning of the message (Page and Duffy 2013).

What's Ahead?

If we can better understand how meanings are produced, we can become smarter consumers of visuals and other communication and more effective creators. As you can see from the previous discussion, how we communicate and interpret visuals is deeply rooted in our cultural worlds and expectations. In the following chapters, we'll explore how and why images communicate effectively, how they can fail to communicate, and how to apply that knowledge as professional communicators.

- Chapter 2 outlines useful approaches to ethical decision-making in creating and consuming visuals.

- Chapter 3 explains a classic way to explore the meanings of images: visual rhetorical analysis, and then introduces the next four chapters that deal with symbols, metaphors, narratives, and imaginative fantasies.

- Chapter 4 teaches semiotics: how visual "signs" and symbols communicate within a culture.

- Chapter 5 covers how the comparative functions of metaphors can be a powerful visual strategy.

- Chapter 6 illustrates the storytelling capacities of visual images.

- Chapter 7 helps you see how visuals can illustrate dramas and meanings within group communication.

- Chapter 8 is the first of four chapters that cover professional practices using visual images. This chapter helps you to understand advertising, its compelling visual qualities, and questions of ethics.

- Chapter 9 continues with strategic communication, featuring the field of public relations and its use of visuals, for example, in crisis, public service, and political communications.

- Chapter 10 features the role of visual imagery in journalism, the image's significance in delivering news, and issues of subjectivity and misinformation.

- Chapter 11 teaches how to "read" and perform an organization's culture from the standpoint of observing and transmitting visual cues.

- Chapter 12 builds on all previous chapters by developing your intercultural literacy when it comes to the use of visual imagery.

CHAPTER SUMMARY

In this chapter we began our exploration of visual culture and its influence in our lives, influence fueled in large part by technological innovations. Professional communicators increasingly use images and video for messaging and persuasion. Moreover, the proliferation of devices and apps allowing almost everyone to create and share images contributes to visual culture. Social media amplify the power of visuals, a power that can be positive, promoting individuals' and communities' wellbeing. Yet, social media may also unleash destructive messages and have negative, unintended consequences. Visual social media's impact extends to every realm of social life and helps shape what we understand as reality.

KEY TERMS

Stereotype   Attitudes people acquire without specific knowledge of an event or individual.
Memes   Cultural images shared between people, often with text and carrying symbolic meaning.
Virtual reality (VR)   Computer simulation of a 3D image or environment which a person can interact with in a seemingly real or physical way through use of special electronic equipment.
Augmented reality (AR)   The superimposing of a computer-generated image into the real world.
Polysemy   Differences in meaning and interpretations; multiple meanings.
Visual culture   The visually-constructed way of life of a people; a way of thinking, feeling, and believing.
Scopic regime   Ways in which both what is seen and how it is seen are culturally constructed.
Decode   The interpretation of the underlying meanings of texts based on varying assumptions and skills, dependent on context and interpreter.
Denotative   Literal definition or description.

Connotative   Meanings drawn from associations, emotions, and cultural expectations.
Semiotics   Study of signs and their meanings.
Visual rhetoric   Persuasive messages carried in visual images.
Narrative analysis   Determining how compositions tell stories.
Metaphor analysis   Determining how images propose comparisons.
Fantasy theme analysis   Determining how messaging converges in groups to develop cohesive understanding.

PRACTICE ACTIVITIES

1. How has changing technology affected the visual culture of your life? Compared to text-based communication, how have the increasing numbers of visuals – and ways to view them – shifted your engagement and experience of media?
2. Locate a contemporary advertisement, short video, or newscast that has a dominant visual component. Consider it individually by examining:
   a. The setting
   b. The visual features
   c. The messages
   d. The persuasive elements

Then, together as a class, share the meanings you individually took away. Note any differences and discuss how social life, popular culture, historical memory, personal circumstance, etc. shape one's understanding of a visual message.

NOTE

1. It should be noted that a similar phrase also appeared in a *New York Times* real estate ad in the early 1900s as "a look is worth 10,000 words" and it is possible that Fred Barnard borrowed or built on the concept.

REFERENCES

Anderson, W. (1990). *Reality Isn't What it Used to Be*. New York, NY: Harper Collins.
Bernazzani, S. (n.d.). The 10 best user-generated content campaigns on Instagram. https://blog.hubspot.com/marketing/best-user-generated-content-campaigns (accessed September 1, 2020).
Central Intelligence Agency. (n.d.) The world factbook. https://www.cia.gov/library/publications/the-world-factbook/docs/flagsoftheworld.html# (accessed 1 September 2020).
Cisco. (2019).Cisco Visual Networking Index: Forecast and Trends, 2017–2022 White Paper. https://davidellis.ca/wp-content/uploads/2019/12/cisco-vni-mobile-data-traffic-feb-2019.pdf (accessed November 12, 2020).

Claveria, K. (2019). Unlike Millennials: 5 ways Gen Z differs from Gen Y. https://www.prdaily.com/wp-content/uploads/2018/02/gen-z-versus-millennials-infographics (accessed November 12, 2020).

Constine, J. (2018). Instagram hits 1 billion monthly users, up from 800M in September. https://techcrunch.com/2018/06/20/instagram-1-billion-users (accessed November 12, 2020).

Duffy, M., Page, J., and Young, R. (2012). It's just a joke: Racist rhetoric and pass-along email images of Obama. In: *Assessing Evidence in a Postmodern World* (ed. B. Brennen), 67–97. Nieman Research Conference Proceedings.

Eco, U. (1978). *A Theory of Semiotics*. Bloomington: Indiana University Press.

eMarketer (2015). What is the visual web? http://www.emarketer.com/Article/What-Visual-Web/1013064 (accessed October 19, 2019).

Geertz, C. (1973). *The Interpretation of Culture*. New York: Basic Books.

Graber, D.A. (1988). *Processing the News: How People Tame the Information Tide*. New York: Longman.

Graber, D.A. (1990). Seeing is remembering: how visuals contribute to learning from television news. Journal of Communication 40: 134–155.

Hall, S. (1997). *Representation: Cultural Representations and Signifying Practices*. Thousand Oaks, CA: Sage.

Hall, K., Goldstein, D.M., and Ingram, M.B. (2016). The hands of Donald Trump: entertainment, gesture, spectacle. Journal of Ethnographic Theory 6 (2): 71–100. https://doi.org/10.14318/hau6.2.009.

Harley, A. (2016). Trustworthiness in web design: 4 credibility factors. https://www.nngroup.com/articles/trustworthy-design/ (accessed November 12, 2020).

Hoaxes. (2015). The gallery of fake viral images. http://hoaxes.org/photo_database/viral_images/P45 (accessed October 25, 2015).

Jirousek, C. (1995). Two dimensional illusion of three dimensional form. http://char.txa.cornell.edu/language/element/form/formillu.htm (accessed September 1, 2015).

Kranse Institute. (2017). 2016 SAT scores were the lowest in the last 20 years. https://www.kranse.com/blogs/news/2016-sat-scores-were-the-lowest-in-the-last-20-years (accessed September 1, 2020).

Lippmann, W. (1922). *Public Opinion*. New York, NY: Harcourt.

Medina, J. (n.d.) Brain Rules. Rule #10: Visual trumps all other senses. http://www.brainrules.net/vision (accessed November 12, 2020).

Morrison, K. (2015). Visual media changes how humans consume information (infographic). http://www.adweek.com/socialtimes/visual-media-webdam-infographic/622827 (accessed October 29, 2015).

Page, J. and Duffy, M. (2013). Big Bird, binders, and bayonets: The persuasive power of social media visual narratives in the 2012 presidential campaign. Presentation at the Association for Education in Journalism and Mass Communication Annual Meeting, Washington, DC.

Raposa, K (2012). In attack ad, Paul Ryan kills grandma in wheelchair. *Forbes*. https://www.forbes.com/sites/kenrapoza/2012/08/12/liberal-group-throws-granny-off-cliff-again/#186fe2cd8286 (accessed September 1, 2020).

Rose, G. (2012). *Visual Methodologies*, 3e. London: Sage.

Safire, W. (1996). On language: Worth a thousand words. *New York Times*, April 7. http://www.nytimes.com/1996/04/07/magazine/on-language-worth-a-thousand-words.html (accessed October 4, 2015).

Sturken, M. and Cartwright, L. (2009). *Practices of Looking: An Introduction to Visual Culture*. New York: Oxford University Press.

Tavin, K. (2009). Seeing and being seen: Teaching visual culture to (mostly) non-art education students. The International Journal of Arts Education I nJAE7.2: 1–22.

Whitehead, C. (2015). What we don't see. *New York Times*, May 28. http://www.nytimes.com/2015/05/31/magazine/what-we-dont-see.html?_r=0 (accessed October 4, 2015).

Willard, S. (n.d.) Topics in Western Civilization: Ideals of Community and the Development of Urban Life, 1250-1700. http://www.yale.edu/ynhti/curriculum/units/1986/3/86.03.08.x.html (accessed October 25, 2015).

Williams, A. (2015). Move over Millennials, here comes Generation Z. *New York Times*, Sept. 18. http://www.nytimes.com/2015/09/20/fashion/move-over-millennials-here-comes-generation-z.html?_r=0 (accessed September 18, 2019).

Williams, R. (1958/1993). Culture is ordinary. In: *Studying Culture: An Introductory Reader* (eds. A. Gray and J. McGuigan), 5–14. London: Edward Arnold.

Wolf, M. (2018). Skim reading is the new normal. The effect on society is profound. https://www.theguardian.com/commentisfree/2018/aug/25/skim-reading-new-normal-maryanne-wolf (accessed September 1, 2020).

Chapter 2
Visualizing Ethics
Revealing Shortcuts and Missteps

Friend or Foe? Hero or Villain?

When you meet a stranger at a bar, you automatically draw conclusions about the person's age, gender, and their differences or similarities to yourself. You process a huge amount of information almost instantaneously and use shortcuts to assign that person to certain categories. Are they a student, professor, office worker, soldier, athlete, other? Of course, you may be mistaken in this process, thinking that an old-looking individual is a teacher when he's actually a student, or the heavily tattooed woman who looks

Visual Communication: Insights and Strategies, First Edition. Janis Teruggi Page and Margaret Duffy.
© 2022 John Wiley & Sons, Inc. Published 2022 by John Wiley & Sons, Inc.

like a Goth may actually be a social worker or a business executive (tattoos are no longer taboo in many corporate offices).

We also use physical and visual cues to identify that a truck is a type of motorized transportation, that an apple falls into the category of fruit, and that a starling is a species of bird. This quick categorization is an evolutionary adaptation and helps us conserve cognitive resources. By that we mean that every time you encounter a phenomenon, you don't need to think a lot about what it is and what it means to you. Trying to understand others' intentions toward oneself is a crucial survival skill, and visual cues are the primary means we use to make evaluations.

Sometimes, however, we are influenced by unconscious bias and make faulty snap judgments, raising ethical concerns. Inferences we make about people may lead us to make bad choices when evaluating them. The ethical questions raised with this impulse to judge begins our study of routines and practices in our daily and professional lives that concern visual ethics.

Key Learning Objectives

After engaging in this chapter, you'll be able to:

1. Understand the ethical dimensions of visual communication.
2. Identify the ethical dimensions of visual manipulation, framing, appropriation, and intellectual property.
3. Apply strategies for evaluating the ethics of visual communication that you or others create.

Chapter Overview

In this chapter, we'll outline useful approaches to ethical decision-making in creating and consuming visuals. You'll see real-world examples including the ethics of using graphic photos and videos, issues related to memes and remixes as well as photo manipulation, and stereotyping. We'll discuss visual framing, the concept that any image or video is created and presented in ways that highlight some aspects of a phenomenon or event while downplaying or eliminating other aspects. These frames thus present readers and viewers with different meanings. A related issue is that of visual metaphors where viewers are invited to see one thing in terms of another. For example, a Nike ad showing a tennis star serving a grenade instead of a tennis ball highlights not only the star's explosive serve, but the Nike brand gear that presumably enables it. Finally, we work through a concrete example of applying an ethical framework to a health communication issue and introduce you to the Potter Box, a well-known and frequently used approach to media ethics questions.

HOW VISUALS WORK: ETHICAL IMPLICATIONS

LO1 Understand the ethical dimensions of visual communication

You can imagine how our quick assessments of others and their possible intentions toward us can be either adaptive or damaging. These instant evaluations are **heuristics**, or shortcuts, in thinking. They may also be forms of stereotyping. We may conclude that an older person is unimportant, an unattractive individual is less competent, or a member of a minority is somehow threatening (Belluck, 2009).

You likely have seen images of American indigenous people appropriated in professional and college sports logos, essentially promoting a warrior identity as well as commodifying it. In their edited volume, *Images that Injure: Stereotypes in the Media*, Ross and Lester provide a compilation of images and critiques on gender and sexuality, race and ethnicity, religion, and nationality (Ross, 2011, p. 3). Sexualized stereotypes of both women and men have been heavily used in advertising.

Significantly, much research on visuals and stereotyping suggests that media depictions are more likely to stereotype African Americans as violent criminals, and people draw negative conclusions from those stereotypes (Welch, 2007). Some studies show that video newscasts are more likely to show African American men as angry and handcuffed, and others conclude that crime reporting often demonizes African Americans (Anderson, 1995; Gerbner, 2003). Welch (2007) writes, "these images are so widespread that it would not be surprising if much of American society has subconsciously come to accept the visual portrayal of Blacks as criminals in contemporary society" (p. 281–282). This doesn't mean that news media workers are purposely portraying minorities in a negative way. It does mean that they are likely interpreting events through stereotypes and shortcuts.

In the same vein, visuals have important political implications, particularly in an age of easily shared photos, symbols, and mashups. Research shows that looks matter. Ballew and Todorov (2007) asked participants to quickly glance at photos of real candidates who were unknown to the participants and then choose their favorites. It turned out that even though people in the study had no knowledge of the candidate they selected, their snap judgments predicted almost 70% of the winners of US House and Senate races. Thus, as Page and Duffy (2018) point out, in a world increasingly dominated by visual messages distributed largely in online settings, we tend to draw critical inferences about people based on very little real information.

The power of images to be interpreted as evidence of what's real and true also can be used for unethical purposes, intentionally, or unintentionally. Visuals embrace us, excite us, strike us, hurt us, lift us up, and make us yearn. The power of visuals and their representation of what looks like reality makes them particularly interesting and important to study from the standpoint of ethics.

Ethical issues in any field – and especially in media – arise when different interests and intentions collide. As Patterson and Wilkins (1997) put it, "Ethics is less about the conflict between right and wrong than it is about the conflict between equally compelling (or equally unattractive) values and the choices that must be made between them" (p. 3).

For example, a journalist may take a compelling photograph or video of a person who has been hurt or injured because they wish to highlight an important event or social issue or simply because it appears to be newsworthy. Some may argue that the most important ethical value in this situation is the journalist's duty to depict the truth. Others may say that showing graphic images is offensive and may invade the privacy of an individual or their family and thus would be ethically questionable.

FOCUS: Images of Tragedy: Afghan Victim

A *New York Times* (NYT) special report told of how an Afghan woman was falsely accused of burning a Koran at a Muslim shrine in Kabul. An enraged mob beat her to death and then burned the body. The story featured a video of cellphone clips depicting the gruesome and bloody assault with the warning it contained scenes of graphic violence (Rubin, 2015).

This powerful NYT piece stitches together cellphone clips posted on social media into a compelling story that emphasizes the apparent bloodlust of the mob, the relative indifference of the police, and the horrific abuse the woman undergoes. A voiceover briefly explains the source materials used in the story. What isn't immediately apparent is that, like all stories whether visual or in other media, the process of the gathering and organizing of story elements is largely invisible to the casual viewer.

Journalists compiled this story thus creating a narrative or plotline based on storytelling conventions, the perceived news value of the story, and the journalists' skills and beliefs about good reporting. In the newsgathering and editing process, various story elements are rearranged, deleted, or given less or more prominence. As Ernest Bormann wrote in describing the coverage of an American hostage crisis, the images create a specific rendering of reality: "The pictures . . . are stitched into dramatically improvised scenes. The viewer sees an artistic, interpretative, organized portrayal of social reality" (Bormann, 1982, p. 145). A different rendering of these very same videos might lead viewers to a different storyline and conclusion about what took place.

What does this have to do with ethics? First, "real" and relatively undoctored images can be presented in ways that draw viewers to different conclusions that may or may not be intended by the presenter. Second, different media outlets, news organizations in particular, have different guidelines about what types of images should or should not be disseminated (Brooks et al., 2020). At one time, media companies could largely control and limit the dissemination of gruesome, sexual, and graphic images. However, with the massive sharing capabilities of social media and non-journalistic outlets, there are few ways to limit or protect viewers from seeing problematic images or protect people's right to privacy. For example, several times when terrorists beheaded captives, mainstream media did not run the video the terrorists took. However, within minutes the videos were widely available on the Internet.

Even the choice as to whether to run a photo or include a video in a news story or other media representation has ethical implications as well. Of course, the issue raised earlier about graphic video and imagery is one that journalists frequently confront. How many, if any, photographs of a tragedy should be included?

Foundations of Ethical Thought

Your grounding in ethics likely emerged from your upbringing – the mores of your family, religious institutions, school, and family – and even the media you use. It may be useful to begin with reflecting on your own beliefs and approaches to dealing with ethical dilemmas. Most of us respond instinctively in such situations and think we "just know" the right thing to do. However, our instincts can lead us down problematic paths. This risk is why a system of reasoning about complex situations is helpful. Ethicists tend to fall into two main camps known as "**deontological**" and "**teleological**" (Figure 2.1).

Deontology

Think of deontological ethics as rules based. Deontology is based on the Greek word for duty. Deontological ethicists insist that regardless of the situation, individuals should adhere to moral rules that either require or prohibit certain types of action, regardless of the consequences. We can also think of these rules-based people as being absolutist in that they often rely on religious tenets or other deeply held values that, in their view, can never be broached. For instance, a photojournalist who believes that they are duty bound to provide photos depicting a "newsworthy" event, regardless of whether others might be injured or shocked in some way, would be an absolutist.

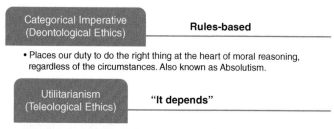

Figure 2.1 **Categorical imperative and utilitarianism.** *Source:* © John Wiley & Sons, Inc.

Deontology, also called absolutism, places our duty to do the right thing at the heart of moral reasoning, regardless of the circumstances. For instance, an absolutist believes that it is never right to lie so presumably if a crazed killer breaks into your house and demands to know where you keep the knives, you would be duty bound to tell the truth. This, of course, sounds extreme, but carried to its ultimate conclusion, that is where deontology takes us and why many people don't think it passes the "real-world" test.

Does the end justify the means? The absolutists will say no. Immanuel Kant is the most famous proponent of this view described as the **categorical imperative**. Kant believed that each of us should start with the premise that people should only behave in ways that they would want others to behave. In other words, we should act as if our own ethical choices were universal law. As Patterson and Wilkins (1997) explain, the test of a moral act is its universality – whether it can be applied to everyone.

Teleology

In contrast to deontology, think of teleological as "it depends." Ethical theories can be categorized in terms of those theories' basic guiding principles (Black and Roberts, 2011). These principles bring different values to the fore and influence our ethical decision-making.

Teleology, also known as consequentialism, focuses on outcomes or ends and is at the root of **utilitarianism**, a well-known philosophical approach to moral reasoning. We ask ourselves "what are the possible results of choosing one decision over another?" "What happens if I favor one value instead of another?"

The core of decision-making for utilitarian thinkers involves what actions will lead to the best outcomes for the most people or will cause the least harm. One of the ways we commonly do this is to focus on outcomes, known in ethicist lingo as "consequential-ism." By that, we mean that we think about what will happen if we choose one course of action over another.

For instance, if an advertising agency's creative director wants to use a video of a person base jumping from a skyscraper to dramatize the thrilling taste of a soft drink, they may indeed be successful in gaining the attention and interest of members of a target audience and thus have greater success in selling the product. On the other hand, they may also want to take into account that depictions of potentially dangerous behaviors may encourage others, especially vulnerable audiences, to emulate that behavior. A 12-year-old boy whose judgment is not highly developed may see the video and believe himself capable of doing the same thing.

While at first blush utilitarianism seems logical and fair, it's often criticized for ignoring the needs and concerns of those who aren't in the majority. Critics also say that utilitarianism lets people off the hook by ignoring our fundamental human responsibility to make ethical choices. And, as Black and Roberts (2011) point out, it's problematic to expect people to be able to accurately imagine and predict the outcomes of these decisions.

Pluralism

The categorical imperative (deontology) and utilitarianism (teleology) are often envisioned as being on the opposite ends of the spectrum of moral thought. The ideas of W.D. Ross provide different perspectives that many people believe bridge the gap between absolutist and consequentialist views of ethics, offering a **pluralistic** viewpoint (Figure 2.2). Ross (1930/2002) argued that we often are faced with competing values as we consider ethical questions. He provides moral guidelines that he calls **prima facie duties**. The term prima facie literally means "on its face" (at first glance) in Latin and refers to the concept that certain duties and obligations come first unless other contingencies or issues come up.

Ross lays out these duties in his book, *The Right and the Good* (1930/2002):

- Fidelity: the need to keep promises and avoid lying and deception.

- Reparation: the requirement to ameliorate or "fix" actions we may have made that were wrong and injured others.

- Gratitude: the duty to be thankful for others' good acts and to act positively in return.

- Non-injury and harm-prevention: the responsibility to avoid hurting other people and to forestall harm where possible.

- Beneficence: the duty to do our best toward others, recognizing that in doing good toward others and holding that there are people in the world "whose condition we can make better in respect of virtue, or of intelligence, or of pleasure."

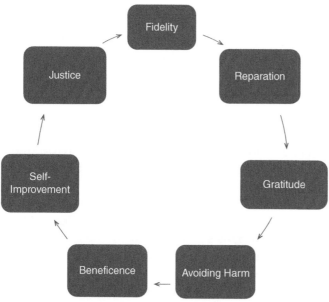

Figure 2.2 Ross's seven prima facie duties (pluralism ethics) "At first glance."
Source: © John Wiley & Sons, Inc.

- Self-improvement: a responsibility to ourselves to foster our own well-being, health, and safety.
- Justice: the duty to behave in ways that ensure happiness and pleasure are distributed fairly among all people. (Ross, p. 21–22).

One way to understand Ross's ethics theory and the role of contingencies is to consider the analogy of a card game. When you look at a newly dealt hand, at first glance you might think that you will win in a "top card wins" game because you have an ace. However, you might end up losing if another player has a trump card. This can be any card in the deck, but the players have determined beforehand that this card will beat, or trump, any other card, even the ace.

Now consider Ross's ideas on a person's moral duties. Most situations will involve more than one duty. Often, they will conflict, causing you to deliberate which one to follow within a specific situation. While this seems confusing, using personal moral judgment to weigh decisions based on the context of a given situation can be more useful than being bound by clear-cut rules and answers. Can you think of a situation involving visual communication that you would decide by weighing Ross's seven duties? Consider what content you'd use to cover a fast-moving news event like a salmonella outbreak, or what images you'd use in a fund-raising campaign to fight childhood malnutrition.

VISUAL DECEPTION

LO2 Identify the ethical dimensions of visual manipulation, framing, appropriation, and intellectual property.

Photographers have altered their images long before digital picture taking and Photoshop. Search for "digitally manipulated photos" and you'll find multiple sources that document and illustrate doctored pictures stretching back to the 1800s. In professional situations, ethical issues still arise as modern media organizations make decisions about how to portray male and female politicians and celebrities.

To Tell the Truth . . . or Not

During the 2008 US presidential election, *Newsweek* magazine ran a cover story on vice presidential candidate Sara Palin featuring a closely cropped photo and following its longstanding policy of not retouching photos (Baird, 2016). The photo caused an uproar because critics said it was cruel, revealing wrinkles and some facial hair. Photographers for *Newsweek* said they had set up for a male candidate, not a female candidate thus using stronger, and some would say harsher, lighting for the shoot. The managing editor commented that *Newsweek* used unretouched photos of men on a regular basis. As Baird (2016) wrote, "*Newsweek* was accused of sexism because we did *not* (original emphasis) airbrush the photo. The truth was, we'd portrayed Ms. Palin just the way we did male candidates." This incident points out how expectations of women's appearances are far different from men's, and people apply different and gender-based ethical judgments.

Figure 2.3 Intentionally cropped photo of President Trump's 2017 inauguration day photo. *Source:* Scott Olson/Getty Images News/Getty Images.

Nearly a decade later, President Trump instructed the National Park Service to remove empty space and make the audience look larger in his 2017 inauguration day photo posted to social media (Figure 2.3). A government photographer admitted to investigators that he intentionally cropped photos to fit the statement of Trump's then-press secretary Sean Spicer, "This was the largest audience to ever witness an inauguration – period" (CNN, 2018).

Visual Manipulation Issues

Technology allows people to easily create visual memes from their own photos or others' images and share them on social media. For example, when Fox Sports reporter Erin Andrews interviewed star NFL player Richard Sherman after a close-fought game, Sherman shouted that he was the best corner in the game, launching scores of memes that called on visual popular culture. The memes, mashups of Sherman photos and images of the Incredible Hulk, an alien, and a bully, tended to characterize Sherman as a scary and frightening individual (Figure 2.4), possibly even threatening to Andrews (Page et al., 2016).

Professionally, from retouched photos in fashion spreads and ads to digital effects in video and motion pictures, enhanced images are part of our daily media consumption. They're not all without harm. Depictions of thin, attractive female models and

Figure 2.4 Meme depicting Richard Sherman as *The Predator* film character. *Source:* Athletize.

celebrities in movies, on television, and in advertising have been shown to lead young women to have unreasonable expectations about their own bodies and to undermine their self- confidence: a negative consequence of seeing those images (Gleeson and Frith, 2006). A magazine retoucher for *Vogue* magazine reported altering 144 pictures in the magazine for fashion articles and for advertising (Orbach, 2011). Some critics might argue that the images thus are not authentic and represent a false "reality" to readers of the magazine. Others might argue that everyone knows that such images are carefully posed, chosen, and fine-tuned to present clothing and other products in the most appealing fashion.

FOCUS: Digital Manipulation

Photo manipulation is a contentious area in journalism, advertising, and other forms of strategic communication. From almost the beginning of photography, it became possible to manipulate, edit, alter, and combine images, thus changing their meanings in subtle or blatant ways. Celebrated US Civil War photographer, Mathew Brady, made a portrait of General William Tecumseh Sherman's top officers – but later added a missing officer who Brady evidently thought should be part of the record (Strauss, 2011). More recently, *Time* magazine edited and darkened a cover photo of African American murder suspect O.J. Simpson in a move that some said had the effect of making him look more menacing (Black and Roberts, 2011).

News organizations and professional photojournalism organizations have specific guidelines regarding manipulation. The Associated Press (AP) policy begins, "AP visuals must always tell the truth. We do not alter or digitally manipulate the content of a photograph in any way" (AP n.d.). However, the policy goes on to say minor adjustments are acceptable including cropping, dodging, and burning, conversion into grayscale and normal toning and color adjustments which should be "limited to those minimally necessary for clear and accurate reproduction" (AP n.d., para. 2).

The *New York Times* also has policies against photo manipulation, however, it acknowledged that fashion photography in its *T Magazine* has different rules (Sullivan, 2013). The magazine's fashion editors argued that fashion is a different genre of photography and that the publication's readers recognize that "fashion is fantasy." Their public editor (an ombudsperson) suggested that fashion spreads should be subject to the same rules as any other part of the publication or at the very least should have a sort of warning label about the different standards for fashion (Sullivan, 2013). Of course, these policies do not govern the photo manipulation that goes on in fashion advertising carried on their pages. Fashion brands and advertisements frequently manipulate photos to make models appear thinner and to eliminate "flaws" they may have. Some critics argue that such alterations give people unrealistic ideas about body images they may aspire to and may even lead to eating disorders (Bissell, 2006; Reaves et al., 2004).

In the past, with film-based, analog photography, it was usually possible to compare film negatives with altered pictures and detect a fake. Today, however, people with even minimal skills can create mashups, edit their own photos, remove or add individuals, and so on. Individuals can easily share images on social networks like Snapchat, Facebook, and Instagram.

Framing that Distorts Reality

Decisions about how tightly a photographer frames their image can make a significant difference in how viewers interpret its meaning. The famous wartime photographer, Robert Capa said, "If your pictures aren't good enough, you're not close enough" (Bird, 2002). For many photographers, deciding how closely a person or event should be shot relates more to the skill and artistry of good photography rather than consideration of how they may be altering viewer perceptions. In an effort to create a more arresting or dramatic photo, the photographer may be presenting an image that distorts the reality of the event.

Similarly, cropping an image, an everyday activity for photojournalists and editors, might also be considered as a form of manipulation. The not-for-profit journalistic publication *ProPublica* reported on photos and videos taken during the US invasion of Iraq in 2003 (Maass, 2011). Videos and still photos of crowds pulling down a statue of dictator Saddam Hussein in a public square rocketed around the world. News organizations reported it as revealing the US victory and the Iraqi people's joy at the defeat of a ruthless dictator. The close-up shots seemed to show a jubilant crowd of Iraqis and US soldiers as they slung a rope around the statue and dragged it from its pedestal: a potent symbol of Saddam himself being toppled from power. But a more distant shot, without benefit of cropping, shows only a scattering of people in a mostly empty square, an image that likely would convey a different meaning from the tight rendering. The choice of the more dramatic image may misrepresent the event it is supposed to document.

The Saddam statue cropping is an example of visual framing. **Framing** theory offers us a way to understand how messages communicate different meanings. A frame, whether it's expressed verbally or visually, highlights certain aspects of a phenomenon or event while eliminating or minimizing others. We can't describe everything about any event – there are just too many factors. For example, imagine that you're describing a lunch with a good friend. You had a lively conversation, laughed about some of the funny things that have happened in the past week, and shared some worries about the future. You dined on Japanese food and drank tea. In talking about the lunch with a foodie friend, you might emphasize the meal and show your Instagram photo of the sushi. For a different friend, you might focus on the enjoyment of the laughs and jokes and post a photo of the good time on Facebook. As you can see, it's the same event, but you make choices about what you want to highlight for the person you're speaking with or what was most important to you.

According to Entman (1993), frames have four main elements: (i) defining aspects of a problem, (ii) identifying causes, (iii) making moral judgments, and (iv) implying solutions. For instance, if policymakers and citizens identify obesity as a public health problem that should be addressed, news stories or campaigns can be told with many different frames, and these frames have moral and ethical implications (Figure 2.5). If the message is "you should eat healthy meals and exercise more," the campaign suggests the individual responsibility frame. With this framing, the problem lies with each person who should have the will and capability to alter his behavior. Such individual responsibility frames,

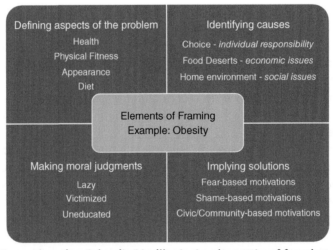

Figure 2.5 **Example using "obesity" to illustrate elements of framing.** *Source:* **Children's Healthcare of Atlanta/NPR.**

some critics say, unfairly victimize individuals. If the message is "people who live in 'food deserts' in urban areas don't have access to healthful foods," the problem is framed to highlight social or economic issues within cities and towns. Another frame could use fear appeals that graphically show the risks of obesity or even shame appeals. Thus, you can see that morals, judgments, and values imbue all human expression.

Effects of Virtual Reality

Emerging virtual reality technologies have potential side effects because, psychologically and physically, the experiences seem to be so real. Early studies already suggest that people's beliefs and ideas are affected by a virtual reality experience. For example, in an environmentally focused experiment where subjects "virtually" cut down a tree in a single episode, participants were more likely to use fewer paper towels to clean up a spill later (Nicas, 2016). Other media and filmmakers have produced work that has had individuals experience traumatic situations such as bombings, a diabetic coma, and even the aftermath of being in the World Trade Center on 9/11. This melding of experiential and visual stimuli has powerful potential ethical implications. This has to do with the issue of choice – that is, we as human beings can choose to use and apply a technology – or not.

Visual Metaphors and Ethics

We all use metaphors every day, mostly without giving them much thought. We say things like "he saw the light" meaning that someone came to understand something, or "in a nutshell," meaning that someone is about to briefly summarize a concept or event. We say, "don't shoot the messenger," "that's the elephant in the room," and "that's a slippery slope." Lakoff and Johnson (1980) suggest that "the essence of metaphor is understanding one thing in terms of another" (p. 5) leading us to different ways of interpreting a message. You'll read more about visual metaphors in Chapter 5.

Brand Mascots and Celebrities

Brands frequently use mascots and celebrities as metaphors for the benefits of their products and services. You may have heard of Q Scores, a research service that measures the appeal of various sports figures, movie stars, and musical performers. The appeal is largely powered by photos, images, and drawings. Even cartoons and images of dead celebrities can be persuasive – learn more on the Q Scores website.[1] For instance, the mascot for Kellogg's Frosted Flakes cereal is Tony the Tiger, now over 60 years old, and Tony has a Q Score.

Many critics think it is unethical to use cartoon characters, like Tony, to sell products, particularly products, such as sugary cereals, aimed at children. "Joe Camel," a cartoon character promoting Camel cigarettes, ran in ads and other venues from 1988 to 1997. Research showed that even young children recognized the character. There is evidence that R.J. Reynolds tobacco company specifically sought to entice younger people to smoke (Stanford, n.d.). Joe Camel was portrayed as cool and smooth: a metaphor pointing the viewer to the idea that Camel cigarettes and their users were desirable and that consuming the product was a smooth and pleasurable activity.

Two insurance company mascots, GEICO's gecko and Aflac's duck, are among the most popular spokes-characters in the last 30-plus years (Phillips, 2014, p. 156). Both characters have scored in the top 10 in terms of Q scores, with fans on social media and appearances on late night comedy TV shows. If a compelling metaphor for a presumably safe product leads to product awareness and a sale, that is a good outcome. On the other hand, if it would lead a vulnerable consumer such as a child to feel more positively about using a dangerous product, then that would indeed lead to an ethical breach.

Favored Strategy in Advertisements

There are lots of metaphors in advertising visuals. A running shoe ad that shows the shoe bursting into flames suggests that the wearer will run extremely fast. An ad for light beer may show a glass full of beer in the shape of a light bulb. Research shows that visual metaphors are often highly persuasive in advertising and contribute to people's quick understanding of complex ideas (Jeong, 2008). In addition, the persuasive messages made through visual metaphors appear to encourage greater agreement than with verbal or textual messages. Thus, to illustrate another common metaphor, using images to persuade may be a double-edged sword in that they can be deployed for a variety of goals and intentions. As you can see, the metaphors we use are an important part of framing our messages.

Advertisers, both in print and video, rely heavily on metaphors because they point us to certain elements – we call this **salience**, or how much something stands out or draws our attention (Kress and van Leeuwen, 1998, p. 210). The salience factors that we are drawn to can include contrast, a familiar or iconic photo, the size and shape of an element, or a top left position in Western cultures. Often, you'll see a familiar image – perhaps a celebrity's photo – in a surprising or incongruous setting or position. The creator of the ad intends that you interpret the image in a specific way, drawing meaning from it.

The poster from the World Wildlife Fund (Figure 2.6) uses a powerful visual metaphor to

Figure 2.6 The World Wildlife Fund uses a visual metaphor for global warming. *Source:* Romolo Tavani/123RF.

highlight the risks of global warming. As you can see, the visual metaphor suggests the earth and ice cream share traits of melting fast. While the small wording below relays the message in the visual, the dramatic presentation of the melting earth cone against a stark black background dramatizes the danger in a memorable way. Again, we can see the power of visuals to persuade and provide real impact.

Visual metaphors may use various approaches including fear appeals of varying intensity that may be effective in changing behaviors. They also may cause psychological distress or harm, such as the use of graphic images illustrating child abuse or car injuries due to impaired driving. Visual metaphors also open the door to puffery: the practice of exaggerating claims in advertising (Richards, 2016; Thorson and Duffy, 2016). Richards discusses the notion that some critics consider puffery to be deceptive. Others say that statements or images such as "Budweiser is the king of beers" or a video showing a man wearing his Skechers shoes outrunning a cheetah aren't deceptive because they are in the realm of fantasy and thus are unlikely to mislead a consumer.

Visual Appropriation

Visual **appropriation**, the intentional borrowing, copying, and alteration of preexisting images and objects, is a strategy long used by artists. For example, in 1962 Andy Warhol painted images of the Campbell's tomato soup can. It led to a great debate about the ethics of such work, and appropriation remains an ethical gray area today.

Visual appropriation has been strategically used in negative political advertising. In 2016, an attack ad by Republican primary candidate Ted Cruz against rival Marco Rubio attempted to visually paint Rubio as the Republican Obama. One of the final images on a campaign video make an analogy between the Obama "Hope" poster by Shepard Fairey (Figure 2.7) and a photoshopped image of Marco Rubio (Figure 2.8). The Rubio image used the recognizable style of the Fairey poster, seeking to short-circuit people's analysis of Rubio's characteristics and policies by heightening his presumed similarities to Obama. In addition, it used the creative work of Fairey in a different context. In this case, a political operative applied a digital filter known as posterizing. Widely available apps allow users to use a limited number of colors on a photo, thus

Figure 2.7 Original image inspiring the Rubio photoshop. *Source:* **Aaron Alex / Alamy Stock Photo.**

Figure 2.8 Photoshopped image of Marco Rubio. *Source:* https://www.youtube.com/embed/uKcQoFSVvGQ?feature=oembed, Ted Cruz.

giving it the effect of a movie or music poster. This brings up the question of visual plagiarism such as using elements of one image combined with others to create a different representation, image, or work of art. Regarding the original Fairey graphic, AP sued the artist in 2011 claiming copyright ownership over the image, as it was closely based on an AP photo. Both sides settled on sharing rights to the image (Kravets, 2011).

Mashups and Remixes

Mashups or remixes are now common, and some say they are simply new cultural practices enabled by technology. **Vidding**, or editing and adding to existing video footage, may be used to comment, satirize, or to offer a fresh perspective on an event or viewpoint. This brings up both legal and ethical implications. Is it proper to use materials that someone else has created? In addition, what legal policies may be applicable to these situations? In these cases, copyright and "fair use" laws are in play. Copyright laws are intended to protect writers, photographers, and videographers from having their work stolen or used inappropriately. It also protects their rights to be compensated (Brooks et al., 2020). However, rules regarding fair use of copyrighted materials allow others to use small portions of those materials when they are properly attributed. In this book, our use of others' work and ideas are examples of fair use or copyrighted use has been sought and granted. Images, especially in the age of digital work, present ever more complex ethical questions.

Homages

There are tensions between stealing another's work and an "homage" to another's creation. An homage is a reference, reconfiguring, and sometimes a recreation of an image or work of art, often done with the goal of honoring and elaborating on that work. Moviemakers frequently will adopt or reference scenes from other movies. For example, director Quentin Tarantino in *The Hateful Eight* uses costumes, snips of dialogue, and scene setups that call on classic western films (Miller, 2015). To use the Obama "Hope" poster by Shepard Fairey in this chapter required that we provide compensation to the copyright holders, in part because it is a complete work and it wouldn't be possible to use only a portion of it.

However, imagine if an individual substantially altered the Obama "Hope" poster, animating it, inserting new characters, settings, or backgrounds. Does it then become a different creation, possibly with copyright protection itself? What if it is then disseminated on social media? Noted visual theorist William J. Mitchell (1994) suggests that easily replicable visual images have profoundly changed how we interact with those images both individual and societally.

> We might best regard digital images, then, neither as ritual objects (as religious paintings have served) nor as objects of mass consumption . . . but as fragments of information that circulate in high-speed networks now ringing the globe that can be received, transformed, and recombined like DNA to produce new intellectual structures having their own dynamics and value
>
> *(Mitchell 1994, pp. 53–54).*

Mitchell and others point out how easily manipulated and shared images seem to have less and less relationship with an "external referent" (p. 55) or to be mirrors of what we think of as our everyday reality. Visuals are never just neutral representations of the world. Instead, they are interpretations that may have different meanings for different people and, intentionally or unintentionally, "argue" for a certain point of view.

APPLYING ROSS'S ETHICS

LO3 Apply strategies for evaluating the ethics of visual communication that you or others create.

Earlier in this chapter, in the section on Pluralism, you read that Ross's first duty is fidelity or the responsibility to keep promises, be truthful, and fulfill contracts and obligations. That means we shouldn't lie. However, another one of Ross's duties is *non-injury*: our responsibility to avoid hurting other people physically, emotionally, or psychologically.

Unintended Effects

Ross's approach can be useful to professionals in advertising, journalism, and other media because of the frequently competing roles they must fulfill (Wilkins, 2016). For instance, a health communication message meant to address a problem of childhood obesity could be considered beneficent since it is a serious public and individual health problem. However, some messages may have unintended effects (Thorson and Duffy, 2016). Visuals are very powerful and can evoke visceral responses, short-circuiting our processes in evaluating the worth of messages (Page and Duffy, 2016). A good example is the Strong4Life campaign from Children's Healthcare of Atlanta that used images of obese children believing that such images would motivate pediatricians, families, and schools to provide supportive actions. However, some critics said that the campaign stigmatized and shamed overweight children (Lohr, 2012).

Thus, the duty to do no harm and duty for beneficence come into conflict and the multiple duties of public health professionals and those creating the campaign arise. According to Wilkins (2016), Ross's typology encourages us to look at the specifics and the context of circumstances and decide which duty outweighs the others in a given situation.

FOCUS: Rethinking Diversity in Visual Narratives

A video series by the nonprofit iBiology showcases researchers who represent overlooked groups. "Background to Breakthrough" features Latino Estaban Burchard's journey from growing up in a poor, single parent home to his adult life as a health expert on asthma. The video's unique perspective frames Burchard not as a marginalized survivor, but rather as an creative achiever drawing from his valuable life experience to become a world-renowned researcher and tenured professor at the University of California, San Francisco.

While many narratives about scientists from underrepresented backgrounds present an "underdog" story, iBiology believes they are stale, overused, and lack contextual depth.

This "surviving the odds" storyline does not fairly represent the scientists and science itself; rather, it is one dimensional. It diminishes the way they are seen and understood, harming the way others like them could envision themselves as scientists. And it obscures the value of diversity in the field and how it shapes breakthroughs.

iBiology's open-access free videos in this series provide a broader picture using a variety of visual storytelling strategies focusing on how the race, identities, cultures, and backgrounds of underrepresented scientists fire up their ingenuity and approaches to problem solving. In Burchard's videos, he's not only seen as a researcher but as a mentor and activist. The essential message is that diversity enhances scientific research so that it helps people of all backgrounds.

Visual Storytelling Strategies

Make a direct connection: Burchard directly asks the viewer, "If you were a parent, would you let your child use this?" "This" is a drug that significantly increases the risk of death in African Americans. With the question, Burchard, an expert on asthma health, builds a one-on-one rapport with the audience, engages them emotionally, and communicates care and credibility.

Use visual comparisons: Race is a "shopping cart that contains lots of information that is relevant for clinical and biomedical research," explains Burchard. An animation illustrates the relationship between race and biology and its complexities – creatively explained in a compelling and accurate way.

Show visual evidence: Rather than defining Burchard as an underdog who rose to the top, the producers explored how he overcame the challenges he faced. They looked at hundreds of old photos to show and tell a more nuanced story of how Latino culture gave him unique perspectives in science research – bringing to life the many mentors who gave him the confidence, support, and guidance throughout his journey

Source: https://blogs.scientificamerican.com/voices/rethinking-the-narrative-of-diversity-in-science

The Potter Box

The Potter Box is a useful tool to guide us in answering ethical questions in visual communication and incorporates the values suggested by Ross. Devised by theologian Ralph Potter, it provides a step-by-step process to weigh varying situations and values. As you can see, the Potter Box (Figure 2.9) visually shows a process that involves four major elements of ethical decision-making. The four steps are:

1. Definition: identifying the facts of a given problem or situation.

2. Values: considering what issues and outcomes are most important to you.

3. Principles: thinking about the ethical philosophies you subscribe to.

4. Loyalties: considering your loyalty to various stakeholders.

Let's take a closer look at each step:

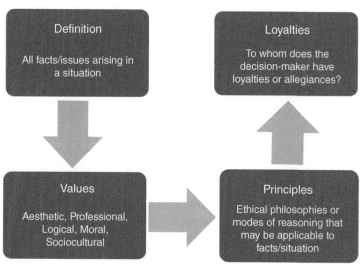

Figure 2.9 The Potter Box. *Source:* © John Wiley & Sons, Inc.

Definition

In the case of the children's anti-obesity campaign, the facts of the situation are that the state of Georgia faces a public health crisis. The children who are obese face the likelihood that they will experience disease and shortened life spans. The state faces the problem of increased health care costs and potentially unsustainable budget expenditures.

Values

The second step is more difficult because the meaning of the concept "values" is often unclear for many people. Patterson and Wilkins (2002) point out that when we discuss ethical values, we need to be clearer about their meanings: "when you value something – an idea or a principle – it means you are willing to give up other things for it" (p. 77). An important value for government leaders is positive health outcomes for the people in the state. Another value would be effectiveness in that state leaders would want to know and be able to tell others that funds invested in this strategy actually worked to improve health and reduce obesity. Some in government might highly value what they perceive as honesty and truth in telling people "like it is" rather than sugarcoating issues to protect their feelings. Still other values could be protecting vulnerable populations such as children from psychological harm from hard-edged or even cruel messages. As Patterson and Wilkins (2002) point out, "values often compete and an important element of using the Potter Box is to be honest about what you really do value" (p. 77).

Principles

The third step is a careful examination of ethical principles that underpin values and ethical decisions. Someone who is a consequentialist might insist that even if someone's feelings get hurt in the process, more people will benefit from tough anti-obesity messages. Someone who is a deontologist or absolutist might argue that it is never acceptable to injure others psychologically or physically regardless of the potential outcome. Someone following Ross's principles on prima facie duties would consider what values are in conflict in this particular case and which should be most important, and these can help you be more systematic in reasoning through ethical dilemmas. Ross's approach is helpful, we think, because it offers guidelines for this reasoning rather than rules that are expected to apply in any given situation.

Loyalties

The fourth step involves loyalties, an area that Christians et al. (1987) suggest deserves the greatest attention because it's easy to deceive ourselves about the loyalties that are most important to us. Assume that you are a Georgia health policymaker. You may have loyalty to your own ethical beliefs, to the people of Georgia, and to your department. You may also be loyal to your own self-interest, to be and to be seen as effective at your job and worthy of recognition and possibly promotions. Other likely loyalties may be to your family's well-being, to your coworkers in the department, and so on. If you're committed to the duty of "non-injury," then you may be weighing the potential harm that campaign images might do against the possibility that such messaging might be effective. Again, having your campaign shown to be effective could also be a strong benefit to you.Last, you come to some conclusions about the proper course of action in this particular case. Reject the campaign because it unfairly targets vulnerable children and may cause them to feel hurt and ashamed? Go forward with the campaign because it is the most likely to result in better long-term health for these same children? Ethical decision-making is a real-world activity with genuine consequences for real people. What is the right decision in the case of the Georgia obesity campaign? Reasonable people can disagree, but at the very least, the choices made would be based on a systematic and thoughtful process.

CHAPTER SUMMARY

You are a creator, consumer, and distributor of visuals in today's world of instantaneous communication and sharing through social networks and digital devices. Your job as a consumer or creator of visuals has never been more challenging from an ethical standpoint. In the future, it will be even easier and cheaper to create and disseminate images, apps, videos, and remixes. Photography once had a more obvious referent to real life in that a photo of an event was relatively difficult to alter, filter, or otherwise manipulate. In the future, we will all be consuming and evaluating many images that are created primarily from people's imaginations and combinations of materials of all kinds. However, regardless of changing technologies, new and unexpected events, and even more instant and sophisticated sharing capabilities, we can still apply systematic ethical reasoning and consider our duties to ourselves and to others.

KEY TERMS

Heuristics Mental shortcuts allowing someone to make a decision, evaluate, or problem-solve quickly with little effort.

Deontological Absolutist ethics that are rule-based; beliefs that standards are always true regardless of contexts or consequences.

Teleological Consequentialist ethics that value the outcome or consequences of an act as most important.

Categorical imperative A concept of deontology; belief that one's own ethical choices are universal law; one should act as we would want others to behave.

Utilitarianism A central concept of teleology; belief that acts should result in the great amount of good for the greatest number of people.

Pluralistic Belief in several ethical perspectives and not one basic one.

Prima facie duties Ethical decisions that should come first; from the Latin "on its face" (at first glance).

Framing Concept that any text or artifact is created – and presented – in ways that highlight some aspects of it while downplaying or eliminating other aspects, thus guiding readers and viewers to draw specific meanings.

Salience   Quality of how much something stands out or draws our attention.
Appropriation   The intentional borrowing, copying, and alteration of preexisting images and objects.
Vidding   Editing and adding to existing video footage.

PRACTICE ACTIVITIES

1. As a class exercise, take an image from the Creative Commons website (creativecommons.org) where you are legally allowed to use work as long as you attribute it. Go to a meme site and "memify" it. In teams, answer the following questions: (i) What meaning do you take from the original image and what frame did it use? (ii) What meaning do you take from the meme and what frame does it use?
2. Either in teams or for individual assignments, find print ads or photos for ethical analysis using the Potter Box.
3. Imagine you're on an advertising agency team with the assignment to design a campaign to discourage 16- to 26-year-old young men from drinking and driving. What frames would you consider in creating a persuasive video?
4. You read earlier that the *New York Times* has one set of guidelines for news photos and another for fashion photos. Do you agree that there should be a distinction? Why or why not? Would a disclaimer or warning label help readers be more informed? In your view, do readers and viewers easily understand that fashion is a different genre and is not expected to be realistic?
5. In small groups, review the codes of ethics of news organizations and/or advertising and PR agencies. Are these codes sufficient in an age of digital communication and highly visual programming? How are the codes different from each other? Which does each group believe is most applicable in today's media world?

NOTE

1   http://www.qscores.com

REFERENCES

Anderson, D. (1995). Crime and the Politics of Hysteria. New York: Random House.

AP. (n.d.). Visuals. https://www.ap.org/about/news-values-and-principles/telling-the-story/visuals (accessed September 3, 2020).

Baird, J. (2016). Sara Palin's mustache. *New York Times*, Feb. 26. http://www.nytimes.com/2016/02/26/opinion/campaign-stops/sarah-palins-mustache.html (accessed February 26, 2020).

Ballew, C.C. and Todorov, A. (2007). Predicting political elections from rapid and unreflective face judgments. Proceedings of the National Academy of Sciences of the United States of America 104 (2): 17948–17953.

Belluck, P. (2009). Yes, looks do matter. *New York Times*, April 24. http://www.nytimes. com/2009/04/26/fashion/26looks.html (accessed December 29, 2015).

Bird, M. (2002). Robert Capa, in focus. *Time*, June 30. http://content.time.com/time/ magazine/article/0,9171,267730,00.html (accessed February 4, 2016).

Bissell, K. (2006). Skinny like you: Visual literacy, digital manipulation, and young women's drive to be thin. Simile: Studies in Media and Information Literacy Education 6 (1): 1–14.

Black, J. and Roberts, C. (2011). Doing Ethics in Media: Theories and Practical Applications. New York: Routledge.

Bormann, E.G. (1982). A fantasy theme analysis of the television coverage of the hostage release and the Reagan inaugural. Quarterly Journal of Speech 68: 135–145.

Brooks, B.S., Horvit, B.J., and Moen, D.R. (2020). News Reporting and Editing. Boston: Bedford/St. Martins.

Christians, C.G., Rotzoll, K.B., and Fackler, M. (1987). Media Ethics: Cases and Moral Reasoning, *2e*. White Plains, NY: Longman.

CNN. (2018). National Park Service edited inauguration photos after Trump, Spicer calls. https://www.cnn.com/2018/09/07/politics/trump-inauguration-photos/index.html (accessed December 23, 2020).

Entman, R. (1993). Framing: Toward clarification of a fractured paradigm. Journal of Communication 43 (4): 51–58.

Gerbner, G. (2003). Television violence: At a time of turmoil and terror. In: Gender, Race, and Class in Media, 2e (eds. G. Dines and J.M. Humex), 339–348. Thousand Oaks, CA: Sage.

Gleeson, K. and Frith, H. (2006). (De)constructing body image. Journal of Health Psychology 11 (1): 79–90.

Jeong, S. (2008). Visual metaphor in advertising: Is the persuasive effect attributable to visual argumentation or metaphorical rhetoric? Journal of Marketing Communications 14 (1): 59–73.

Kravets, D. (2011). Associated Press settles copyright lawsuit against Obama 'Hope' artist. https://www.wired.com/2011/01/hope-image-flap (accessed September 3, 2020).

Kress, G. and van Leeuwen, T. (1998). Front pages: (The critical) analysis of newspaper layout. In: Approaches to Media Discourse (eds. A. Bell and P. Garrett), 186–219. Oxford: Blackwell.

Lakoff, G. and Johnson, M. (1980). Metaphors We Live By. Chicago: University of Chicago Press.

Lohr, K. (2012). Controversy swirls around harsh anti-obesity ads. https://www.npr. org/2012/01/09/144799538/controversy-swirls-around-harsh-anti-obesity-ads (accessed September 21, 2020).

Maass, P. (2011). The toppling: How the media inflated the fall of Saddam's statue in Firdos square. *ProPublica*, Jan. 2. http://www.propublica.org/article/the-toppling-saddam-statue-firdos-square-baghdad (accessed February 4, 2016).

Miller, J. (2015). How Quentin Tarantino paid homage to Hollywood with his *Hateful Eight costumes*. Vanity Fair, Dec. 29. from http://www.vanityfair.com/hollywood/2015/12/ quentin-tarantino-the-hateful-eight-costumes (accessed March 2, 2016).

Mitchell, W.J. (1994). The Reconfigured Eye: Visual Truth in the Post-Photographic Era. Cambridge: MIT Press.

Nicas, J. (2016). What happens when virtual reality gets too real? Jan. 4. https://cacm.acm.org/news/196187-what-happens-when-virtual-reality-gets-too-real/fulltext

Orbach, S. (2011). Losing bodies. Social Research 78 (2): 387–394.

Page, J.T. and Duffy, M.E. (2018). What Does Credibility Look like? Tweets and Walls in U.S. Presidential Candidates' Visual Storytelling. Journal of Political Marketing 17: 1, 3–31, doi: https://doi.org/10.1080/15377857.2016.1171819.

Page, J.T., Duffy, M., Frisby, C., and Perreault, G. (2016). Richard Sherman Speaks and Almost Breaks the Internet: Race, Media, and Football. Howard Journal of Communications 27 (3): 270–289. https://doi.org/10.1080/10646175.2016.1176969.

Patterson, P. and Wilkins, L. (1997). Media Ethics: Issues and Cases. Boston: McGraw-Hill.

Patterson, P. and Wilkins, L. (2002). Media Ethics: Issues and Cases, 4e. New York: McGraw-Hill.

Phillips, B.J. (2014). Spokes-characters. In: Brand Mascots: And Other Marketing Animals (eds. S. Brown and S. Ponsonby-McCabe), 165–174. New York: Routledge.

Reaves, S., Bush-Hitchon, J., Park, S., and Yun, G.W. (2004). If looks could kill: Digital manipulation of fashion models. Journal of Mass Media Ethics 19 (1): 56–71.

Ross, S.D. (2011). Introduction. In: Images that Injure: Stereotypes in the Media, 3e (eds. S.D. Ross and P.M. Lester), 1–4. Santa Barbara, CA: Praeger.

Ross, W.D. (1930/2002). The Right and the Good, 1e (ed. P. Stratton-Lake). London: Oxford University Press.

Rubin, A. (2015). Flawed justice after a mob killed an Afghan woman. https://www.nytimes.com/2015/12/27/world/asia/flawed-justice-after-a-mob-killed-an-afghan-woman.html?_r=0 (accessed September 3, 2020).

Stanford. (n.d.). Research into the impact of tobacco advertising. Stanford School of Medicine. http://tobacco.stanford.edu/tobacco_main/images.php?token2=fm_st138.php&token1=fm_img4072.php&theme_file=fm_mt015.php&theme_name=Targeting%20Teens&subtheme_name=Joe%20Camel (accessed February 1, 2016).

Strauss, D. L. (2011). Doctored photos: The art of the altered image. https://time.com/3778075/doctored-photos-the-art-of-the-altered-image (accessed September 3, 2020).

Sullivan, M. (2013). Tattoo removal on the photo desk. New York Times. May 18. http://www.nytimes.com/2013/05/19/public-editor/photo-manipulation-on-the-fashion-pages.html (accessed February 4, 2016).

Thorson, E. and Duffy, M. (2016). Marbles in the Soup and Crushed Volvos: Ethical Choices on the Advertising Ethics Battlefield. In: In Persuasion Ethics Today, eds Margaret Duffy and Esther Thorson. New York, NY: Routledge.

Welch, K. (2007). Black criminal stereotypes and racial profiling. Journal of Contemporary Criminal Justice 23: 276–288.

Wilkins, L. (2016). Advertising Ethics: Applying Theory to Core Issues and Defining Practical Excellence. In: Persuasion Ethics Today (eds. M. Duffy and E. Thorson). New York, NY: Routledge.

Chapter 3
Ways of Seeing
Visual Rhetoric

What's in a Wink?

Many people have observed that the candidacy and election of Donald Trump in 2016 marked the rise of the celebrity politician. Both critics and supporters of Trump observed that he prized visual messaging, often posing with supporters with

Source: AP Images/J. Scott Applewhite

a thumbs up gesture, hugging the American flag, and tweeting a Photoshopped image of himself as Rocky, the boxer in the popular films (Street, 2019; Wheeler, 2013).

Visual Communication: Insights and Strategies, First Edition. Janis Teruggi Page and Margaret Duffy.
© 2022 John Wiley & Sons, Inc. Published 2022 by John Wiley & Sons, Inc.

But even before that, the 2008 race for the White House saw its candidates transform before a global audience into popular culture celebrities. This was especially true in the weeks and months following the nominating conventions. On the Democratic side, Barack Obama became the first African American to win the presidential nomination and named Senator Joe Biden, a senior politician and purported champion for the middle and working class, as his running mate. On the Republican side, Viet Nam War hero and presidential candidate John McCain chose a little-known Alaska governor, Sarah Palin, to run as his vice president – a candidate who instantly became a media star. Her performance at the Republican Convention energized the party's base and her down-home comments about hockey moms and pit bulls caught the public's imagination.

In October, the American public eagerly awaited the 2008 vice presidential debate performance of McCain's surprise pick for running mate. However, the debate quickly grew beyond a serious political exchange into a spectacle, with people following it on social networking sites, adding comments on the candidates' poise, clothing, hair, and performance. An online bingo game tracked Palin's oft-repeated talking points such as "maverick," "real American," and "middle class." In defending McCain's statement that the fundamentals of the economy are strong and that Main Street's workers are safe, Palin winked, as she did at least six times at 70 million viewers during the debate: history's most-watched vice presidential debate.

An early Monty Python comedy sketch that introduced the saying "nudge nudge, wink wink" gave the wink a popular understanding of sexual innuendo. Fiore (2008) suggests the word's origin, ". . .from the word 'hoodwinked,' which may have stemmed from the custom of placing a hood over the heads of those about to be hanged (p. 1). The Bible warned against it in Proverbs: 'Whoever winks the eye, causes trouble.'"

The act of the wink also has common understandings in contemporary American popular culture: flirting, slyness, code for a conspiratorial "we're in on this together," or a slightly darker, "you know I'm not serious about what I'm saying."

Research shows that ambiguous gestures like a wink are risky on a medium such as television, particularly when aimed at an audience that the speaker wants to persuade, according to Erik Bucy, coauthor of *Image Bite Politics: News and the Visual Framing of Elections*. Because visuals invite the viewer to participate in meaning construction with symbolic imagery, viewed behaviors help to direct sense-making. The wink enters murky rhetorical waters because it triggers a closer evaluation of the source, sometimes turning negative (Grabe and Bucy, 2009). Considering the possible connotations of this visual rhetoric, Palin's wink – and a subsequent SNL parody with Palin look-alike Tina Fey – suggested she herself may be playacting as a vice presidential candidate.

1. Demonstrate an understanding of theory, rhetoric, and methodology when conducting visual criticism.
2. Understand visual rhetoric as both an object and a perspective and identify rhetorical actions.
3. Compare four theories useful for conducting visual rhetorical analyses.

Chapter Overview

In this chapter, we describe key terminology: theory, methodology, and visual rhetoric and then explain a classic way to explore the meaning of images: the visual rhetoric perspective. With knowledge, you can then better understand how visuals tell stories, how they propose comparisons, how they express fantasies, how they function as signs and symbols, and how they cross cultures. We then introduce the theories or perspectives that will guide your visual literacy experience throughout the rest of this book: semiotic theory, metaphor theory, the narrative paradigm, and symbolic convergence theory. These approaches help to explain how aspects and elements of visual imagery work in different ways to suggest meaning. This allows you to better navigate the visual messaging you experience, and to use visual messaging strategically.

THREE KEY TERMS

LO1 Demonstrate an understanding of theory, rhetoric, and methodology when conducting visual criticism.

To use visuals wisely in all types of communication, it's also wise to understand the potential for their meaning, why they should be used, and how to actually use them. As an example, consider you're building a small airplane. You need to know the science of what makes it fly, what gives it speed, and so on: **theory**. You need a design that allows you to combine the science into an artful and reliable-looking product: **rhetoric**. And, you need instructions to follow, to assemble all of its parts: **methodology**. Below we explain those three terms as related to communication.

What Is Theory?

The term theory may be intimidating to some of you. Even many people who work in the communications field fail to understand or appreciate theory. You may have heard the phrase, "It's just a theory," implying a hunch or a guess. True, a theory can be considered a hunch, yet a fuller definition is "a set of systematic, informed hunches about the ways things work" (Griffin et al., 2015, p. 2). Another helpful definition of theory is "a set of assumptions used to explain how a process works and to make predictions as to what will result from that process" (Bobbitt and Sullivan, 2014, p. 5). These are assumptions that have survived over time and been tested and proven through research.

There are many theories of communication. Think of theory as a pair of eyeglasses, or a camera, with different lenses which allow you to see the world in different ways. With a specific theory, we focus on some features while putting other features into the background.

Rhetorical Theory

This book concentrates on a type of communication theory called rhetorical theory. "Rhetoric" is another commonly misused term, often with negative connotations, for example, implying trickery or empty, pretentious language with no substance. Government leaders in challenging situations may be called upon for "action, not rhetoric," (Foss, 2009, p. 3). Actually, "rhetoric" refers to the use of symbols in communication that's crafted to modify the perspective of the receiver, whether by informing or persuading. Symbols can be either verbal or nonverbal, for example, speeches, conversations, essays, comic books, websites, television programs, films, art, music, advertisements, and even clothing are all forms of rhetoric (Foss, 2009, p. 5). Clothing can be rhetorical as costumes in plays help develop a character. Even how you're dressed today carries some expression of your identity, personality, frame of mind, or life situation. If guided by material culture theory, we would conduct a rhetorical analysis to learn what this self-expression could mean.

Rhetorical theories, then, help us make sense of symbolic communication – and also help us use symbolic communication for strategic purposes. Turning the tables, a clothing brand might develop a fashion line that pointedly addresses the fantasies of young professionals.

Methodology

When theory provides a lens into the rhetoric of symbolic communication, we need a map, or a "methodology," to guide us through the process of understanding the symbols and how they operate to propose meaning. This process is called "rhetorical analysis" or "rhetorical criticism." In later chapters, we provide explanations, examples, and exercises that will help you to critically analyze visual material as you look through a lens of theory. Using different ways of seeing visual elements – as telling stories, as comparisons, as fantasies, or as signs – will empower and add value to your professional practice of visual communication.

FOCUS: Visual Rhetoric in Fake Facebook Accounts

Heart of Texas

Among the thousands of Russian-linked ads and images that bombarded Facebook users in the months leading up to the 2016 presidential election was one, the "Heart of Texas," that sought to capitalize on the Texas secessionist movement, according to documents released by Democrats on the US House Intelligence Committee (Moritz, 2018).

The site was well received within the state. "Russians pretended to be Texans – and Texans believed them" according to the *Washington Post* (Michel, 2017). The "Heart of Texas" Russian-controlled account grew to be the most popular Texas secession page on Facebook: one that boasted more followers than the official

---

(Continued)

Texas Democrat and Republican Facebook pages combined. When it was taken down by Facebook in fall 2017, it had a quarter of a million followers.

At one point the page's organizers even managed to stir up its followers into staging an armed, anti-Islamic protest in Houston. This image uploaded days before the 2016 presidential election used inflammatory language and visual rhetoric to incite its followers about the corrupt media, a criminal Hillary Clinton, and "establishment robbers."

Source: The Mike Rothschild.

Rhetoric of the Image

Doctoral student Elizabeth Kaszynski (2017) provides an analysis. In the image, Texas is visually separated from the rest of the continental United States. In the silhouette of Texas, there is a family, in red t-shirts and blue jeans, holding guns. The rest of the continental United States are filled in by rainbow flags in the West and radicalized Islam in the East. The background to these divisions is a faded Texas flag and the shadowed silhouettes of cowboys on horseback, calling out a deeply held affinity for the western character, who is often realized in real life in Texas, due both to the large numbers of cattle farms and stockyards, as well as to culture. The associations indicate a larger disruptive goal, to which Texas could play a part, in assuming that Texans will recognize lesbian, gay, bisexual, transgender, and queer (LGBTQ) and Muslim identities as always already both extreme, and the enemy.

The Texas secession movement calls for aggressive self-defense against imagined or presumed aggressors like the US Federal Government, international terrorists, or campaigns for equal human rights. This aggression, visualized here by the armed Texas family against the rest of the United States, promotes a distrust of government, of democracy, and of civil and civic discourse with fellow citizens.

VISUAL RHETORIC

LO2 Understand visual rhetoric as both an object and a perspective and identify rhetorical actions.

Visual rhetoric refers to the study of visual imagery within communication. The pervasiveness of the visual image today, its impact on contemporary culture, and how it provides access to a range of human experience not always available through words alone all inspired Sonja Foss to develop a theory of visual rhetoric.

Two Meanings of Visual Rhetoric

The term "visual rhetoric" is sometimes used interchangeably between: (i) the object or article itself and (ii) the perspective of studying visual data.

1. **Visual rhetoric as object.** Here, the visual rhetoric might be paintings, sculpture, architecture, advertisements, cartoons, fashion, and so on. However, not every visual object is visual rhetoric. To be considered visual rhetoric, it must have (i) symbolic action, (ii) involve human intervention, and (iii) be presented to an audience for the purpose of communication.

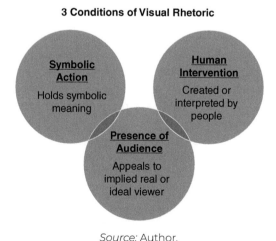

Source: Author.

Take a closer look at each of these characteristics:

- *Symbolic action.* Foss explains, "visual rhetoric, like all communication, is a system of signs" (Foss, 2005, p. 144). In the simplest sense, a sign communicates when it is connected to meaning outside itself. For example, a stop sign is connected to the act of stopping a car while driving. There is no natural relationship between the shape and color of the stop sign and a car stopping. The relationship has been invented by those who regulate traffic. This sign, then, counts as visual rhetoric because it involves arbitrary symbols to make meaning. Just as there is no natural relationship between the length of a nose and the act of lying – the relationship was invented by the author of a children's novel, *Pinocchio.*

- *Human intervention.* Foss explains, "visual rhetoric involves human action of some kind . . . in the process of creation or in the process of interpretation" (p. 144). Humans are engaged in the process of image creation, for example, when they consciously decide how and what to paint or to photograph, deliberating strategies of color, form, media, and size. Another type of visual rhetoric involving people is when visual objects are used as symbols, as in bringing a fir tree into a home to suggest "Christmas," or using an oak tree's image in an ad to suggest longevity.

- *Presence of an audience.* Foss again explains, "visual rhetoric implies an audience and is concerned with an appeal either to a real or an ideal audience" (p. 144). Beyond the possible motive of self-expression, visual rhetoric is created for an audience. The only audience may be the creator alone or it may be others. In either case, the artifact is purposefully produced to communicate. And this communication is symbolic in that the relationship between the image and its meaning is arbitrary – it was created for interpretation, carrying a message that can be received and studied.

2. **Visual rhetoric as perspective.** Here, visual rhetoric refers to the theory that guides analysis of the symbolic and communicative aspects of visual data. To avoid confusion with visual rhetoric as an object, we use the term **visual rhetoric perspective**. This perspective offers a way to view images, to understand how they are suggesting meaning, and to identify the meaning.

   It is a broad perspective that considers visual imagery in its multiple forms, with limitless application on how they might operate symbolically. Later chapters demonstrate the various applications of visual rhetoric through different ways humans make meaning: signs, comparisons, storytelling, fantasies. The key focus is on how the images function rhetorically to evoke a response in the beholder, beyond aesthetic appreciation (enjoying the color or texture, etc.). A rhetorical response, however, attributes meaning to images – inferences of emotions, values, ideas. In this book we will be learning how to better *understand* rhetorical responses to images.

Three Aspects of Visual Images

Foss's visual rhetorical perspective considers three aspects of visual images: (i) nature, (ii) function, and (iii) evaluation.

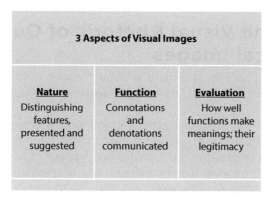

3 Aspects of Visual Images		
Nature	**Function**	**Evaluation**
Distinguishing features, presented and suggested	Connotations and denotations communicated	How well functions make meanings; their legitimacy

Source: Author. © John Wiley & Sons, Inc.

1. **Nature**. An image's "nature" refers to its distinguishing features, of which there are two types: presented elements and suggested elements. Analysis of these elements helps the critic locate the image's meaning likely received by the audience. Let's look at each component:

   - *Presented elements.* Major physical features such as the size of the image, its colors, and the forms featured in the image.

   - *Suggested elements.* Foss (2005, p. 146) explains, ". . . concepts, ideas, themes, and allusions that a viewer is likely to infer." For example, a Brooks Brothers suit might suggest wealth, privilege, and power.

2. **Function.** An image's "function" refers not to the creator's intended or desired effect, as we may not know the creator's intentions. We view the object as independent of the creator's intention; rather, we are interested in what is there for the audience to take away. So, the "function" is the action the image communicates with its elements (Foss, 1994). A painting of New Mexico's majestic Organ Mountains warmed in morning sunlight may serve to remind the viewer of an enjoyable vacation. An ad showing a jeep conquering rugged mountain terrain may encourage the viewer to explore (or at least dream about) a more daring lifestyle.

3. **Evaluation.** An image can be evaluated in different ways: first, evaluate whether it accomplishes the functions suggested by the image itself. How are the denotative (literal) and connotative (suggested) meanings presented in the visual to influence and impact each other? Second, evaluate whether the functions themselves are legitimate based on their implications and consequences: perhaps questioning their ethics or emancipatory potential. For example, if analyzing an ad that uses women in sexually suggestive posturing to sell bathroom fixtures, one might conclude it stereotypes or degrades women.

FOCUS: The Visual Rhetoric of Quirky and Magical Images

Humorous, outlandish, and fantastical visual rhetoric in tourism marketing campaigns has the power to draw people in. Consider these examples:

Travel Oregon, the agency run by the Oregon Tourism Commission, is exemplary of how state tourism earned approving media and consumer attention. During a campaign in 2017, on the landing page of its website, a video panned breathtaking scenery while a deep male voice intoned, "Oregon . . . Vast . . . Pristine . . . Experience it now . . . with a robot fish."

Yes, a robotic, talking salmon tells you about it. In Travel Oregon's goofy and popular campaign, viewers experienced a full 360° view of Oregon's many natural environments and fun activities like dune riding and fly fishing, plus came away with an impression of the state as both spectacular and with a little bit of a comedy too – *Portlandia*-style.

Source: TravelOregon.com

Tourism Ireland used the medieval fantasy *Game of Thrones* television series as a hook to draw people in. The "Doors of Thrones" campaign, a collaboration between Tourism Ireland and HBO, won a gold medal at Cannes Lions, the "Oscars" of the advertising and creative industry. Tourism Ireland's campaign used the visual rhetoric of The Dark Hedges, a 400-year-old tunnel of beech trees that **Game of Thrones** used to represent "Kingsroad." Remnants of battered trees from the road were carved into 10 intricate doors, each resembling one episode from season six of the show. Besides being featured in the media campaign, each door was placed on a pub in Northern Ireland to create a 10-stop bar crawl paying homage to both The Dark Hedges and Northern Ireland's connection to the show. The campaign weaved pop culture into the architecture of local watering holes to create a unique tourist attraction.
Source: Pasotti 2018.

Basics for Analyzing Visual Rhetoric

Any introduction to visual rhetoric would be incomplete without mentioning the classic **Aristotelian triad** – the three means by which communicators persuade – as well as the contributions of French researcher Jacques Durand in testing and developing a **visual rhetoric matrix**.

Ethos, Pathos, Logos

The ancient Greek philosopher, Aristotle, identified three strategies that communicators use to persuasively appeal to their audiences: **ethos**, **logos**, and **pathos** – known as the Aristotelian triad. It is also commonly referred to as the rhetorical triangle of rhetor, message, and audience, and can be extended to the visual:

- *Ethos (trustworthy)*: Credibility of the author
  - *Rhetor*: Form and manner of communication
  - *Visual signifiers*: Well-designed, ethical, high-status implications
- *Logos (logical)*: Use of reasoning
  - *Message*: Communicated ideas; the argument
  - *Visual signifiers*: Unity, balance, evidence
- *Pathos (emotional)*: Force, feelings
  - *Audience*: Appeals to audience's emotion and sympathies
  - *Visual signifiers*: Friendly, pitiful, indignant (or any desired state)

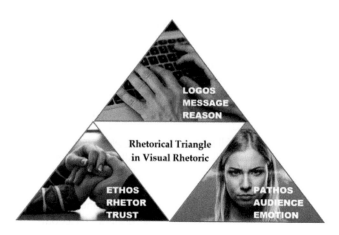

Infographic source:
Author. Image sources: Pathos jpg: Pixabay.
Ethos jpg: Milan_Zokic/iStock/Getty Images.
Logos jpg: Pixabay.

Durand's Visual Rhetoric Matrix

In 1970, Jacques Durand reported on his extensive and systematic study of the use of visual rhetoric in advertising (Zakia, 2013). He showed that not just some, but all of the classical figures of rhetoric can be found in advertising images, and that most of the creative ideas behind the better advertisements can be interpreted as conscious or unconscious transpositions of the classical figures of rhetoric.

Philosopher Roland Barthes was first to propose a method of analyzing advertising images based on rhetorical concepts. Barthes's in-depth analysis of an advertisement led him to outline the foundations of a "rhetoric of the image" in 1964, suggesting that contemporary advertisements make use of the figures described by the ancient rhetoricians, and transpose these in visual terms. He added that this rhetoric could only be established on the basis of a quite considerable inventory (Barthes, 1977).

It is this kind of inventory Durand attempted to study, in fact, several thousand ads. His analysis produced a very useful visual rhetoric matrix for analyzing the composition of an ad, photograph, or any visual statement. It also shows how easily one can alter pictures and words to modify or change meaning.

The visual rhetoric matrix suggests how variations in visual composition – the *operations* of addition, suppression, substitution, and exchange – work to shape an image's meaning in particular directions. Within these operations, *elements* can be used to further alter an image's message in a certain way: elements that are identical, similar, different, opposing, or ambiguous/paradoxical. The result is 16 different rhetorical actions.

While it looks quite complicated, it's meant to offer all possible operations and elements of visual rhetoric. Following the matrix, see examples of visual images. Note we identify a few rhetorical operations/elements not only to understand how meaning is rhetorically constructed, but also to find a basis for understanding their persuasive intent.

Table 3.1 Durand's visual rhetoric matrix.

		Rhetorical operation			
		A. Addition	**B. Suppression**	**C. Substitution**	**D. Exchange**
1.	**Identity**	Repetition	Ellipsis	Hyperbole	Inversion
2.	**Similarity**	Like, yet not identical. An agreement or comparison	Salient features suppressed	Allusion (indirect), impersonation (mimic other's appearance), metaphor (implicit comparison)	Concrete object gives meaning to abstract idea: Symbol
3.	**Difference**	Unordered elements that are propositional	Suspension; resolution delayed; meaning uncertain	Metonym (attribute stands for thing itself; crown = king) Synecdoche (part suggests the whole; red lips = woman)	Fragmentation; without connectors

Table 3.1 (Continued)

| | Rhetorical operation | | | |
	A. Addition	B. Suppression	C. Substitution	D. Exchange
4. Opposition	Anachronism Juxtaposition of contrasts creating surprises, intrigues, irony, satire	Expressions of doubt or reticence	Roundabout expression Euphemism	Impossible situations; illogical sequences; routine order followed by order inversion
5. False homology				
Ambiguity	Repetition that plays off opposition, suggesting double meaning (perception/reality)	Repetition in proximity, but with different meaning	Puns (one or two elements suggesting different meanings; humorous)	Repetition of ideas in inverse order
Paradox	Seeming absurd but possibly true	Feigning a secret; false modesty; slight mention while professing omission; trompe l'oeil	Use of element in sense opposite of its meaning	Contradiction

Source: Author, drawn from Zakia (2013) pp. 302–335.

Applying the Visual Rhetoric Matrix

The internet meme in Figure 3.1 uses the rhetorical operation of *substitution*, replacing a bandit's face with that of President Barack Obama who says, "Birth certificate? I don't need no stinkin' birth certificate!" The caption directly refers to Obama's earlier refusal to provide a copy of his birth certificate. The original meme uses a scene from the popular 1948 film *The Treasure of the Sierra Madre* in which a Mexican bandit terrorizing the countryside and impersonating a federal policeman speaks nearly similar lines, "Badges? I don't have to show you any stinking badges!" It was later widely popularized through parodic use in TV shows, films, cartoons, songs, books, video games, and news stories (probably the most popular being the 1974 film *Blazing Saddles*). So embedded in popular culture, this image's references should immediately evoke humor. Yet a deeper construct through the substitution is *similarity*, the mimicking of appearance through correspondence of traits from one likeness, the bandit, to another, Barack Obama; and from the imitation policeman to the allegedly illegitimate president.

The image in Figure 3.2 appears on The Cult of Kek, a neo-Nazi website. It appropriates the fourteenth-century religious painting by Duccio di Buoninsegna, "Military Parade

Figure 3.1 Internet meme inspired by the 1948 film *The Treasure of the Sierra Madre. Source:* Baloo-Rex May/Cartoon Stock.

Figure 3.2 Cult of Kek image illustrating rhetorical manipulation. *Source:* lifo.gr.

At Campo Di Marte," which features the Virgin Mary and Christ child perched on a gothic throne, flanked by angels and saints. The appropriation manipulates the meme character, Pepe the Frog, which has been classified as a hate symbol by the Anti-Defamation League.

First, meaning is proposed by the rhetorical strategy of *substitution* in which the elements create a relationship of *similarity*. Characters mimic others' appearances through *impersonation*. The Statue of Liberty substitutes for the Virgin Mary and Trump for the Christ child.

Moving away from the center of interest, the Pepe characters substitute for the angels and saints. Here, we also see the rhetorical operation of *addition* evident in a relationship of *repetition*: all the Pepe characters, saintly with halos and respectful gestures. The relationship between the Pepes is also one of *similarity*; they are "like" but not identical, suggesting some agreement. They may represent the relatively homogenous community of white supremacists.

In many religious paintings of Christian architecture, often letters are inscribed on the walls. The letters here require intuitive understandings within the Kek community and appear as "inside" jokes. The letters BTFO and CUCK create a *false homology* or relationship:

echoing the typical Latin parables or Biblical quotes. This rhetorical operation is *substitution* and creates a *paradox*: the use of elements in a sense opposite of their expected meaning. BTFO can mean "blow the f--- out" (landslide victory); CUCK is a derogatory term for a weak, effeminate man.

FOCUS: Visual Rhetoric Glossary

Allusion A covert or implied reference.

Anachronism The use of an image referring to a different period than those in the remainder of the text.

Ellipsis The omission of one or more images in a visual statement which would be needed to express the statement completely.

Euphemism A figure by which a less distasteful visual expression is substituted for one more exactly descriptive of what is intended.

Fragmentation Broken into separate parts.

Inversion Use of images in a sense opposite to their proper meaning.

Homology A similarity often attributable to common origin; a likeness in structure.

Hyperbole A figure of speech consisting in an exaggerated visual statement used to express strong feelings or produce a strong impression and not intended to be taken literally.

Juxtaposition Two things being seen or placed close together with contrasting effect.

Metonymy An attribute is substituted for the thing meant.

Repetition The use of repeated images.

Salient Primary or most important.

Symbol Something that stands for something else.

Paradox A visual statement seemingly self-contradictory or absurd, though possibly well-founded and essentially true.

Propositional Suggestive of something to be considered and accepted.

Pun A humorous suggestion that a visual may have two or more meanings. They may derive from verbal puns or they may be purely visual.

Suspension A figure keeping the listener or reader in a state of uncertainty.

Synecdoche A figure by which a part stands for the whole, or whole for the part.

Trompe l'oeil French for "trick the eye," an art technique that uses realistic imagery to create the illusion of a three-dimensional object.

Source: van Leeuwen (1983).

THE DIFFERENT LENSES OF VISUAL RHETORIC

LO3 Compare four theories useful for conducting visual rhetorical analyses.

In this book, you will use specific rhetorical theories to guide your visual analyses. You will be introduced to and use these theories – theories of signs and symbols, metaphors, storytelling, and imagination – in combination with visual rhetoric. These theories offer unique lenses to guide you through the visual artifacts. In some cases, we will take the position that the visuals tell a reliable or unreliable, story. In other cases, we will see how the visuals tell collective and imaginative fantasies, helping to draw individuals into a cohesive group, and so on. They are all introduced with examples in the following sections.

Sign Language (Semiotic Theory)

Have you heard the song, "Tie A Yellow Ribbon Round The Old Oak Tree"? Written more than four decades ago, in 1973, it became a worldwide hit for Tony Orlando and Dawn. In 2018, *Billboard Magazine* listed it as 43rd in its 100 greatest songs of all time, ahead of The Beatles' "I Want to Hold Your Hand" and Whitney Houston's "I Will Always Love You."

The many meanings of the yellow ribbon help us to understand what we call sign language: semiotics. It's the study of signs and their meanings. It's the first theory we introduce in this book because, within semiotics, anything that is used for human communication is defined as a sign. Semiotics (and visual rhetoric) provide a foundation for your knowledge of visual analysis and visual creation.

In popular culture, the meaning of the yellow ribbon sign has changed over time and circumstance. In the nineteenth century it stood for "remembrance," worn by women to signify their devotion to a husband or loved one serving in the US Cavalry. In the hit song, it stood for "acceptance and a welcoming home" to someone who has done his time, implying prison or military service. During the 1991 Gulf War (operation Desert Storm), yellow ribbons wrapped around trees, posted in store windows, and pinned to clothing signified "support for US troops and the war effort." After 2001, America's long engagement in a war on terror resulted in use of the yellow ribbon with the meaning "we are proud of you." Today, various health-related causes, including bone cancer and obesity, have awareness ribbons that are yellow.

As you can see, the yellow ribbon has multiple meanings, depending on historical or cultural context, and the intent and knowledge of those who engage with it. The yellow ribbon is a sign in semiotics, as is anything that can stand for something else. In Chapter 4 you'll learn about three types of signs: symbol, index, and icon.

What's a **symbol**? Signs that themselves bear no resemblance to the actions, ideas, and objects to which they refer. Green lights mean "go," a thumbs-up gesture means "okay," and alphabetical lines, circles, and curves spelling "spoon" mean a slender stick with a concave shape at one end.

And **index** (or indexical sign) directly connects to what it references: it alludes to it. Examples help to better explain: smoke is an indexical sign of a fire, the circular shatter on glass with a hole in its middle is an indexical sign for a bullet, handprints in wet sand are signs of real (or fake) human hands and thus the past presence of a person.

Finally, an **icon** is a sign having some perceived resemblance with the object it portrays. For example, a clip art tree might represent a real tree and figures on washroom doors usually represent males and females. Souvenirs are often iconic; you may bring home a miniature Eiffel Tower from a trip to Paris.

With semiotic analysis, a method introduced in Chapter 4, you will learn to identify how pictorial signs produce meaning and how to interpret them through cultural knowledge.

Figure 3.3 A semiotic sign can have multiple meanings depending on context. *Source:* Veroush/Shutterstock.com.

Analysis allows you also to detect any inconsistencies or contradictions in the visuals, and to determine if something is presented as "common sense" when it really should be questioned as imposed by some ideology.

Some semiotic signs can be complex. Consider the many possible meanings of Figure 3.3. Pirate? Danger? Poison? Death? A cult or gang? Meaning may change according to context. For example, if this were on a bottle of liquid, the meaning might indicate a warning and possibly lethal danger.

This Means That (Metaphor Theory)

This is an easy one. Or is it? We learned in grammar or high school that the metaphor is a comparison between two unlike things without using the words "like" or "as." Yesterday, the gym was a circus. The quarterback was throwing bombs in the field. David is a real worm. Imagine these are not just written or spoken but are visually presented.

As you read earlier in this chapter, Durand's visual rhetoric matrix is the result of his analysis of thousands of ads. He identifies that the element of similarity in the rhetorical operation of substitution has qualities of: allusion (indirect), impersonation (mimicking another's appearance), and metaphor (implicit comparison). Durand's recognition of metaphor is just one of 16 possible rhetorical actions. Chapter 5, however, takes the simple metaphor and goes beyond simply X = Y to explain how humans *think* metaphorically based on concepts like journeys or spatial orientation.

For example, consider journey conceptual metaphors about love: it's a long and winding road, we hit a dead end, we're at a crossroads, and so on. Now consider these examples of spatial orientation conceptual metaphors: my spirits rose, I'm on top of the situation, he is under my control. Imagine the visual representations.

You'll learn how both verbal and conceptual metaphors can be conveyed visually. It's best to use examples from advertising to introduce visual metaphor. A common use in advertising is surrealism or the violation of some aspect of physical reality, transforming the qualities of one object to another. An anti-smoking ad may feature a hand holding a cigarette in a certain angle, casting a shadow on the wall of a hand holding a gun. Consider this ad from the "Stinky" campaign created for the Health Education Board for Scotland (Figure 3.4), countering the tobacco industry's images of beautiful, sexy women with a visual metaphor. Substituting for her hair is a dense and tangled mass of stained cigarette butts (Messaris, 1997, p. 13).

Figure 3.4 **This ad uses visual metaphor to emphasize the negative qualities of smoking.** *Source:* **Kevin Donlin/Marketing Multipliers.**

Whether in advertising, public relations, marketing, digital or broadcast journalism, or areas of corporate communication, visual metaphors allow you to influence your target audiences. Metaphor analysis gives you the wisdom to be critical consumers of messaging as well as creators of it.

FOCUS: Visual Rhetoric in Activist Campaigns

The 2018 Oscar-winning film *Three Billboards Outside Ebbing, Missouri* resonated with protest groups around the world, who adopted the style of the billboard campaign from the film into their own repertoire. The film tells the story of Mildred, a mother (played by Frances McDormand) who rents three billboards to campaign about the unsolved murder of her daughter.

The film inspired similar campaigns (Jenzen, 2018). Billboards called for a probe into the murder of investigative journalist Daphne Caruana Galizia in Malta and humanitarian organizations used the tactic to press for UN Security Council intervention in the Syrian civil war. Motivated by the school shooting in Parkland, Florida, the guerrilla artists collective INDECLINE vandalized a billboard for the Battlefield Vegas firing range, replacing ".50 caliber" with "school kid":

Source: Ethan Miller/Getty Images News/Getty Images.

These campaigns strive to capitalize on the media coverage of a successful film by linking their off-screen activism to it. But also, the style of billboard protest is something that can be easily replicated and this analog mode of protest communication – the billboard – in an age of digital culture and social media dominance has an unusual appeal.

Activists have been using other Hollywood products as a springboard, appropriating themes of struggle for social justice issues. For example, the 2009 sci-fi blockbuster *Avatar* and its message of eco-activism led to many blue-painted protests, referencing the tall, blue-skinned aliens fighting for their home in the film.

In 2018, demonstrations for women's rights often featured activists dressed in red robes and white bonnets, referencing the television adaptation of Margaret Atwood's *The Handmaid's Tale*. These contemporary protests refer to the drama's dystopian future of patriarchal rule over women and their reproductive rights. The visual impact of these red robes and white bonnets is powerful: the anachronistic dress is stark and simple, the outfits cloak women in blood-red anonymity, but with connotations of a rebellious army in uniform. By simply appearing dressed as handmaids, as some did to attend a legislative debate at the Ohio Statehouse on the removal of abortion rights, the protesters' silent presence itself was a clear communication of their activism, and a ready-made, visually-dramatized image for the press.

It is not just that these campaigns gain some attention through referencing popular culture; they also illustrate how contemporary protest movements combine the visual composition skills typically found in the creative industries, and then carry them into social media with a keen understanding of online modes of expression such as memes and hashtags.

Storytelling (Narrative Paradigm Theory)

People are essentially storytellers. All human communication is story. Life is a series of ongoing narratives with conflicts, characters, beginnings, middles, and ends. And narrative is rhetorical, and thus persuasive, in nature. These are foundational beliefs behind Walter Fisher's Narrative Paradigm Theory (NPT) which is comprehensively detailed by Cragan and Shields (1995). (Note: "paradigm" means universally accepted.) So naturally, as we are constantly telling and hearing stories, we make decisions based on good reasoning: stories we know from history, culture, characters, and our own biographies.

Thus, communication that's believable and acceptable must have the basic elements of story (character, setting, action), and make sense based on our understanding and experiences with past stories. The characters must act in their "setting" in a reliable fashion. In this sense, the story hangs together. The plot must also resonate as truthful and humane, imbued with values and emotions, allowing us to "connect" to it. All the world is a set of stories, and we must choose from them as they constantly recreate our lives.

Our stories take the form of **myths**, often subtle and beneath the surface. Myths are traditional stories that serve as primordial types in a culture's world view. These stories contain beliefs and values that are significant and long-lasting – vital to the mindset of the culture which holds them – and that are widely accepted as being true. In NPT, myths fall into two general categories: materialistic – including individualism, entitlement of abundance, heroic achievement, entrepreneurial spirit, and so on; and moral/idealistic – including family, success of the amateur, harmony, virtue, celebration of community. As myths are told and retold (shown and reshown), they become naturalized and powerful. Myths also contain archetypes: universal symbolic patterns of characters, situations, symbols that are constant in our stories (Campbell, 1988).

With narrative criticism, a method introduced in Chapter 6, you will discover how pictorial stories perform persuasively. Narrative criticism is a respected way of studying visual stories that embody a range of values: enduring beliefs that include character virtues and vices, socially preferable behaviors, and lessons about life. You will understand how to identify and answer questions of narrative "**probability**" (does it hang together?) and "**fidelity**" (does it ring true?).

For example, Home and Garden Television (HGTV) programs, such as *Property Brothers* or *Flea Market Flip*, are best viewed as story (Figure 3.5). We can analyze the pictorial narrative for its believability, asking if the stories are logically consistent with stories we know to be true.

Often, they are deeply embedded, archetypal, situational myths of our culture such as the task, the journey, the ritual, with archetypal characters such as the hero or the sage. Chapter 6 will guide you in conducting a visual analysis to identify rhetorical devices that, through their persuasive nature, are employed to engage viewers and direct sense-making.

Figure 3.5 HGTV programs like *Property Brothers* can be viewed as visual narratives based on archetypal myths. *Source:* MSA/Splash News/Newscom.

Visual Voices (Symbolic Convergence Theory)

Sometimes it's difficult for a group to come to an agreement, right? And sometimes it's not. Ever wonder what the difference is? It could be the structure of your meeting or what's on the agenda. A brainstorming session is likely to deliver some agreed-upon items. A formal meeting consisting of a dominant speaker and listeners may not. What's missing in the latter case can be called "imaginative language."

When you consider group communication through the lens of symbolic convergence theory (SCT), you seek and identify the creative interpretations made by group members of past, future, or outside events. One group member excites another, and then the next, with what SCT calls a "dramatizing" message. Soon there's a lively conversation and a reached agreement.

In Chapter 7, however, we're not talking about verbal speech in group meetings, but rather how visual communication can be imaginative and dramatizing and be a vehicle for group collaboration and consensus. Think of online memes about political figures, celebrities, movies, and even fluffy kittens and cute kids (Figure 3.6) that can take on new meanings. We call these "visual voices." SCT's terminology is more exotic: fantasies, dramas, chains, symbolic cues, sanctioning agents, rhetorical visions.

SCT's method of criticism, fantasy theme analysis, has been used to study communication in many settings and forms from websites to films, advertising, and public relations campaigns. For example, Cragan and Shields (1995), in their classic book,

Figure 3.6 Memes can take on new meanings when altered and shared online.

Symbolic Theories in Applied Communication Research, recount a study using SCT to evaluate components in PR campaigns for three large-city fire departments. One campaign depicted its "giving back to the community" through charity drives, donation baskets, and hosting children for tours. It was judged to serve a standard stereotype of service workers with too much time on their hands: not necessarily the case, but the overall impression it gave. The second campaign communicated the heroic image of the firefighter saving lives and protecting property, judged as proactive and reflecting the emotions and values of its community. The third campaign was devoted to a crisis the department had experienced with an illegal strike and subsequent loss of property. The components of the campaign created a dominant drama for failure, having very negative effects (1995, p. 189).

Another example of practical application: college and university websites are essential for recruiting students. One university used SCT to examine its three most common elements for recruitment: the viewbook, a travel page, and the search-for-majors page. Results found both academics and sports shared the school's dominant vision. Themes of a family environment where learning flourishes, campus friendliness, and an invitation to become connected in some way with sports was evident in all three of the publications, creating a dominant vision that balanced community, academics, and sports (Agozzino, 2008).

FOCUS: Visual Rhetoric Analysis: One Student's Example

Source: Kolle Rebbe GmbH.

What do we know about the image? It is created by Misereor, a nonprofit that benefits war orphans. Its purpose is to raise funds.

What do we see (the literal)? A woman dressed in head covering holding a sleeping infant. The woman is slightly smiling. The colors are soft blues and yellows. A large black bullet hole appears in place of her left eye and multiple smaller bullet holes are scattered on and around her face and head. Large black words in the lower left-hand corner read "War leaves many scars." The word "Misereor" is spelled in smaller white letters. Much smaller white letters are hard to read, but upon close look they ask for donations.

What is the importance of these elements? Why chosen? How do you feel? What do you think? The image, presented with calming colors, depicts the love of a mother for her baby. These elements are contradictory to the apparent violence of the bullet holes. People naturally are more sensitive to violence against women and children, influencing Misereor to use a mother and child. Altogether the elements evoke fear. I feel empathy for the people who go through this in real life.

What is the image's visual message? Its overall goal? Families are being destroyed leaving innocent children. The image's goal is to bring the reality of war to the viewers, making them realize there are innocent victims who need help, and encouraging viewers to donate money. It is achieved through an emphasis on pathos. The words have an impact; however, they are smaller in scale to the image so that they do not distract from the visual's powerful message.

Now, who do you feel is the ideal audience? Anyone globally who is removed from war situations and feel they have a moral responsibility to help.

For further consideration: Would the impact have been the same if the image were smaller and the wording larger?

CHAPTER SUMMARY

You've been introduced to an important way of seeing that will aid your progress throughout the upcoming chapters: the visual rhetoric perspective. For example, the concepts you learned here, such as "presented elements," help to explain concepts in later chapters, for example, icons in semiotics, targets in metaphor, and descriptive content in narratives. And the concept of "suggested elements" helps explain the semiotic index, metaphor's source, and form conventions in narratives. Reviewing Aristotle's triad in relation to the rhetorical triangle gave you a foundation in understanding the logical and emotional requisites of narrative theory. And the visual rhetoric matrix offered tools for interpreting — and using — figurative imagery as you become accomplished consumers and creators of visual messaging.

KEY TERMS

Theory   A set of assumptions used to explain how a process works and to make predictions as to what will result from that process.

Rhetoric   Use of symbols in communication that's crafted to modify the perspective of the receiver, whether by informing or persuading.

Methodology   Specific steps or techniques used to identify, select, process, and analyze information about a topic.

Visual rhetoric perspective   A theory that guides analysis of visual images to understand and identify their meaning.

Aristotelian triad   The three means by which communicators persuade: ethos, logos, pathos (also known as the rhetorical triangle of rhetor, message, and audience).

Visual rhetoric matrix   A schema for analyzing how variations in visual composition work to shape an image's meaning.

Ethos   Trustworthiness; credibility.

Logos   Logic; reasoning.

Pathos   Emotions; force and feelings.

Symbol   A sign that stands for something else; bears no resemblance to its reference.

Index   A sign that shows physical evidence of the concept or object in reference, e.g. a footprint in mud.

Icon   A sign having resemblance with the object it portrays.

Myths   Traditional stories in a culture's world view containing beliefs and values that are significant and long-lasting.

Probability   A story's coherence judged by its internal consistency, how it compares and contrasts to other stories known to be true, and if its characters behave reliably.

Fidelity   A story's truthfulness based on a logic of good reasons: fact, relevance, consequence, consistency, and social value.

PRACTICE ACTIVITIES

1. Using the student analysis of the Misereor image as an example, analyze an award-winning photo from the World Press Photo Contest at https://www.worldpressphoto.org/collection/photocontest/winners/2020/39192/2020-Photo-Contest.

2. Go to a meme generator, choose a popular meme, and create a persuasive visual message by applying at least one of the functions in the visual rhetoric matrix. Create two more versions using different visual rhetoric functions.
3. Working in small groups, do a visual image search online for a cereal box like Kellogg's Frosted Flakes, Trix, or Fruit Loops. Drawing from the lessons in this chapter, do a visual rhetorical analysis of it.

REFERENCES

Agozzino, A. (2008). Recruiting the right class: Analysis of admissions publications. National Communication Association. 21–24 November. San Diego, CA.

Barthes, R. (1977). *Image. Music. Text.* (trans. S. Heath). London: Fontana Press.

Bobbitt, R. and Sullivan, R. (2014). *Developing the Public Relations Campaign.* New York City: Pearson.

Campbell, J. (1988). *The Power of Myth.* New York: Doubleday.

Cragan, J.F. and Shields, D.C. (1995). *Symbolic Theories in Applied Communication Research.* Cresskill, NJ: Hampton Press.

Fiore, F. (2008). Sarah Palin stirs up controversy in the wink of an eye. http://www.latimes.com/world/la-et-wink14-2008oct14-story.html (accessed 4 September 2020).

Foss, S.K. (1994). A rhetorical schema for the evaluation of visual imagery. Communication Studies 45: 213–224.

Foss, S.K. (2005). Theory of visual rhetoric. In: *Handbook of Visual Communication* (eds. K. Smith, S. Moriarty, G. Barbatsis and K. Kenney), 141–152. Mahwah, NJ: Earlbaum.

Foss, S.K. (2009). *Rhetorical Criticism.* Mt. Prospects, IL: Waveland Press.

Grabe, M.E. and Bucy, E.P. (2009). *Image Bite Politics: News and the Visual Framing of Elections.* Cambridge, MA: Oxford University Press.

Griffin, E., Ledbetter, X., and Sparks, G. (2015). *A First Look at Communication Theory.* New York City: McGraw-Hill.

Jenzen, O. (2018). From billboards to Twitter: Activist campaigns capitalising on media buzz. https://themediaonline.co.za/2018/06/from-billboards-to-twitter-activist-campaigns-capitalising-on-media-buzz (accessed 4 September 2020).

Kaszynski, E. (2017). Visual scholars read the fake Russian ads – Part 2. https://www.readingthepictures.org/2017/12/fake-russian-ads-part-2 (accessed 4 September 2020).

Messaris, P. (1997). *Visual Persuasion: The Role of Images in Advertising.* Thousand Oaks, CA: Sage.

Michel, C. (2017). How the Russians pretended to be Texans—and Texans believed them. https://www.washingtonpost.com/news/democracy-post/wp/2017/10/17/how-the-russians-pretended-to-be-texans-and-texans-believed-them/?utm_term=.6737cccd9d2f (accessed 4 September 2020).

Moritz, J.C. (2018). 2016 Russian Facebook ads targeted Texas secessionist movement, documents show. https://www.caller.com/story/news/local/texas/state-bureau/2018/05/10/russian-facebook-ads-targeted-texas-secessionists-democrats-say/598726002 (accessed 4 September 2020).

Pasotti, N. (2018). 5 killer tourism marketing campaigns that make us want to travel. https://trendyminds.com/blog/5-killer-tourism-marketing-campaigns-that-make-us-want-to-travel (accessed 4 September 2020).

Street, J. (2019). What is Donald Trump? Forms of 'Celebrity' in Celebrity Politics. Political Studies Review 17 (1): 3–13.

van Leeuwen, T. (1983). Rhetoric and the advertising image. Australian Journal of Cultural Studies 1 (2): 29–61.

Wheeler, M. (2013). *Celebrity Politics: Image and Identity in Contemporary Political Communications*. Cambridge: Polity Press.

Zakia, R.D. (2013). *Perception and Imaging*. New York City: Focal Press.

PART TWO

Basic Ways of Seeing, Interpreting, and Creating

Chapter 4
Sign Language
Semiotics

The $20 Controversy

Source: El Nuevo Diario.

In the spring of 2016, the US Treasury Department announced that Harriet Tubman, African American former enslaved person and antislavery activist, would displace US President Andrew Jackson on the twenty-dollar bill, and revealed a

Visual Communication: Insights and Strategies, First Edition. Janis Teruggi Page and Margaret Duffy.
© 2022 John Wiley & Sons, Inc. Published 2022 by John Wiley & Sons, Inc.

proposed design. This action brought praise but also ignited a furious debate on the appropriateness of consigning Jackson to the back of the bill. Some critics said that such a move was divisive or was simply a concession to political correctness (Yglesias, 2016).

Tubman escaped slavery and, despite great danger to herself, led hundreds of slaves to freedom as part of the Underground Railroad during the US Civil War. She was a scout and spy for the Union Army as well. The Underground Railroad was, of course, not comprised of real trains, but was a network of activists, both white and black, seeking to abolish slavery and provide passage to freedom for the enslaved (History.com, 2019).

Jackson, the seventh US president, was a notable and controversial military figure and a reformer in his political career. He was also a slave owner who acquired most of his substantial wealth from his 1,000-acre plantation that had enslaved 100–150 people of African descent. He rose from an impoverished childhood to become a war hero and successful lawyer. His legacy, however, is mixed not only because of his slave ownership, but also because under his administration, 15,000 Cherokee tribe members were compelled to leave Georgia and walk for hundreds of miles to designated territories west of Arkansas. This became known as the "Trail of Tears" and thousands of American indigenous people died during the forced march (History.com, 2019).

Why the twenty-dollar bill controversy? We don't tend to think about the visuals on our money – they are taken for granted as "the way things are" – or should be. Most of us think it's normal that virtually all currency features white men from the distant past. Images of women have rarely appeared on any US currency. Many of you may be thinking, "what does any of this matter?" Semiotics answers this question, explaining how we find both *denotative* and *connotative* meanings of signs we see. Denotative meanings are the literal elements: a twenty-dollar bill features numbers identifying its value in purchasing goods and services. Artwork showing its official nature includes the great seal of the United States, elaborate borders, and a serial number. Connotative meanings are messages that are implied or that people infer from images.

Regarding the Harriet Tubman twenty-dollar bill example, an individual may draw a connotative meaning of value (I can buy 20 songs on iTunes). Others may draw connotative meanings of injustice whether they regard the change in images as positive or negative. There is considerable research revealing that images (signs) in entertainment, advertising, and other media affect perceptions of the self and others. An early study of television content (Gerbner, 1972) was among the first showing how minority groups were substantially underrepresented or shown in negative stereotypical ways. The absence of minority and female images and video tends to normalize perceptions of people's "natural" roles in society (The Opportunity Agenda, 2011). The absences of women and minorities in official and unofficial images downplay those groups' visibility in society and reinforces the status quo. Research shows that media content "usually promotes White privilege and the idea that Whites occupy the top of a racial hierarchy wherein Blacks are largely and naturally relegated to the bottom" (Entman and Gross, 2008, p. 97).

The twenty-dollar bill redesign and associated controversy reveals how people interpret signs and draw different connotations from images. For some, the image of Tubman on such an official document evoked pride in the recognition that an African American female hero was finally being recognized for her accomplishments and for overcoming adversity. For others, the proposed "demotion" of Jackson represented a blow to tradition and represented a rebuke to American history. In 2019, Treasury Secretary Mnuchin announced that the design of the bill would be delayed for technical reasons by six years and might not include Tubman (Rappeport, 2020).

Key Learning Objectives

After engaging in this chapter, you'll be able to:

1. Understand the science of semiotics to recognize how elements of communication can be viewed as signs with meanings below the surface.
2. Evaluate the different approaches to semiotic analysis.
3. Recognize signs in the communication professions.
4. Learn how to discover deeper meanings through analysis.

Chapter Overview

In this chapter, you will learn about semiotics, the study of how "signs" communicate within a culture. If you've traveled internationally or even to different regions of your own country, you encounter signs that give you clear directions but you may also find signs that are ambiguous or confusing. Semiotics is a way of understanding all texts (visual images, music, words, fashion, architecture, etc.) as signs with meanings. The meanings may be below the surface and you must work to find them. You'll learn a new vocabulary for discussing semiotic meanings, see how semiotics helps you make sense of visual messaging in the communication professions, and practice both analyzing and creating visual images influenced by semiotics.

SEMIOTICS: THE SCIENCE OF SIGNS WITH MEANINGS

LO1 Understand the science of semiotics to recognize how elements of communication can be viewed as signs with meanings below the surface.

Semiotics is the science of signs and their meanings. We interpret the meanings of signs experientially since they are often commonly used. They are so normal that we don't stop to consider how they may have a preferred intention that leads us to think in certain ways. In fact, these everyday signs can cause us to interpret some phenomena that are quite extraordinary as simply "the way things are."

Source: Stephan Pastis/GoComics/Andrews McMeel Syndication.

What Is a Sign?

It can be a mark, a gesture, a material object, a sound, an event, and so forth, all indicating some meaning. To begin at its simplest function, some signs are surprisingly literal. We should stop our motor vehicles or bikes in the United States when we see an octagonal red traffic sign – it doesn't mean anything else. An "A" on a term paper means superior work. The image of an envelope on an iPhone app means e-mail.

Other signs require deeper cultural awareness. The yellow ribbon (see Chapter 3 for more detail) has had several meanings throughout history, including remembrance, hope, forgiveness, a welcoming, protest, and patriotism, depending on the era and the country. Today the pink ribbon, due to publicity campaigns, is globally recognized for breast cancer awareness. But do you know what a lime green ribbon stands for? Our knowledge on how to interpret signs often comes from personal contexts and experience. With specialized information, we could recognize that the lime ribbon signifies lymphoma.

We take for granted the meaning of many symbols in our everyday lives. Let's consider the more widely recognized stop sign and the pink ribbon, both with well-known meanings, but certainly predetermined by public works departments and advocacy groups. Are their meanings below the surface? Yes, because on the surface one is just a red octagonal shape and the other a simple looped pink ribbon, both void of meaning without prior introduction to the actions or issues they represent. We come to realize their predetermined meaning through interacting with them, whether responding to the signal to stop our car, or choosing to wear a pink ribbon to promote awareness of breast cancer.

These examples lead us into a discussion about signs and the study of semiotics. Semiotics is a way of understanding things in our everyday lives (visual images, music, words, fashion, architecture, etc.) as signs with meanings.

Semiotic Knowledge Expands Visual Awareness

Roland Barthes, an influential French semiotician in the twentieth century, suggested the newspaper photograph is "an object that has been worked on, chosen, composed, constructed, treated according to professional, aesthetic or **ideological** norms which are so many factors of connotation" (Barthes, 1977, p. 19), that is, of implied meaning. A newspaper is a perfect candidate for semiotic analysis as it has visual signs composed linguistically (headlines) and photographically, often along with illustrations and infographics. Those elements are contained and read in the context of a two-page spread or just a single page. The elements communicate not only with the public but create meanings through their placement and relationship, as semiotic analysis explains.

Source: Author.

While printed newspapers are no longer the common way to consume news, they offer an easy-to-grasp format for demonstrating how semiotic meaning is constructed. Consider the following analysis of a university newspaper. Changing reader preferences and new options for getting news have shaken newspapers worldwide, including student newspapers. For instance, *The Maneater*, established in 1955 as the official, independent student news source of the University of Missouri, Columbia, now appears online daily and only produces a printed version one day a week. But for decades, freshly printed papers were stacked daily throughout the campus in the entryways to buildings. On any day, its front page typically followed general newspaper design guidelines: a nameplate at the top, a story of the day headline under the logo, and then news stories determined as worthy of front-page prominence and photos sized by importance.

A Troubling Story on the Front Page

Imagine the visual presentation of the front page on one significant day. It displayed three dominant visuals: (i) the large green *Maneater* nameplate at the top, (ii) the lead headline strongly announcing "Student shot, killed at weekend party" (Schweiger, 2003), and (iii) the page's largest photo featuring four young Black men standing against a stark shadowy background: the closest man with his arm and fist extended in front of him.

Smaller, secondary images included a middle-aged White man carrying a sign reading, "THOU SHALT NOT KILL," a map graph of the killing's location, and a head-on shot of the university's six columns, each 43 ft tall, standing in a row on the Francis Quadrangle. There was also an infographic showing the number of admissions applicants with a ghosted photo of football players in the background.

Due to size and proximity, the signs and associated meanings on this front page proposed a linkage between the student's killing and the four Black men in an ambiguous background (note one is making an aggressive gesture). Within this context, a photo of the iconic University of Missouri columns, typically representing history and tradition, also implied a protective or restrictive barrier, perhaps even evoking prison cell bars.

The small gray type of the news articles fills the gaps between the powerful visuals as the viewer "reads" each visual and connects them with the others. An implied causal relationship arises between the jarring headline and the photo of the Black men (only identified in a small caption as members of a Greek organization performing on stage). *The Maneater* nameplate, too, adds tension in its evocation of a vicious man-eating tiger. Finally, the bottom photo of the columns may predictably just represent the university, but as an end statement to the page's dominant signs, its pride is ironic and its imagery even suggestive of graveyard monuments. When one notes it is aligned with a welcome to new University of Missouri applicants, within the context of this front page the image becomes a paradox.

Thus, the dominant and secondary images on this particular front page suggest not only contradictions within the paper's editorial decision-makers, but perhaps also within the university itself. This way of "reading" the front page of a newspaper is called a "semiotic" reading. We learn about semiotics from various scholars who developed ideas on the meanings of signs.

FOCUS: Perception = Interpretation

Visual composition is often influenced by the theory of **gestalt,** explaining that we perceive meaning by first automatically grouping elements to make sense of the whole. This process can be important in creating and critiquing visual communication, as how we group visual elements leads to determining their semiotic meanings.

The gestalt concept comes from psychologist Max Wertheimer's conclusion in 1910 that the whole is different from the sum of its parts (Zakia, 2013, pp. 26–27). In other words, meaning results from a combination of sensations and not of individual sensations. Consider this poster for the movie *The Ides of March.* What do you see at first? The "whole" looks like one person. However, on closer look, who else do you see? Your first impression is very different from when you stop and analyze the parts. Yet, gestalt theory says that people get meaning from the whole of a set of stimuli rather than any individual stimulus.

Source: Sportsphoto/Alamy Stock Photo.

Many gestalt principles have been identified since Wertheimer's early insight: simplicity, closure, symmetry and order, figure/ground, connectedness, common regions, proximity, continuation, common fate, parallelism, focal points, and similarity. Descriptions with examples can be found at many Internet sites. Let's look more closely at six commonly used principles:

1. *Common fate* causes a viewer to mentally group items that appear to point in the same direction.

2. *Proximity* induces the eye to more closely associate objects that are near to each other more than it does objects that are set apart. We see them as together making some common sense.

3. The *continuation* principle recognizes that the eye prefers directional continuity over sudden or unusual changes in direction.

4. *Similarity* causes the viewer to concentrate on the most stable grouping of things that are similar in various ways (color, size, shape); that is, they appear as a single unit amid disparate shapes. We perceive that there is some relationship or unity among them.

5. *Figure/ground* induces us to look for a dimensionality, a foreground and background, which can be ambiguous in some designs. A frequent example is a white shape (suggesting a footed goblet) that's defined by black areas on either side (suggesting the side profiles of two faces).

6. *Closure* involves content with missing parts: parts that rest within the viewer who is then called to draw upon memory, latent knowledge, or impressions or desires collected from cultural experiences to complete the idea or image. The eye is compelled to complete the image by suggestion of a familiar shape or partially recognizable object, or to try to make sense of a missing element needed to make a picture "whole." A simple example might be a face with a missing mouth, violating everyday reality and summoning the viewer to "see" the mouth and draw conclusions about the meaning of its absence.

Source: Zakia (2013); Soegaard (n.d.).

Question "Common Sense"

The taken for granted realities of everyday life, the way things are, were identified as ideological by scholars of British cultural studies (Burgin, 1982, p. 46), meaning those everyday experiences reinforce a dominant way of thinking. Ideology is generally defined as a body of beliefs and representations that sustain and legitimate current power relationships thus promoting the values and interests of dominant groups within society (Eagleton, 1991, pp. 5–6).

This perspective is also held by semiotic theory: signs steer us to think in certain ways. Several theorists, including Roland Barthes, Ferdinand de Saussure, Umberto Eco, and Charles Sanders Peirce, each suggested analytic methods to understand communication "signs."

Semiotic analysis begins with the recognition that there are no neutral signs; they function to persuade as well as to refer. Yet their intent is often veiled as common sense, the status quo in society. Think about the serious implications of a semiotic perspective: if signs do not merely reflect reality but are involved in constructing and reinforcing it, then those who control the sign systems control the construction of what we know as reality (Chandler, n.d.).

Semiotic analysis, then, questions *how* a visual image works to construct meaning, an accepted "truth." The analyst searches for what is hidden beneath the obvious. This discovery can lead to insights on whose view of reality is being privileged, and what may be challenged. Let's look at another example.

Roland Barthes, French critic and semiotician, considered the cover of a magazine (Figure 4.1) and its built-in meaning shaped by culture, myth, and/or ideology; in other words, by common sense knowledge, historical legend, and/or society's dominant beliefs. His method of semiotic analysis, drawn from Saussure's work, uses the terms **signifier** (visual image) and what's **signified** (its meaning). These elements carry both **denotation** (literal meaning) and **connotation** (meaning that's implied).

Figure 4.1 Barthes's semiotic analysis found this image represented French imperialism. *Source:* IZIS/Paris Match Archive/Getty Images.

A Classic Example

In Barthes's famous book, *Mythologies,* he analyzed the cover of the French magazine, *Paris Match* (Figure 4.1). His analysis is considered a classic example of semiotic analysis. The cover carried a photo of a young black soldier in a French uniform, appearing to salute the French flag. Barthes found it signified Frenchness, militariness, and ethnic difference, but taking these in combination with France's history of colonialism in Africa hidden under the obvious, he identified the image as a sign for French imperialism. Imperialism refers to the social, political, and financial domination of one nation over another less powerful nation.

FOCUS: The Semiotics of Cultural Appropriation

Saussure, the originator of semiotics, said a sign is composed of a signifier (the visual you use to communicate, for example a "thumbs up") and a signified (the meaning of the visual, like "yes" or "I approve"). The meaning of a sign doesn't live in the signifier itself (thumbs up) nor in the signified itself (approval). The *real* sign is the relationship between the two – if no one knows what the hand gesture is trying to signify, it might just be a random hand twitch that's meaningless.

To convey meaning, you need cultural knowledge.

Take the example of dreadlocks, which can be a complex sign. They aren't just hair but may be deeply meaningful hair to a Rastafarian of Jamaica. The dreadlocks are not complete without the meaning they carry, imbued in history. Consider the Confederate flag as another cultural sign – it has a history. Both signs do not exist in themselves without context. When we try to strip away that context, we are trying to break the sign and its meaning. Meanings can be anything from religious devotion, to family links, to lineage, to honor, mourning, and so on. Culture lives in signs. When signs are appropriated, the signifiers (meanings) are removed. Think of Native American cultural images used as sports mascots. When what holds cultural meaning is appropriated for other purposes, the meanings are lost.

Understanding and respecting cultural signs and reading them *in their context* is a moral practice. As ethical communicators, we have an obligation to seek to read signs in their full signification – even the sad, uncomfortable parts, the slavery parts, and all the parts that make us rethink not only our hairstyles and public monuments, but our place in history and our accountability to others.

MEET THE SEMIOTICIANS

LO2 Evaluate the different approaches to semiotic analysis.

Ferdinand de Saussure, a Swiss linguist, is regarded as the founder of semiotics (which he called semiology) along with American philosopher Charles Sanders Peirce (Lester, 2014). As you read earlier in the *Paris Match* example, to Saussure a sign consists of two elements: the "signifier" (the visual image itself) and the "signified" (the meaning it conveys).

Denotation and Connotation

Saussure's conception was enhanced by Roland Barthes, along with British critical cultural theorist Stuart Hall, who more fully defined the terms. The signifier has a denotation function, offering direct, specific, or literal meaning; the signified has a connotation function, having meaning that is subjective, that is, dependent on individual interpretation, biases, and cultural meanings attached to words or visuals.

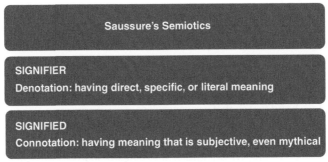

Source: Author. © John Wiley & Sons, Inc.

To further explain denotation and connotation, consider the meaning that spins out from the following example. Picture a tall palm tree against a brilliant blue sky. It denotes a tropical destination (a literal meaning we understand based on our knowledge), but it may also connote a wished-for vacation (triggering a desire we may have), and it becomes mythical when it's taken to mean the essential college spring trip (understood as the ideal and necessary break from school).

Icon, Index, and Symbol

Peirce's semiotics takes a more structured approach to understanding the meaning of signs by categorizing them into three types. Peirce's semiotic triad includes the icon, index, and symbol. An **icon** is a sign that conveys similarities to the object. It is a likeness of an object, or an image denoting the same qualities of the object or shares relations or structures with the object (e.g. a map of a hiking path is a diagram of the path itself). An **index** is a sign that appears to have a factual connection with a missing object (e.g. a handprint in the sand). Although absent, the object is suggested. A **symbol** is a sign that associates with knowledge drawn from interpretation, and not through perceptions of similarity or factual connections. For example, a dancing bear is symbol for the classic American rock band The Grateful Dead.

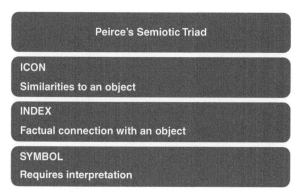

Peirce's Semiotic Triad
ICON Similarities to an object
INDEX Factual connection with an object
SYMBOL Requires interpretation

Source: Author. © John Wiley & Sons, Inc.

Icon

The "Kitchen Sink" is a 40-year-old specialty ice-cream dish at Colonial Café in suburban Chicago. This giant replica (Figure 4.2) is an iconic sign representing its mouthwatering ingredients and actual appearance (although quite enlarged). Without any prior experience at the restaurant, a viewer may understand the meaning of this sign.

Figure 4.2 Example of an iconic sign.

Index

A photo taken in front of a former political prisoner detention center in Santiago, Chile, shows a close-up view of footprints on a sidewalk (Figure 4.3), presenting an indexical sign. Now a public memorial, the footprints suggest a factual connection with those imprisoned there. They also evoke the people who must have walked by, worked, or lived in the neighborhood at the time, and in the context of contemporary Santiago, the passersby who become involved in this puzzle and search for its meaning.

Figure 4.3 Example of indexical sign.

Figure 4.4 Example of symbolic sign. *Source:* http://www.sanalbino.org/1BasCOA.html.

Symbol

While we may recognize elements in Figure 4.4, as a symbolic sign, the meanings require interpretation based on a particular knowledge that goes beyond identifying a bird or a building. If we lived in Mesilla, New Mexico, belonged to the Catholic faith, and attended mass at the Basilica of San Albino, we might recognize its coat of arms. A deeper study of its elements would reveal signification of the Zia Pueblo Indians, the New Mexico state flag, the nearby Organ Mountains, the French ancestry of St. Albinus, and many principles of the Catholic faith.

Social Semiotics Explores "What's Going On?"

Communicative events often reflect the mood, ideas, and beliefs of a place's moment in history. For understanding such events, we turn to "social semiotics." The meanings that arise from specific social settings, at a particular place in time, guide how we interpret visual (and verbal) messaging (Kress and Van Leeuwen, 2006, p. 266). Simply, we pay attention to situational contexts.

What May Lie Beneath Tradition

For example, a social semiotic visual analysis of a university commencement address would certainly study the imagery (the caps, gowns, and staging). But consider the setting: this particular evangelical university has experienced year-long budget cuts, campus demonstrations for lowering tuition, and fast growth of an LGBTQ underground movement. These are specific social circumstances that will guide a critic to better understand the meaning of the ceremony. Maybe some of the attendees' fashions will communicate identities, gestures will reveal political views, or certain props will signify power (or powerlessness).

News Images

The public relations efforts of advocacy and issue campaigns can also provide rich material for social semiotic analysis. One research project considered the online activity of anti-**ACTA** (anti-counterfeiting trade agreement) protesters in Poland (Nowak, 2016). The study used social semiotics to conclude the images appropriated pop culture and counterculture references with the purpose of opposing this attempt at global copyright enforcement. The researcher also found the participants' online posting and sharing were essentially a reconstruction of "piracy." The study concluded that the Internet was depicted as a public "commons" endangered by ACTA.

SIGNS ARE ALL AROUND US

LO3 Recognize signs in the communication professions.

Building your knowledge and understanding of semiotics will allow you to choose, create, or critique images used throughout the communications professions, including marketing, journalism, public relations, advertising, business, government, nonprofit and advocacy work.

Figure 4.5 The Harley visual branding serves to replace, substitute for, or supplement identity. *Source:* ermess/Shutterstock.com.

Marketing and Movies

What do motorcycles and roses have in common? Semiotics will tell you. Consider Harley-Davidson motorcycles. A researcher explored the power of the Harley brand to replace, substitute for, or supplement one's identity (Trendafilov, 2015). Looking at Harley's storytelling process told visually through its ads, he concluded that because this legendary global brand responds to cultural values of freedom, tribal belonging, and nonconformity, its story resonates with customers who find personal meaning, status, and identity within it (Figure 4.5). The imagery in the ads creates this meaning through depictions of camaraderie in group rides, the pleasure and freedom of cruising through majestic landscapes, and clothing that emulates aspects of the motorcycle itself, marking the owner as a powerful and distinct.

In *American Beauty,* a film about a midlife crisis, semiotic analysis finds that recurrent rose imagery carries multiple meanings including sexuality, lust, and death, but also freedom: a freedom to change and experience a "second blooming" (Zauderer, 2015).

FOCUS: Semiotics in Marketing

A Semiotic Retail Strategy for Domino's

Increased consumer mobility has increased demand in carryout service, a practice that experienced huge growth during the Covid-19 virus pandemic that emerged in late 2019. This cultural change has created demand for carryout service that meets consumer needs for pleasure and convenience. Domino's anticipated this need and

---

hired Marketing Semiotics (n.d.), a Chicago-based firm that applies semiotics to strategic brand development, to reinvent the carryout experience at its stores.

Cultural perspectives have significant effects on brands, and conversely, brands impact culture. Brands research and develop cultural codes that influence their physical and visual attributes, as well as their beliefs and values, serving to differentiate them in the marketplace. For example, while we may think two makers of sports apparel may be similar, Nike and Adidas have different cultural values: Nike has competitiveness; Adidas has authenticity (Maden, 2013).

In the case of Domino's, semiotic research identified emergent cultural codes in the out-of-home dining sector that emphasized parallels between food service and entertainment. The result: a design strategy for Domino's based on theater semiotics. Domino's rolled out their "Pizza Theater" concept stores nationwide in 2013. See it at marketingsemiotics.com/portfolio_item/dominos-pizza-theater/. They had indoor seating and a viewing area where customers can watch their pizza being made as well as track their carry-out orders electronically on a lobby screen. Dominos was one of the few restaurant chains that thrived during the pandemic and its advertising emphasized delivery innovations dramatized in still images and video.

Originally, Marketing Semiotics' research provided both a platform for Domino's rebranding and redesign project and created a new service paradigm that incorporates entertainment, visual pleasure, and convenience to carryout service. The strategy also called for integrating the physical and digital spaces of retailing in a multimedia service experience.

News

The choices made by photojournalists and photo editors can reflect an imposition of their values and opinions in what we customarily consider "objective" media. These news images thus are good choices for semiotic analysis. For example, a researcher used semiotics to study two iconic news images of the Iraq War (Dunleavy, 2015). These images had become iconic through their wide distribution, intense public attention, and accepted meaning, thereby allowing them to define the war and its repercussions. However, upon close analysis, Dunleavy found the images, one depicting a hooded Iraqi prisoner being tortured at Abu Ghraib, and the other depicting a tired US Marine, revealed conflicting ideals and helped to perpetuate and reinforce normative values and moral biases of Western society.

Advertising

Today semiotics is an important tool to use with much of our mediated communication, as visual messaging is so widespread and prolific. But for decades, semiotics was mainly applied to advertising, both creation and interpretation. This is because, by nature, ads so outwardly aim to influence through persuasive imagery, with a not-so-evident intent to stimulate desire, fear, self-dissatisfaction, the need to belong, and other motivations, all moving the viewer to say "yes" to the ad's offer. Especially in analysis, semiotics allowed critics to understand how the ad worked, what was happening, and if it was ethical or not.

Semiotics continues to be an excellent tool to understand ads, as a study of Old Spice campaigns reveals. Old Spice is an American brand of male-grooming products manufactured since 1934. Its "Smell Like a Man, Man" campaign, launched in 2010, and its "Smell is Power" campaign, launched in 2012, produced 13 commercials targeting masculine identity construction in young men. One study found the latter relies on men's insecurities, while the former constructs men as patriarchic and masculine objects of female desire (Kluch, 2016).

FOCUS: Semiotics of Visual Appropriation

Since 1984, digital imaging has exploded, not only in electronic cameras but in computer programs that can manipulate images. Widely accessible photo editing software, along with the Internet, provide easy opportunities for changing images and sending them out to friends or to everyone. Manipulating an existing image often results in visual appropriation: the borrowing of a familiar visual reference. Thousands of advertisers effectively use provocative images and video in viral campaigns to gain awareness for diverse brands.

A classic manipulated image appeared in the August 1989 issue of *TV Guide*. Its cover photo featured an image with the head of Oprah Winfrey on the body of 1960s movie star Ann-Margret. Neither woman had been asked permission (Garber, 2012). Likely a stunt to sell its magazines quickly at supermarket checkout lines, *TV Guide* manipulated its cover composition further by perching her on a pile of dollar bills alongside the headline, "Oprah! The Richest Woman on TV?"

Source: iPrima zoom.

Using the interpretant matrix (Table 4.1), we can propose how the creator constructed the cover to connote multiple meanings.

Table 4.1 Interpretant matrix.

Semiotic form	Signifiers	Signifiers
Iconic	Jewelry and fashion	Pile of money
Indexical	On cover of *TV Guide*	Source of wealth unknown
Symbolic	Oprah as starlet	Direct gaze; body position
Meaning	*Celebrity*	*Powerful*

Source: Author. © John Wiley & Sons, Inc.

Public Relations

With communication now widely digitized, semiotics plays a big role in public relations (PR), allowing practitioners to be more creative and more targeted in developing visual communications. Visual components of campaigns can strengthen relationships as publics connect more emotionally to the organization or brand. The key lesson is that meaning is created in the mind of the receiver, as publics decode images according to their own personal, cultural, or social terms of reference. Important to PR, semiotics makes one think about how people use the information that's sent – text, image, color – to construct their own versions of the message. A primary responsibility of PR practitioners is to be aware of the varying publics they reach and their varying reactions to a message. They learn this by conducting research through interviews, focus groups, and linguistic analysis.

Activist Art and Installations

The winning design among 600 entries in *Ad Age's* 2018 global contest for young creatives addressed a highly topical issue: school gun violence. The contest's challenge was to put their creativity toward "good." The design featured an analog clock. At the tip of the hour hand, placed at the 11 o'clock position, is a small child with a backpack. The clock's minute hand follows behind at the 10. This hand is shaped as an automatic weapon resembling an assault rifle. Using a semiotic lens, the two hands are the signifiers. The use of the analog clock versus a digital image heightens the sense of continuous and inexorable movement. With this image, the designer Dany Alberto Sosa Gálvez suggests that time is running out and inevitably more schoolchildren will become victims of gun violence.

The Brady Center to Prevent Gun Violence took its mission directly to Daley Plaza in downtown Chicago with its "Metro Gun Share Program," an installation structured to look like the city's Divvy bike-sharing stations (Figure 4.6). The Brady station holds replicas of AR-15 rifles. As a semiotic sign, it illustrates how easy it is for an ordinary citizen to obtain an assault weapon through the connotation of renting a bike. The meaning is personally relevant to the city with its high incidence of gun violence, but as the imagery spread via media across the United States, its interpretations likely linked its relevance to broader issues.

Figure 4.6 "Metro Gun Share Program" installation in Chicago.

DOING SEMIOTIC ANALYSIS

LO4 Learn how to discover deeper meanings through analysis.

Roland Barthes's method for semiotic analysis is particularly useful for students new to the theory, as it guides you through six steps. Once a visual image is selected, Barthes suggests beginning by clearly listing the meanings of objects in the image that are apparently neutral (e.g. an apple: a fruit). This is what the object denotes; the literal. Then, consider their deeper social and historical meanings (good health, temptation and sin, poison, even New York City). A defining feature of signs is that they stand for or represent other things. Analysis ultimately asks what concepts the composition stands for. It is particularly useful to critically analyze photographic images in that they are typically judged to be the most "realistic." This realism helps to naturalize the underlying symbolic message. The basic questions to ask and answer in semiotic analysis are:

1. Why choose this image to analyze? What is its significance?
2. What are the denoted elements in the sign?
   - What is dominant?
   - What is of secondary importance?
   - What is the significance of the elements?
3. What are the connoted messages?

4. What story does this scene suggest?

5. Does the composition evoke any other images?

6. What conclusions can you now make?

Example Analysis

This semiotic analysis is part of a class assignment completed by one of this book's authors when a graduate student. After some revision, it became part of a research study presented at the annual conference of the Association for Education in Journalism and Mass Communication. Finally, with some helpful reviewer feedback, the study was published in *Visual Communication Quarterly* (Page, 2006).

Introduction

The objectification of women in advertising has a long history. In *The Erotic History of Advertising,* author Tom Reichert (2003) documented 150 years of using sex in American advertising. He noted late nineteenth-century ads for tobacco featuring buxom topless women and early twentieth-century ads for building materials featuring completely naked women, up to more blatant sexual innuendos of the early twenty-first century. In 2016, Badger and Winters, a New York ad agency specializing in female consumers, posted a two-minute video #WomenNotObjects on YouTube. It exposed ads that showed up when Google-searching for the phrase "objectification of women." The video generated nearly two million views in about three months. Its popular critical message resonated with numerous brands that reached out to the agency to share their support for female-empowering messages (Stein, 2016).

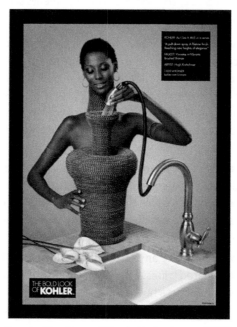

Source: Courtesy of Hugh Kretschmer, ©2021.

1. **Why choose this image to analyze? What is its significance?**
This image is one in a series of four made by surrealist photographer Hugh Kretschmer. It was commissioned by the Kohler Company for the "As I See It" ad campaign promoting high-end plumbing and bath fixtures. Since the campaign began in 1988, the company has chosen globally recognized photographers and artists to create memorable ads supporting its brand positioning, "the bold look of Kohler." The company's mission is to contribute to "a higher level of gracious living for those who are touched by our products and services." Kohler (n.d.) defines gracious living as "marked by qualities of charm, good taste and generosity of spirit. It is further characterized by self-fulfillment and the enhancement of nature." With this mission in mind, this photograph, which appeared in home magazines during 2003 and 2004, was chosen because it seemed to propose not gracious living, but something much more disquieting.

2. **What are the denoted elements in the sign?**
   - *What is dominant?* A woman of African ancestry, in a short "Afro" hair style, appears to be standing naked in a kitchen. Her neck looks unnaturally elongated, encircled with 20 brass chokers. A large brass urn with a tall neck stands in front of her. Her hand holds a pull-down sprayer, its black hose drawing from a tall, arched kitchen faucet.
   - *What is of secondary importance?* She appears to be filling the urn with water. She wears large hooped earrings and bracelets on her upper arms. There is an empty white square sink. Three white laceleaf flowers, with long pink pistils, lie on the gray counter. There is no background.
   - *What is the significance of the elements?* These elements seem purposefully staged to highlight the function of the faucet in (ful)filling the needs of the woman.

3. **What are the connoted messages?** The exotic treatment of the woman suggests the product itself is exotic. The woman appears to become the urn, suggesting she is ancillary or subservient to home products. There are also sexual connotations, as the faucet and hose suggest phallic shapes filling the woman's bronze body/container. The phallic-shaped pistils of the flowers also contribute to the connotation of sexual desire and perhaps satisfaction, as the flowers are intended for the vase.

4. **What story does this scene suggest?** Female viewers of this ad can also receive the "magic" of fulfillment with a Kohler faucet. Magic helps explain the unusual transformation depicted in this story. It presents the classic formula of a spell: there is a special gold vessel, sparkling liquid, and an act of consumption (Williamson, 1987, p. 148).

5. **Does the composition evoke any other images?** It evokes images of African women in male-dominated tribes, wearing heavy neck rings to mark faithfulness to husbands or when seeking a husband.

6. **What conclusions can you now make?** It is far easier to say things with visual images that would be unacceptable in words. With no obvious wording, the ad uses

the female body as an instrument for product desire combined with sexual desire: evidence of our culture's patriarchal ideology that fetishizes the female anatomy and persona and regards women as sexual commodities. Because of the ideological dominance of patriarchy in American society, we find ourselves socialized to reproduce forms of oppression without questioning or opposing it. Ethical evaluation must be made prior to creative strategy and execution to ensure an organization isn't associated with ambiguous or unintended messages that miscommunicate its brand.

Applying Semiotic Analysis in Your Work

This section calls on you to build your analytic and creative skills. You will choose visual artifacts that interest you, analyze them, and then create your own visual messages guided by semiotics to create meaning. While you won't be expected to conduct complex research and analysis, these projects allow you to sample and experience these processes.

REC Challenge: Research – Evaluate – Create

Step One: Research

Choose a single-frame advertisement on which to conduct a semiotic analysis. It should be something you find puzzling, intriguing, or appealing. Now identify the organizational source, or brand source, of the ad and determine its mission/positioning. Some good sources for ads are *Adweek* and the Ad Council, or simply doing a Google image search.

Step Two: Evaluate

Analyze the ad by following the six steps given in semiotic analysis.

1. Why choose this image to analyze? What is its significance?
2. What are the denoted elements in the sign?
   - What is dominant?
   - What is of secondary importance?
   - What is the significance of the elements?
3. What are the connoted messages?
4. What story does this scene suggest?
5. Does the composition evoke any other images?
6. What conclusions can you now make?

Step Three: Create

Based on your discoveries in the research and evaluate stages, use the following creative brief template to write instructions for *new* visual messaging for the ad's organization or brand. Then, follow the brief to produce an ad to promote the product, support organizational identity, or an organizational perspective on the issue.

Produce two deliverables:

1. *Creative brief template:*
   - *Client:*
   - *Project:*
   - *The challenge:* (What is the need?)
   - *The solution:* (How and why will you successfully meet the challenge?)
   - *The audience:* (Who will your messaging target?)
   - *The intention:* (What does the audience need to understand/feel?)
   - *The specifics:* (How should the visual message look and function?)

2. *Executed tactic.* Now follow your brief to create a new visual artifact.

   You may create it in any digital platform, for example Publisher, PowerPoint, Photoshop, InDesign, Word, and so on. Use your own photos or illustrations, or images downloaded from the Creative Commons or a similar copyright-free source. If you choose to use copyrighted images, remember they may only be used for classroom assignments and may not be publicly published (including posting/sharing online).

CHAPTER SUMMARY

While learning how to reveal the meanings of communication signs, you met the significant theorists who contributed to our understanding of semiotics. You also learned about gestalt theory and how groupings of elements in a visual image contribute to meaning. Examples of semiotic analysis showed the broad range of its applications: in news articles, magazine covers, movie posters, advertisements, physical environments, art installations, and even our personal appearances. Finally, you practiced applying semiotic analysis to learn how to be a better critic and to learn how to use semiotics to be a better image creator.

KEY TERMS

Semiotics   The study of how "signs" communicate within a culture

Ideology/Ideological   Ideology is generally defined as a body of beliefs and representations that sustain and legitimate current power relationships thus promoting the values and interests of dominant groups within society.

Gestalt   A concept that the whole is different from the sum of its parts.

Signifier   In semiotics, a visual image.

Signified   In semiotics, the meaning people derive from an image.

Denotation   In semiotics, the literal meaning of a sign.

Connotation   In semiotics, the meaning implied or taken from a sign.

Icon   In semiotics, a sign that has similarities to the object (e.g. a map of a hiking trail).

Index   In semiotics, a sign that has a connection to a missing object (e.g. a footprint in the sand).

Symbol   In semiotics, a sign that associates with knowledge drawn from interpretation.

PRACTICE ACTIVITIES

1. Search for "ads that objectify women" and note the range of products. Why do you think certain products use sexual imagery to sell? What do you think the "signs" mean? Now, search for "ads that objectify men" and draw some comparisons with your first search.

2. Look at your favorite news feeds and choose a news photo that you find particularly compelling. Ask yourself a few sense-making questions: What is going on here? What is the message this image conveys? Is this message supportive of the news story, or does it carry other implications or questions? Can you identify iconic, indexical, or symbolic elements in the visual? Why do you think the photo editor chose this image?

3. The TEASA (technique, effect, audience, symbolize, alternative) structure of semiotic analysis offers five steps. Choose any popular culture image and answer the following:
   1. What is the technique? (visual qualities)
   2. What is the effect? (values suggested by above)
   3. What is the effect on the audience? (how audience likely interprets above)
   4. What else could this symbolize? (other meanings)
   5. Consider an alternative viewpoint (possible oppositional interpretations)

4. Find a web page, news photo, video (keep it short), or any visual message that you find puzzling, intriguing, or appealing. First, identify the organizational source of your visual and determine its mission. Then conduct a semiotic analysis. Based on your analysis, use the creative brief template in this chapter to guide new visual messaging. It may be a redesigned webpage, a news infographic, an ad, or other. It should authentically support an organization's identity or perspective on its problem or opportunity.

REFERENCES

Barthes, R. (1977). *Image, Music, Text*. London: Fontana Press.

Burgin, V. (1982). *Thinking Photography*. London: Macmillan.

Chandler, D. (n.d.). Semiotics for beginners. http://visual-memory.co.uk/daniel/Documents/S4B/?LMCL=KaowtY (accessed September 7, 2020).

Dunleavy, D. (2015). A search for meaning in iconic news images of the Iraq war. *Visual Communication Quarterly* 22 (4): 197–205.

Eagleton, T. (1991). *Ideology: An Introduction*. Brooklyn, NY: Verso.

Entman, R.M. and Gross, K.A. (2008). Race to judgement: Stereotyping media and criminal defendants. *Law and Contemporary Problems* 71 (93): 94–133.

Garber, M. (2012). Oprah's head, Ann-Margaret's body: A brief history of pre-Photoshop fakery. https://www.theatlantic.com/technology/archive/2012/06/

oprahs-head-ann-margarets-body-a-brief-history-of-pre-photoshop-fakery/258369 (accessed September 7, 2020).

Gerbner, G. (1972). Communication and social environment. *Scientific American* 227: 152–160.

Gerbner, G. and Gross, L. (1976). Living with television: The violence profile. *Journal of Communication* 26: 172–198.

History.com editors. (2019). Harriet Tubman. http://www.history.com/topics/black-history/harriet-tubman (accessed September 7, 2020).

Kluch, Y. (2016). "The man your man should be like:" Consumerism, patriarchy and the construction of twenty-first-century masculinities in 2010 and 2012 Old Spice campaigns. *Interactions: Studies in Communication & Culture* 6 (3): 361–377.

Kohler. (n.d.) http://www.corporate.kohler.com/#mission (accessed September 7, 2020).

Kress, G.R. and Van Leeuwen, T. (2006). *Reading Images: The Grammar of Visual Design*. London: Routledge.

Lester, P.M. (2014). *Visual Communication: Images with Messages*, 6. Boston: Wadsworth.

Maden, D. (2013). The concept of brand culture: A qualitative analysis directed to Turkish airlines. *Mediterranean Journal of Social Sciences* 4 (10): 42–49.

Marketing Semiotics. (n.d.). Domino's Pizza Theater. https://marketingsemiotics.com/portfolio_item/dominos-pizza-theater (accessed September 7, 2020).

Nowak, J. (2016). The good, the bad, and the commons: A critical review of popular discourse on piracy and power during anti-ACTA protests. *Journal of Computer-Mediated Communication* 21 (2): 177–194.

Page, J.T. (2006). Myth and photography in advertising: A semiotic analysis. *Visual Communication Quarterly* 13 (Spring): 90–109.

Rappeport, A. (2020). Despite unrest, Treasury Dept. has no plans to speed Tubman to the $20 note. https://www.nytimes.com/2020/06/11/us/politics/treasury-department-harriet-tubman-bill.html (accessed September 7, 2020).

Reichert, T. (2003). *The Erotic History of Advertising*. Amherst, NY: Prometheus Books.

Schweiger, M. (2003). Student shot and killed at weekend party. http://www.themaneater.com/stories/2003/11/18/student-shot-killed-weekend-party (accessed September 7, 2020).

Soegaard, M. (n.d.) The Laws of Figure/Ground, Prägnanz, Closure, and Common Fate – Gestalt Principles (3). https://www.interaction-design.org/literature/article/the-laws-of-figure-ground-praegnanz-closure-and-common-fate-gestalt-principles-3 (accesssed October 4, 2020).

Stein, L. (2016). *#WomenNotObjects ignites crucial advertising industry conversation. Ad Age*, https://adage.com/article/agency-news/womennotobjects-ignites-crucial-ad-industry-conversation/302379 (accessed September 7, 2020).

The Opportunity Agenda. (2011). Media Representations and Impact on the Lives of Black Men and Boys. https://www.racialequitytools.org/resourcefiles/Media-Impact-onLives-of-Black-Men-and-Boys-OppAgenda.pdf (accessed December 24, 2020).

Trendafilov, D. (2015). Chasing the myth: A Harley-Davidson story(telling). *Semiotica* 204: p. 315–339.

Williamson, J. (1987). *Decoding Advertisements: Ideology and Meaning in Advertising.* London: Marion Boyars Publishers.

Yglesias, M. (2016). The controversy over Harriet Tubman, Andrew Jackson, and the $20 bill, explained. *Vox,* April 21. http://www.vox.com/2016/4/21/11477568/20-bill-harriet-tubman-party-alexander-hamilton (accessed May 8, 2016).

Zakia, R.D. (2013). *Perception and Imaging: Photography – A Way of Seeing*, 4. New York, NY: Focal Press.

Zakia, R.D. and Nadin, M. (1987). Semiotics, advertising, and marketing. *Journal of Consumer Marketing* 4 (2): 5–12.

Zauderer, E. (2015). Is a rose is a rose is a rose? Appropriating polysemy in film: The case of rose imagery in *American Beauty. Semiotica* 205: p.191–205.

Chapter 5
This Means That
Metaphor

Life is a Puzzle

Life *can* be puzzling – not knowing where to go in a new place, wondering how you will fit with all the different shapes, sizes, and colors of things you encounter,

Source: https://visualhunt.com

and trying to make sense out of what sometimes seems like a jumbled mess.

Our tendency to make comparisons to aid understanding is common in communication. More than just uttering these similarities or **analogies**, we tend to *think* that way. Our knowledge about the world is largely "metaphoric" – knowing

Visual Communication: Insights and Strategies, First Edition. Janis Teruggi Page and Margaret Duffy.
© 2022 John Wiley & Sons, Inc. Published 2022 by John Wiley & Sons, Inc.

one thing in terms of something else. Metaphors are frequently used in our daily speech, writing, and visual communication.

The identification of a metaphor dates to Aristotle, with the notion that metaphor works through analogy, transferring meaning from one concept to another: "As old age is to life, so is evening to day. Evening may therefore be called, 'the old age of the day', and old age, 'the evening of life'" (Aristotle *Poetics*, in Harmon 2003).

Advertisements often use metaphorical images because visual comparisons can be quickly evident, understood, and accepted. Absolut Vodka ads have a long history of using visual metaphors to suggest a relationship between its vodka and popular or desired lifestyles – often using **imagery** that violates physical reality. The Absolut bottle has taken the shape of a guitar, has been suggested by a spiraling lemon peel, has been represented as an Andy Warhol painting, and has appeared on a man's back as the *only* skin not tattooed – all to evoke tastes, attitudes, identities, and popular culture. Our eternal passion for springtime is captured in one ad in which the Absolut bottle is constructed with wildflowers – a metaphor comparing the scents and sensations of spring with an Absolut recipe for a mixed drink.

Key Learning Objectives

After engaging in this chapter, you'll be able to:

1. Understand the construction of conceptual metaphors and their verbal and visual expressions.
2. Recognize how visual metaphors work in the mediated world: fine arts and entertainment media, news and social media, and the business and strategic communication fields.
3. Develop a proficiency in visual metaphor criticism.

Chapter Overview

This chapter introduces the figurative properties and functions of the metaphor and explains how it is a valuable tool in strategic visual communication due to its facility to express ideas, convey emotions, and engage viewers. First, you will review verbal metaphors and then become familiar with conceptual metaphors: a groundbreaking development in understanding metaphor as a way of thinking and not solely a matter of words. Importantly, you'll learn how both verbal expressions and concepts can be conveyed visually. You'll also build a new vocabulary to accurately discuss, identify, analyze, and create visual metaphors. To strengthen your command of visual metaphor, you'll be guided to identify them in a variety of media we encounter, including fine art, commercial photography, gaming, illustrations, ads, logos, memes, infographics, videos, and book and magazine covers. Examples of metaphor analysis provide illustrations to increase your knowledge and critical abilities. Finally, you'll be challenged to locate and analyze visual metaphors, and then to create your own communication tactics using this powerful visual strategy.

METAPHOR: WHEN *THIS* STANDS FOR *THAT*

LO1 Understand the construction of verbal, conceptual, and visual metaphors

Metaphor: A word or phrase for one thing that is used to refer to another thing in order to show or suggest that they are similar. (Merriam-Webster [www.merriam-webster.com])

Most students learned about metaphor in high school English class while studying the figurative imagery evoked by the wording in poetry or Shakespearean plays. In the poem, "Nature," (Aspiz, 1983) Longfellow compares nature (constant, lovely) to a mother (nurturing, loving). William Shakespeare wrote abundantly in metaphor. Romeo says to Juliet, "Night's candles are burnt out, and jocund day stands tiptoe on the misty mountain tops," comparing dawn with a joyful dancer.

Yet it wasn't until the early twentieth century that metaphor was studied, elaborated, and formalized as a theory – first only concerning word choice (linguistic), but later understood as the way humans think (conceptual). Richards (1965/1936) first introduced an influential definition of metaphor as an aspect of *language* in 1936, developing the **interactive theory of metaphor** (further developed by Black 1962, 1979). The two parts of the metaphor were labeled "tenor" (the topic) – Longfellow's nature – the underlying situation referred to, and "vehicle" (the framing word or phrase) – a mother. Later in the twentieth century, a new understanding of metaphor based on conceptual thoughts, and not words alone, radically changed the study and use of metaphors. This chapter will cover **conceptual metaphor theory** in detail as it is essential to your understanding of how metaphors work visually.

FOCUS: Visual Metaphors Have Dramatic Effects on Your *Own* Creativity

Why are metaphors so compelling? Andrew Tate, a neuroscientist and writer for Canva, the graphic design website, says it likely starts in infancy. The world is ultimately abstract to us when we're young and we must try and convert strange ideas into something more tangible: "putting two and two together" and getting ... well, not always four. But, the act of trying new things, learning what fits, and bootstrapping off those ideas makes us such good learners. Metaphors are ways of taking weird things in the world and relating them to ideas we already understand.

You've likely been told to "think outside the box" when challenged with brainstorming solutions. Many of us are familiar with the "Aha!" moment this brings, when we suddenly get a spark of insight and can solve a problem that's been bugging us. We've seen illustrations of a lightbulb popping on when a new thought comes, illuminating understanding. But consider if imagining a lightbulb came first. A study by Slepian et al. (2010) found that exposure to an illuminating light bulb activates insight, suggesting we are so used to the idea that a bright lightbulb is linked to clever thinking that we cannot help but think smarter when we see one.

Source: Pixabay

Another research team looked at the metaphor "think outside the box" and creative thinking. They literally built a box for their participants to sit either inside or outside of. In the creativity test afterward, the people lucky enough not to get put in the box, but sat outside it, were more creative.

Recent research explored how simple visualizations of metaphors could increase, or decrease, creativity. While taking an online creativity test, some participants saw a neutral image – a fish, for example – in a banner across the top

(Continued)

Metaphor is All Around Us

When Princess Diana tragically died in 1997, her public identity as a combination royal figurehead, fashion model, and pop star triggered global mourning and inspired singer-songwriter Elton John to metaphorically commemorate her as "England's Rose" (Mirzoeff, 1999, p. 231) in his tribute song, "Candle in the Wind".

Every metaphor has a topic – Diana – which is the underlying situation referred to, and a framing word, phrase, or image – England's Rose. Meaning enters in the *interaction* of these two components, and context influences a metaphor's interpretation. In the combining of topic and frame, meaning is transferred from one to the other – enriching, transforming, or constituting and creating understanding.

Nicknames of popular athletes and politicians often use animal, food, or body-related metaphors. For example, the late Mohammed Ali was known as the "Louisville Lip," a nickname connecting the Louisville-born boxer to an outspoken personality. Boxer Jake Lamotta was deemed "Raging Bull," and NFL lineman William Perry the "Refrigerator" (Figure 5.1). In the world of politics, George Washington was known as the "Old Fox," and Richard Nixon as "Iron Butt." One can just imagine the visual interpretations of these nicknames. However, knowing the context of these associations is critical to understanding their meaning. For example, whereas Nixon earned his from long days of studying during law school, Chicago Bear Perry earned his nickname due to his immense size. With such vividly descriptive nicknames making metaphoric comparisons, it's easy to visualize them and even imagine how they might be characterized pictorially.

Conceptual Metaphors

The essence of metaphor is understanding and experiencing one kind of thing in terms of another. (Lakoff and Johnson, 1980, p. 6)

Metaphor, then, isn't only about the words or images we select. Rather, it's how we think. All people naturally and unconsciously think in terms of metaphor; it is pervasive in everyday thought, say George Lakoff and Mark Johnson. With this claim in 1980, the two scholars started a revolution in the study of metaphor by extending its understanding

Figure 5.1 This explicit metaphor conveys William Perry's size as well as a causal interpretation – the handfuls of sausages and turkey leg. *Source: PinClipart.com Inc.*

beyond spoken words. Lakoff and Johnson argue that metaphors construct meaning through tapping into our ideas and concepts; "human thought processes are largely metaphorical" (1980, p. 6). With their introduction of conceptual metaphor theory, the authors established new terminology: **target** (the topic) and **source** (the frame). Today, the word "metaphor" refers to this comparison of ideas or concepts, and the phrase "metaphorical expression" refers to the expressed words or images.

Love Is a Long and Winding Road

Metaphorical concepts structure our understanding of experiences, events, and the actions we perform. "Most concepts are partially understood by other concepts," Lakoff and Johnson explain (p. 56). For example, one might say of a love affair "it's been a long and winding road." This is an ordinary, everyday expression, yet it is readily understood because the concept of love as a journey is a fixed part of how we think.

Table 5.1 Conceptual metaphor example. © John Wiley & Sons, Inc.

Target	Source	Metaphorical expression
Love affair	Type of journey	Is a long and winding road Hit a dead end At a crossroads Turned onto a bumpy road Heading in the same direction

Source: Author.

How else do we think about love? It can be a crazy journey, we can find ourselves at a crossroads, or it can be a dead-end street. Lakoff and Johnson suggest other journey metaphors that people may use in describing their experience in a relationship, such as "bumpy road," or "heading in the same direction" (p. 44) (Table 5.1).

In fact, conceptual metaphors become so embedded in a culture that they become fixed by convention: an unconscious common sense. For example, the conceptual metaphor "argument is war" is reflected through a wide variety of sayings, including, "he shot down all of my arguments," "he attacked every weak point . . .," and "his criticisms were right on target" (Lakoff and Johnson, 1980, p. 4).

Types of Conceptual Metaphors

There are various types of conceptual metaphors. Understanding some of the predominant types – structural, orientational, embodiment, and conduit – will help you analyze, select, or construct meaningful visual metaphors.

Structural

The most common metaphor category is the **structural metaphor** (Table 5.2), in which somewhat complicated and abstract experiences (the target) are understood based on simple, specific experiences (the source). For example, in the metaphor "life is a puzzle," the target "life" is given meaning by the source "puzzle." The selection of the framing source is crucial to the inferred meaning. The metaphor "life is a picnic" presents a different perspective. Likewise, if we describe politics as a game or politics as a witch hunt, we are establishing quite different realities with each. Metaphors are important tools in conveying meaning as they evoke ideas (and visual images) the recipient can easily grasp. Consider the metaphorical potency and the visual imagery in the words of a homeowner fleeing a fast-spreading forest fire, "I was driving through hell."

Table 5.2 Structural metaphor examples. © John Wiley & Sons, Inc.

Target	Source	Metaphorical expression	Possible visual expressions
Life	Challenge	Life is a puzzle	Situations shaped into puzzle pieces
Politics	Game	The candidate is playing hardball	Candidate hurling a ball at challengers
Argument	War	He took aim at my claims	Word graphic in the shape of a gun
Time	Money	I'll invest an hour	Money sack with a symbol of an analog clock

Source: Author

Table 5.3 Conceptual metaphor examples.

Orientation	Framing idea	Metaphorical expression
Up	Happy	My spirits rose
Down	Sad	My spirits sank
Embodiment	**Framing idea**	**Metaphorical expression**
Eyes	Personal perspective	How I see the world
Hands	Learning	Grasping the basics
Ears	Empathy	I hear you
Conduit	**Framing idea**	**Metaphorical expression**
Communication	Sending	Ideas came across clearly
Lack of communication	Blockage	Can't get ideas across

Source: Author

Orientational

Among the other dominant conceptual metaphors – orientational, embodiment, and conduit (Table 5.3) – many of our fundamental ways of thinking are organized in terms of spatial comparisons called **orientational metaphors** (Lakoff and Johnson, 1980, p. 18). Orientational metaphors have to do with direction and positioning in space, for example, *"I'm feeling up today"* ("up" is happy) or *"I'm feeling down today"* ("down" is sad). Other orientational metaphor relationships are inside–outside, front–behind, shallow–deep, center–periphery, and so forth.

Embodiment

Metaphors can also be structured by the features and function of our bodies; from bodily sensations – how the world is physically experienced through our movement and interactions – for example, balance and near–far relationships (Johnson, 1987). These are formally known as **embodiment metaphors**. Studies have found participants lean forward when thinking about the future (*future is ahead*), and those holding heavier clipboards judged the material to be more important (*important is heavy*) (McNerney, 2011).

Conduit

Finally, language (in all its symbolic manifestations) functions to communicate and to transfer thoughts from one person to another. Michael Reddy (1979) conceived of the conduit metaphor, understanding that ideas are objects, expressions are containers for those objects, and communication is the sending of those containers. Examples of the **conduit metaphor** include *getting a message across* and *her feelings came through*. In Table 5.3, try imaging the visual expression of these various conceptual metaphors.

Metaphor's Extended Family

A metaphor is a thing that is like something else, and this representation can take many forms.

Synecdoche

If you don't recognize this term as a figure of speech, you may remember the 2008 film of the same name. *Synecdoche* the movie starred Philip Seymour Hoffman as an ailing theater director who blurred the boundaries between fiction and reality – prompting his cast to act out their lives. As a metaphor, **synecdoche** means the use of a physical part of something to stand for the whole, or less commonly, the use of the whole to stand for a part. An example of the former is the expression "all hands on deck," hands standing for sailors. An example of the latter is "Argentina won the game," Argentina standing for the country's team members.

Metonym

This metaphoric construction uses a close association with a concept – and not a physical part of it. In America, the "Oval Office" refers to the function or position of the president, and not the person of the president or his literal office. Similarly, "Hollywood," when used as a **metonym**, refers to the American film industry and not the Californian city. News coverage is prone to use metonyms, such as referring to the US financial markets as "Wall Street."

Personification

This metaphor is when a physical object or entity is referred to or presented as a person, thereby suggesting human motivations, characteristics, and activities (Lakoff and Johnson, 1980, p. 33). **Personification** can be found in many types of metaphors, all helping audiences make sense of things through human terms. For example, overheard on a shopping trip, "That dress likes you." Or, imagine this metaphor illustrated on a travel blog post, "The forest told me to stay."

Irony

Alanis Morrissett's song "Ironic" may come to mind along with the debate about its meaning. Some conclude it's not about irony, but its title implies it – and that's ironic. **Irony** is a deliberate metaphorical expression that signifies an oppositional meaning – often implying sarcasm or seen as insulting. Certain types of irony exaggerate or understate:

Hyperbole. This literary device is often found in song lyrics. Roberta Flack sang "Killing me softly with his song," which combines the metaphor of "song" as seducer and the hyperbole of "killing" for being overcome with emotion. When a metaphor uses extreme exaggeration, this is use of **hyperbole** – often unrealistic or literally unbelievable – serving to emphasize an implied meaning. It can both praise or scorn. For example, saying "she's a giant in the industry" about someone who is well respected, or "he's a real brain" about a fellow student who's failing statistics.

Litotes. This figure of speech uses diminishment and negativity to gain positive attention toward something, thus the resulting effect is ironic. It usually is the use of double negatives that function to affirm something as positive. For example, "It's not too shabby" and "It wasn't a terrible movie." **Litotes** can be very effective in visual imagery. Consider an early ad introducing the Volkswagen Beetle combining a curiously small car with the negative "Lemon" label. The body copy then explains that only a small blemish on the glove compartment prevented it from passing inspection, not the outstanding quality of its design and function.

Visual Metaphors

The preceding section gave you a good foundation in understanding the concepts *behind* visual metaphors and how they cluster in categories such as structural, orientational, and more. Now that you know of the many avenues available for transferring meaning from one concept to another, this knowledge will help you better recognize how metaphors work visually.

Paul Messaris offers a definition of the visual metaphor, "the representation of an abstract concept through a concrete visual image that bears some analogy to that concept" in his classic text, *Visual Persuasion* (Messaris, 1997, p. 10). According to this definition, a preschool might use the image of an acorn (Figure 5.2) as a visual metaphor for the concept of future magnificence because of the implied comparison between a small seed developing into an oak tree and small children becoming mature and confident students.

Recognition and study of the visual metaphor is relatively recent. Charles Forceville introduced the concept of pictorial (visual) metaphor in his article "Pictorial Metaphor in Advertisements" (Forceville, 1994). He explained how to identify its elements – newly labeled as the "literal" or "primary subject" (target) and the "figurative" or "secondary subject" (source) – and how meaning transfers between them. He noted

Figure 5.2 This visual metaphor suggests the school will nurture children to become strong and wise. *Source:* Pixabay.

elements such as physical, spatial, and size resemblances, as well as other properties, can play a more important role in pictorial metaphors than in verbal ones. Plus, relationships to known imagery, cultural codes, and popular culture references also help to transfer meaning.

FOCUS: Funny . . . and Sometimes Creepy

Visual puns are humorous visuals that have two or more meanings. They've been called metaphors having fun (Moore, 2017). Visual puns reflect something universal about human expression as they appear in so many forms and cultures throughout history. Humor is welcoming, engaging, and often carries messages that would be awkward, slightly disturbing, or less well-received when verbally expressed. Sometimes, however, due to poor design and content choices, they just aren't that funny.

What's Humorous . . . or at Least Clever

Playing on the elegance of the classic perfume, Chanel No 5, Boston's public radio and television station, WGBH-TV Channel 2, created an ad featuring the familiar perfume bottle with the small headline, "For those unforgettable evenings." However, with the bottle's slightly modified label reading "Channel No 2," it created the metaphoric proposal that both the perfume and the station offer a sophisticated evening experience.

For a cover of *WIRED* magazine, to signal a story entitled "How the NSA nearly killed the internet," Christoph Niemann played on finding the visual pattern and similarity between the "at" symbol and a human skull, merging the two, to satirically illustrate the struggles of internet freedom (Levy, 2014).

What's Not So Funny: Some Logos

A rich trove of visual metaphors can be found in organizational logos, as visual brand connotation is essential in this graphic that's used so extensively to support marketing strategy. For example, adjacent to the organization's logo a light bulb signals a new idea, a triangle implies balance, an upward direction promises positive growth or change. Often the design is influenced by gestalt theory (see Chapter 4, pp. 82–83). Gestalt principles explain how people instinctively perceive visual stimuli by automatically grouping elements.

But for every great logo there are plenty of bad ones. Consider IHOP's logo (www.ihop.com) with its skewed face that's more creepy than happy. The logo for Sherwin Williams Paint Store (www.sherwin-williams.com) is a world globe with blood red paint being poured on top of it. The round Pepsi logo has been memefied into a overweight man in various postures, many communicating the harmful effect of drinking it (e.g. https://www.utne.com/arts/new-pepsi-logo-is-a-joke).

(Continued)

The 2012 London Olympics logo was quite controversial and met with criticism and even hatred. Some said it looked like it hit the floor and broke into pieces, but the designers decided to use it anyway. Others called it a dog's dinner of a logo – a slapdash mess (O'Sullivan, 2012). Critics wondered if it was playing up Britain's quirkiness and mild eccentricity, that the country seems to have decided the world finds adorable. Its design firm defended its intention to get away from the formulaic look of previous games, break rules, and make people think about this Olympics in a different way (noting London's brand is also about discovering new dimensions).

Source: Tommy (Louth)/Alamy Stock Photo

Intentional or Not

Visual metaphors often hold cultural common knowledge and are often used, or understood, without consciously thinking of them. For example, the dollar sign ($) is almost universally known in Western cultures as not only the unit of US currency, but frequently as a symbol for wealth or the economy (Bolognesi, 2015). Familiar symbols may also be used deliberately, rather than unconsciously, to invite viewers to take a certain perspective.

Ambiguity

It is important to remember that while visual metaphors can be strongly persuasive, they almost always have an element of ambiguity depending on the viewer

Figure 5.3 Some visual metaphors are ambiguous: Is the United States wealthy or money-driven? *Source:* LHF Graphics/Shutterstock.com.

or audience. Consider the dollar sign again, this time with red, white, and blue colors and the stars and stripes of the American flag (Figure 5.3). For one person this could convey criticism of the United States as driven only by money, but to another person it could be understood as a proud symbol of the country's wealth and power.

Violations

A subcategory of visual metaphor involves a violation of physical reality, such as the print ads for Absolut Vodka that manipulate the form of its bottle. Forms that alter reality create visual metaphors by giving an object attributes outside of its given or known traits. For example, a cloud that takes the shape of a sheep leaping across the sky. Called morphics, Figure 5.4 describes six different types. In moving imagery, the violation of reality can be particularly arresting. Whereas still imagery guides a viewer's understanding with design and content, video adds the magnetism of motion, animating images to propose meaning.

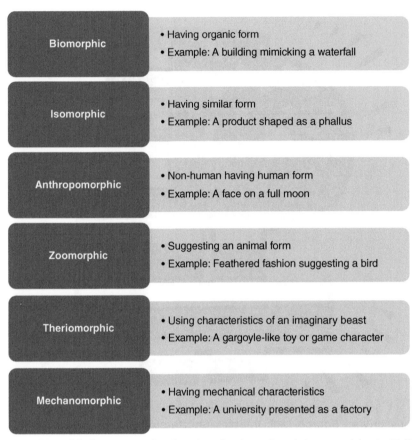

Biomorphic	• Having organic form • Example: A building mimicking a waterfall
Isomorphic	• Having similar form • Example: A product shaped as a phallus
Anthropomorphic	• Non-human having human form • Example: A face on a full moon
Zoomorphic	• Suggesting an animal form • Example: Feathered fashion suggesting a bird
Theriomorphic	• Using characteristics of an imaginary beast • Example: A gargoyle-like toy or game character
Mechanomorphic	• Having mechanical characteristics • Example: A university presented as a factory

Figure 5.4 Morphic forms create visual metaphors by giving an object attributes outside of its given or known traits. *Source:* Zakia (2007, pp. 201–207) and author (examples).

FOCUS: Culture Clash: When Visual Metaphors Can Misfire

You've heard that a picture tells a thousand words, but studying pictorial metaphors reveals how much background knowledge is needed to make sense of, and evaluate, visuals. Commercial print advertising and billboards make for good case studies because their goal is unambiguous: to sell consumer products and services. However, there are some pitfalls found in visual metaphors illustrated by the example below suggesting how they may misfire when interpreted by members from a culture other than the one for which they were designed.

One of the vital questions to ask when using or analyzing a metaphor is what knowledge and background assumptions the targeted audience must draw from to be able to interpret the metaphor, especially in the manner that its sender *wants*.

Source: Alex Howe/AVIA International.

Visual metaphor theorist Charles Forceville (2017) provides an example analysis. Understanding what is going on in this German ad requires quite a bit of background knowledge. We first need to figure out what product is advertised. The picture of the plastic bottle in the right-hand bottom corner and the words "Advanced synthetic motor oil by Avia" provides the answer. But what has this oddly postured horse to do with motor oil? To make sense of the horse, viewers must know that the capacity of motors is measured in terms of "horsepower." The following metonymic chain must thus be recognized: MOTOR OIL (helps function) MOTORS (whose capacity is measured in horsepower, which is visually suggested by) HORSE. But this horse is depicted in an unusual position, looking at and playing with a ball of yarn. Clearly, we're to understand the metaphor HORSE IS CAT. We are helped in the identification of the source domain by the words next to the bottle, "Makes your horses purr." Purring is a sound typically associated with cats, more specifically with *happy* cats. We further must know cats like playing with balls of yarn being dangled above them. Now we are there: HORSE IS CAT means something like "happily playing," which, when applied to the motor, becomes something like "unproblematically running."

While the envisaged audience undoubtedly has no problem going through these interpretation stages, it is important to realize that the central metaphor depends on specific connotations evoked by the cat as primarily a pet. People in cultures and subcultures where the first, or even only, connotation of CAT is "useful for catching mice" or "edibility" may be confused by the metaphor.

VISUAL METAPHOR LESSONS FROM THE MEDIA

LO2 Recognize how visual metaphors work in the mediated world: fine arts and entertainment media, news and social media, and the business and strategic communication fields.

The creative mind works according to metaphors because they help us to understand one idea through another (Gardner, 1993, pp. 23–24). The creative imagination is one of fantasy and playfulness; a combination of the childlike and the adultlike where nonlinear thinking results in new constructs and new solutions. Visual metaphors are both the process and result.

Three Categories of Visual Metaphors

Let's consider our vast world of visual stimuli to see how routinely and frequently visual metaphors enter our lives. The following selection is purposefully diverse to illustrate the widespread use of visual metaphors and is organized into three general categories: metaphors created with **adjacent images**, **unified images**, and **implied images**.

Adjacent Images

In visual metaphors using adjacent images, both the target (primary) image and the source (secondary) image must be presented in some proximity to each other. They may not be superimposed.

Video Gaming. The "life is a journey" conceptual metaphor guides videogames that involve an avatar's movement toward a destination (Kromhout and Forceville, 2013). In one of the games these researchers studied, Half Life 2 (Figure 5.5), the overarching quest is to repel alien invaders from planet Earth. The player must self-propel themself along a physical path through the game, meeting micro movement challenges like overcoming locked doors, and moving from one quest to another.

Unified Images

This type of metaphor blends two different concepts into a single image. It is often found in organizational logos and ads; however, a classic early example is surrealist photographer Man Ray's *Le Violon d'Ingres*.

Artworks. At a glance, the famous photomontage, *Le Violon d'Ingres* (1924) by Man Ray (Figure 5.6), combines the target (woman) and source (a violin's F-holes) into a unified image. Its title provides a hint to Ray's inspiration: the sensuous nudes of Jean-Auguste-Dominique Ingres, the early nineteenth-century neoclassical painter. Ray's inclusion of a headscarf also mimics the turbaned nudes in Ingres's paintings of female servants or concubines in Turkish harems. If one is familiar with Ingres, a

Figure 5.5 In this adjacent metaphor, both the players' avatars and the aliens are shown in proximity to each other. *Source:* WillhelmKranz.

Figure 5.6 This famous Man Ray photomontage presents a unified metaphor; the violin's F-holes are merged with the female model. *Source:* Peter Horree/ Alamy Stock Photo.

possible interpretation might be "Ingres's masterpieces are violins" or even "violins are Ingres's masterpieces" – transferring connotations from one to the other (Carroll, 1994, p. 192). However, without knowledge of Ingres, the interpretation might be "a woman's body is a violin," comparing traits of physical contact, caressing, being cared for or being mastered.

Implied Images

This category of metaphor makes us work a little harder by not showing the source but providing us with clues in the context in which it's presented. For instance, the opening scenes of Cartier jewelry ads show only a sleek leopard in a luxurious, dramatic setting along with the Cartier logo. The viewer thus is intended to infer that Cartier offers exotic, expensive, and thrilling products.

Ads. Most print and moving advertisements function as metaphor due to the historical shift from answering "what does the product do?" to "what does it mean to me?" We find metaphoric propositions that link products to identity or desire. Causal relationships aren't exactly stated, but are implied, for example, connecting drinking Coke to an active lifestyle, or linking eating a Big Mac to happiness.

Coca-Cola Germany's "Together" campaign won a Gold Lion at the 2015 Cannes Lions International Festival of Creativity (Figure 5.7). In the creative process, designers experimented with a series of photographic interpretations of two hands forming the contour of a Coke bottle with a bottle cap on the fingertips. This award-winning ad proposes the metaphor "Coke is Togetherness." It's one of a series using two hands from different people representing various races, religions, and nationalities.

Figure 5.7 The Coke bottle is absent in this implied metaphor. *Source:* Carnyx Group Ltd.

FOCUS: Verizon's "Better Matters" Campaign Showcases Visual Metaphors

"It better work." It's what everyone expects from any product or service every time they use it. That's the message of Verizon's "Better Matters" ad campaign, as "better" is how Verizon differentiates its brand in the marketplace (PR Newswire, 2015).

According to *Adweek,* the campaign's central analogy, illustrated with a series of colorful metaphors in a dozen TV ads from agency Wieden + Kennedy, holds that a higher-quality network leads to a better quality of life, especially when it comes to everyday convenience (Coffee, 2015). It was a challenge to explain dry facts in a way that would resonate, and the varied creative ideas were a huge challenge. Yet, as seen in the following examples, the campaign's theme is impossible to miss: Verizon's network allows for a more unencumbered flow of data than those of its competitors.

In "Scuba", a French instructor compares the flow of wireless data to that of oxygen through a series of tubes. The message is clear: Verizon's product is a "lifeline."

Source: YouTube.

In another spot, an unnamed student admirer of the high school "it" couple, Corey and Samantha, speaks of how Verizon's coverage is as constant and reliable as their relationship. She speaks of how strong and smooth the couple is in similarities to Verizon's network, noting she's never even seen them blink.

A cartoon spot uses the metaphor of humanoids trying to squeeze through a narrow door to explain its "better" network. It answers the question: What good is a door if it doesn't have the capacity to handle large amounts of data? The spot ends showing bodies freely moving through Verizon's "big door."

Comparisons are clear in another ad where "their" hourglass can move data, but slowly; the Verizon version of the hourglass morphs into a wide cylinder that when turned upside down, data literally flows instantly. In another, Verizon

(Continued)

VISUAL METAPHOR CRITICISM

LO3 Develop a proficiency in visual metaphor criticism.

To create and use visual metaphors strategically in professional practice, you should first develop a proficiency in visual metaphor criticism. You need to understand how images are suggesting meaning and to identify that meaning. You must be able to diagnose how the image functions rhetorically to evoke a response in the viewer; a rhetorical response that attributes meaning to the image: inferences of emotions, values, ideas.

There are four steps necessary to analyze and evaluate visual metaphors. For beginners in metaphor analysis, the choice of image is important: Select an image in which you observe some incongruity, strangeness, or inappropriateness between the objects or elements in the composition.

- *Step one.* Examine the image as a whole for a general sense of its dimensions and context. Context is important as the meaning may be influenced by the setting, occasion, intended or ideal audience, and author/creator of the image.

- *Step two.* Identify and sort the elements of the metaphor into topic and frame (for interactive metaphors) or target and source (for conceptual metaphors). Remember, one or the other may not be present, but only implied.

- *Step three.* Draw conclusions to discover an explanation for this visual image. What is the shared connotation or characteristic? Did the metaphor employ widely-known connotations and shared (often popular culture) references? What does the image want you to see, understand, or act upon? You may also consider the potential effect of the visual metaphor on its intended or ideal audience: how the metaphor might have functioned or failed to function in conveying the idea(s) intended.

- *Step four.* Summarize the metaphor(s).

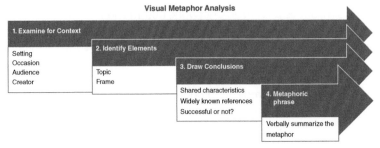

Source: Author.

Example Analysis

During the presidential campaign of 2016, numerous Republican presidential debates took place throughout the fall of 2015. Many media accounts, in both the conservative and liberal press, noted the debates' vitriolic atmosphere and heated moments. This citizen-generated response to the debates is an image-macro meme that circulated online.

In visual metaphor analysis the first task is to choose an image in which you observe some incongruity between the objects or elements in the composition. The incongruity in this image is the scene from Michael Jackson's "Thriller" music video and the written reference, "GOP Debate."

Source: Constance Daire/NEON.

1. *Context.* The context is a popularly-known "Michael Jackson Popcorn Eating" meme, a scene captured from Michael Jackson's 1982 "Thriller" music video. Jackson is eating popcorn with a mesmerized expressed while watching a horror movie in a darkened theater. It both appropriates popular culture ("Thriller") and is itself a piece of popular culture as a well-known meme (see http://knowyourmeme.com/memes/popcorn-gifs).

2. *Elements.* The target (literal) term of the metaphor is not presented pictorially but by the words identifying and characterizing the Republican debate. The source (figurative) element is the scene from "Thriller."

3. *Conclusions.* The visual metaphor is explicit for those who recognize the image as a frame shot from "Thriller," in which Michael Jackson is enjoying a horror movie. The potential effect on the audience is likely one of amusement at the shared connotations. The horror movie genre elicits fear, alarm, and disgust in its audiences, but can also thrill and entertain viewers. The metaphor asks us to understand the Republican debates as horror shows, but with a grotesqueness the public enjoys

as entertainment. The employment of a widely-used meme template reinforces the aspect of an audience watching it, accepting it, enjoying it, and sharing it.

4. *Metaphor(s)*. "The Republican Presidential debates are horror shows" and "The Republican Presidential debates are entertainment."

Applying Visual Metaphor Criticism in Your Work

This section calls on you to build your analytic and creative skills. You will choose visual artifacts that interest you, analyze them, and then create your own visual messages that use metaphors to create meaning. While you won't be expected to conduct complex research and analysis, these projects allow you to sample and experience these processes.

Challenge: Research – Evaluate – Create

Step One: Research

Select a visual image that uses an explicit, obvious metaphor. For your first venture into metaphor criticism, look for a still image and not anything too ambiguous. Some good choices would be an advertisement, a magazine cover or illustration, an editorial cartoon, a book jacket cover, or a movie poster or still.

Next, conduct some general research on the image's subject matter. This may include looking into the current economic state of an industry, societal matters, or political considerations. This background knowledge gives you a better understanding of the literal, primary subject itself and situational contexts. Write a brief summary of your findings.

Try to conclude what knowledge and background assumptions the targeted audience must draw from to be able to interpret the metaphor, especially in the manner that its creator may intend.

Step Two: Evaluate

Analyze your image using the four-step process of visual metaphoric criticism introduced in this chapter.

1. Examine the image as a whole for a general sense of its dimensions and context. Meaning may be influenced by the setting, occasion, intended audience, and author/creator of the image.

2. Sort the elements into target (literal) and source (figurative). Remember, one or the other may not be present, but only implied. If using multiple images, examine the metaphors for patterns.

3. Draw conclusions to discover an explanation for this visual image. What is the shared connotation or characteristic? Did the metaphor employ widely-known connotations and shared (often popular culture) references? What do the images want you to see, understand, or act upon?

4. Summarize the metaphoric expression in words.

Step Three: Create

Drawing from insights gained in steps one and two, plan and create a similar artifact using a *new* visual metaphor strategy. For example, if you chose a car ad that uses an exotic animal to suggest a car's agile and rugged performance, you would create an automotive ad using a visual metaphor *different* from the wild animal in your example, yet still suggesting agility and ruggedness (perhaps an athlete, or a winding mountain road).

Produce two deliverables:

1. *Written plan.* (This explains what will guide your creative work.)

   - *Identify the tactic:* For example, ad, poster, book jacket, and so on.

   - *Identify what's literal:* What is the primary subject of the metaphor?

   - *Identify what's figurative:* What is the secondary subject of the metaphor?

   - *Propose the end meaning:* What are the projected properties?

   - *Identify the ideal audience:* Who will your message target?

   - *Describe the desired response:* What does the audience need to understand/feel?

2. *Executed tactic.* (Now follow your plan to create a new visual artifact.)

   You may create it in any digital platform, for example Publisher, PowerPoint, Photoshop, InDesign, Word, and so on. Use your own photos or illustrations, or images downloaded from the Creative Commons or a similar copyright-free source. If you choose to use copyrighted images, remember they may only be used for classroom assignments and may not be publicly published (including posting/sharing online).

CHAPTER SUMMARY

This chapter introduced metaphor as communication strategy to lend new meaning to routinely understood visual images. It explained how both verbal and visual metaphors work, clarifying the various types of metaphors with illustrations. It then provided an example analysis demonstrating how visual metaphors propose meaning. Here you found that the *context* of the visual metaphor may directly engage some audiences and fail to engage others. A step-by-step method of visual metaphor criticism challenged you to identify, analyze, and then create visual metaphors for specific strategic purposes.

KEY TERMS

Analogy   The comparison of one thing to another in order to provide insight: "life is like a box of chocolates: you never know what you're going to get."

Imagery   Pictorial elements in language or visual expression.

Interactive theory of metaphor   Identification of the two parts of a metaphor: the "tenor" or topic, and the "vehicle," a framing word or phrase.

Conceptual metaphor theory   The theory that all human thought is essentially metaphorical.

Target and source   Terminology in metaphor that identifies "target" as the topic and "source" as the frame. Similar to the terms "tenor" and "vehicle."

Structural metaphor   A type of metaphor where an abstract idea is compared with a simpler and easier to understand action, event, or scene.

Orientational metaphor   A type of metaphor characterized by spatial comparisons: "He was feeling down."

Embodiment metaphor   A type of metaphor that draws on humans' movements: "I grasped his idea."

Conduit metaphor   A type of metaphor that focuses on the transfer of thoughts: "Her feelings came through."

Synecdoche   The use of a physical part of something to stand for the whole: "The patient is in good hands."

Metonym   A figure of speech that uses a close association with a concept: "The pen is mightier than the sword."

Personification   A type of metaphor in which a physical object is portrayed with human characteristics: "That last piece of pie was calling my name."

Irony   A metaphorical expression that signifies an opposite meaning: A person coming in from a violent storm saying "nice weather."

Hyperbole   Extreme exaggeration: "I'm so hungry I could eat a horse."

Litotes   A figure of speech that uses diminishment and negativity to gain positive or differential attention toward something: "He's not the sharpest knife in the drawer."

Adjacent images   Adjacent images, both the target (primary) image and the source (secondary) image must be presented in some proximity: a fast car pictured with a road on fire.

Unified images   This type of metaphor blends two different concepts into a single image. An example would be the "hidden" arrow in the FedEx logo that suggests movement.

Implied images   A category of metaphor doesn't show the source but provides clues in the context in which it's presented: "The con man slithered over to his target" (man as snake).

PRACTICE ACTIVITIES

1. Jump-start your creativity with this fun exercise. Make two stacks of index cards; each card in one stack lists a different animal; each card in the other stack lists a common household object. Students draw one card from each stack, resulting in combinations like a cat and a pair of scissors or a mouse and a pretzel. Then, visually connect the two, creating a humorous metaphor. Example: merge a giraffe's long body with the handle of a fork (Moore, 2017).

2. Often, many local nonprofits haven't invested in a sophisticated logo. In a small group, do a website search to identify a local nonprofit that needs a more effective logo. Discuss how the laws of gestalt and your understanding of visual

metaphor can offer direction for a new, more appropriate logo. Do a quick sketch of your design idea and then explain your design choices in terms of gestalt and metaphor theory.

3. Find a print magazine (often your local library will give away older copies) and tear out five full page ads. Or do a Pinterest search for magazine ads and print five of them. Show a classmate or friend the ads, asking them to organize them by "most appealing" to "least appealing." Then, ask them what made the most appealing ad their top choice, and what made the least appealing ad their bottom choice. Use this insight to guide your suggestions on how to improve the least appealing ad. Incorporate some type of visual metaphor into your solution. You may want to sketch it or even draft a digital design, but a written description will be sufficient. Be sure to explain your choices.

4. Ask a classmate, roommate, or relative which television commercials they "tune out." Once they identify one they *hate* to see, ask them what would make them want to watch it. Use that knowledge to sketch *one frame* from the TV commercial, employing some type of visual metaphor. Explain your process in a short paragraph.

REFERENCES

Aspiz, H. (1983) Longfellow's Nature, The Explicator, 42:1, 22-23, doi: 10.1080/00144940.1983.9939378

Black, M. (1962). *Models and Metaphors*. Ithaca, NY: Cornell University Press.

Black, M. (1979). *More about metaphor*. In: *Metaphor and Thought* (ed. A. Ortony), 19–43. Cambridge, UK: Cambridge University Press.

Bolognesi, M. (2015). Visual metaphors: An academic project. https://www.youtube.com/watch?v=aAaAheCKOng (accessed June 1, 2016).

Carroll, N. (1994). *Visual metaphor*. In: *Aspects of Metaphor* (ed. J. Hintikka), 189–218. The Netherlands: Martinus Nijhoff Publishers.

Coffee, P. (2015). Wieden + Kennedy waxes metaphorical in first full campaign for Verizon. *Adweek*. https://www.adweek.com/brand-marketing/wieden-kennedy-waxes-metaphorical-first-full-campaign-verizon-166791 (accessed September 21, 2020)

Forceville, C. (1994). Pictorial metaphor in advertisements. *Metaphor & Symbolic Activity* 9 (1): 1–29.

Forceville, C. (2017). Visual and multimodal metaphor in advertising: Cultural perspectives. https://www.researchgate.net/publication/317175212_Visual_and_Multimodal_Metaphor_in_Advertising_Cultural_Perspectives (accessed September 22, 2020).

Gardner, H. (1993). *Creating Minds*. New York: Harper Collins.

Harmon, W. (ed.) (2003). *Classic Writings on Poetry*. Poetics. Aristotle, 53. New York, NY: Columbia University Press.

Johnson, M. (1987). *The Body in the Mind*. Chicago: University of Chicago Press.

Kromhout, R. and Forceville, C. (2013). Life is a journey: source-path-goal structure in the videogames "half-life 2," "heavy rain," and "grim fandango.". *Metaphor and the Social World* 3 (1): 100–116.

Lakoff, G. and Johnson, M. (1980). *Metaphors we Live by*. Chicago: University of Chicago Press.

Levy, S. (2014) How the NSA almost killed the internet. WIRED. https://www.wired.com/2014/01/how-the-us-almost-killed-the-internet (accessed September 21, 2020).

McNerney, S. (November 4, 2011). A brief guide to embodied cognition: Why you are not your brain. *Scientific American*. http://blogs.scientificamerican.com/guest-blog/a-brief-guide-to-embodied-cognition-why-you-are-not-your-brain (accessed September 22, 2020).

Messaris, P. (1997). *Visual Persuasion: The Role of Images in Advertising*. Thousand Oaks, CA: Sage.

Mirzoeff, N. (1999). *An Introduction to Visual Culture*. London: Routledge.

Moore, C. (2017). Seriously Funny: Metaphor & the Visual Pun. https://medium.com/@catherineannemoore/metaphor-the-visual-pun-1cd7ec7bd044 (accessed September 21, 2020).

O'Sullivan, F. (2012). Are London's 2012 Logos the worst in Olympic History? https://www.citylab.com/design/2012/04/are-londons-2012-logos-worst-olympic-history/1838 (accessed September 22, 2020).

PR Newswire. (2015). New ad campaign from Verizon highlights why better matters. http://www.prnewswire.com/news-releases/new-ad-campaign-from-verizon-highlights-why-better-matters-300140568.html (accessed September 22, 2020).

Reddy, M.J. (1979). The conduit metaphor – a case of frame conflict in our language about language. In: *Metaphor and Thought* (ed. A. Ortony), 284–324. Cambridge: Cambridge University Press.

Richards, I.A. (1965/1936). *The Philosophy of Rhetoric*. New York: Oxford University Press.

Slepian, M.L., Weisbuch, M., Rutchick, A.M. et al. (2010). Shedding light on insight: priming bright ideas. Journal of Experimental Social Psychology 46 (4): 696–700.

Zakia, R. (2007). *Perception and Imaging: Photography – A Way of Seeing*, 3e. Burlington, MA: Focal Press.

Chapter 6
Storytelling
Visual Narratives

Simple Stories

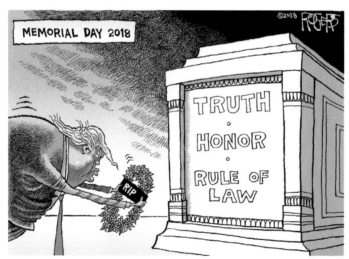

One of the ways people negotiate a chaotic or troubling situation is through humor. Satire, parody, and dark humor help to bring relief from tensions. Cartoons, especially, can

Visual Communication: Insights and Strategies, First Edition. Janis Teruggi Page and Margaret Duffy.
© 2022 John Wiley & Sons, Inc. Published 2022 by John Wiley & Sons, Inc.

quickly communicate across cultures. Wry humor explains the extraordinary popularity of "The Simpsons," winning an Emmy the first year it aired and eventually becoming the longest running comedy on TV. Sometimes, its drawings suggested the faces of celebrities, evoking the art of caricature with exaggerated features. Other times, the tradition of the political cartoon surfaced in situations that commented humorously on political issues.

The political cartoon has often been used to represent and garner attention to the general issues, important events, and political figures in society. In eighteenth-century America, political cartoons were one of the first forms of political satire, often used to criticize English rule in the colonies, appearing in the printed press or as wall posters.

Although not meant to be literal representations of politicians or issues, these cartoons are a vehicle for the creator's opinions, meant to work as a critique by exaggerating and distorting the individual or event. By emphasizing some features or characteristics over others, they aim to lead the viewer to certain conclusions. Political cartoons have used buzzwords and depictions to clearly express an underlying meaning of a topical event or issue. Caricatures, metaphors, and humor appeal to and engage an audience often using popular culture as a frame of reference. The use of known cultural references particularly strengthens the influence and believability of the messages.

In the political cartoon "Memorial Day 2018," cartoonist Rob Rogers uses satire and dark humor to suggest the death of truth, honor, and rule of law during the Trump administration. This was a time when immigration issues had moved squarely into the political scene. As a matter of policy, the US government was separating families who sought asylum in the United States by crossing the Mexican–US border illegally. Children were taken from their parent(s), labeled "unaccompanied minors," and sent to government custody or foster care. The parents often were labeled criminals and sent to jail. When this cartoon appeared, nearly 2,000 children had been separated from their parents in just the past six weeks.

This single-frame image uses allusions to the past and present, along with dark humor, to visually present the elements of story: character, plot, and setting. The setting alludes to the Tomb of the Unknown Soldier where the US president traditionally places a wreath to honor the sacrifice of America's veterans. Another setting is also established outside the cartoon's frame: an America that's engaged in an immigration battle on its southern border. This setting is evoked by the words on the monument "Truth, Honor, Rule of Law:" founding principles of the United States that many critics felt were disparaged by Trump's immigration policy.

The plot is constructed by his action of placing the wreath, proposing he has an approving role in the abandonment of these values. The Trump caricature depicts a cynical purpose through its sneering mouth and closed eyelids. With Trump as the dominant character in this setting and plot, the cartoonist subverted the meaning of this annual ritual: America's values have died. Viewers may accept or reject the message and representation of the president, but in either case, the cartoon

quickly and efficiently communicates a specific perspective.
(Thanks to University of Illinois-Chicago undergraduate student
Sydney Richardson for contributing to this analysis.)

Key Learning Objectives

After engaging in this chapter, you'll be able to:

1. Understand human communication as storytelling.
2. Recognize how visuals construct narratives.
3. Learn how to analyze and create visual narratives for professional communication

Chapter Overview

In this chapter, we introduce and explain the narrative paradigm that sees human beings primarily as storytelling creatures. Through stories and dramas we make sense of the world, assign meanings to people's actions, identify heroes and villains, and share experiences and emotions. When viewing all human communication as story, we can use the method of narrative criticism to evaluate if news, advertising, political speech, and other communication forms are believable or not, discern their guiding values, and discover their relationship to myths and archetypes. You then extend your knowledge of narrative theory to visual messaging, taught through examples and exercises.

PEOPLE ARE STORYTELLERS

LO1 Understand human communication as storytelling.

All forms of human communication are best viewed as story.

(Fisher, 1987, p. xi)

People tell stories across the globe. Throughout history and in every culture, stories instruct, they teach moral lessons, they bring people together, they provide inspiration, and so on (Figure 6.1).

Narrative – a story with a setting, characters, and some plot either visible or imagined, in a sequence of represented or suggested images – is a powerful way that we commonly make sense of the world (Foss, 1994). Anthropologists look at a culture's storytelling to help them understand what the culture's values are and what guides behavior. The fields of psychiatry and literary studies both recognize the sensemaking capacity of narrative, particularly seen through visual images.

Look Below the Surface

Stories often have both a surface structure and a deep structure. For example, in the novel *Moby–Dick; or The Whale* (Melville, 1851), the surface structure is a story of an obsessed ship's captain's pursuit of a white whale (Figure 6.1). But in its deep structure the narrative represents power and the struggle against evil.

Figure 6.1 Moby Dick: In its deep structure lies a power struggle with evil.
Source: ratpack2/123RF.

Looking for the deep structure of stories also reminds us to ask questions about fact versus fiction. Consider the commonly told biblical story of Adam and Eve in the Garden of Eden, losing paradise for eating an apple from the tree of knowledge. However, did Eve really pick an apple? Was there even an apple in the biblical story? No, only the term "forbidden fruit." Yet this is a powerful story and a powerful image depicted in art throughout the ages. Does it matter that it may not be true but just a moral story teaching a lesson? It's important to keep in mind that stories do not always report actual events but often are ways to communicate meaning, values, and ideologies.

Interesting stories have tension. Mother has baby boy, mother loses baby boy, mother gets baby boy back. Plots create different kinds of disturbances that lead to a feeling of uncertainty. This is one of the most popular techniques of drama: engaging audiences to seek some equilibrium in a final resolution. Can you see this dynamic in your engagement with marketing or advertising stories? Do they tease or puzzle you, trigger your involvement to solve the mystery, complete the puzzle, or discover the solution to a perplexing situation? For example, an ad will often pose a problem and then reveal the solution in a dramatic, moving, or funny way. A mortgage company shows a couple frustrated and confused by the tangle of paperwork, regulations, and choices they're faced with. The ad's conclusion shows someone literally cutting through the clutter.

Urban legends, on the other hand, are stories that are not true but are told as if they were true: through jokes, sayings, gossip, rumors, folklore, and more, giving them false credibility. In their popular book *Made to Stick: Why Some Ideas Survive and Others Die*, Chip and Dan Heath (Heath and Heath, 2007) use the example of the Kidney Heist tale as a story that "sticks," meaning we can visualize it, remember it, and retell it later. And if we believe it's true, it might change our behavior. The story goes like this: a business traveler is slipped a mickey at a bar by a young woman he meets, and the next thing he knows he's lying in a hotel bathtub, his body submerged in ice. A note on a nearby cellphone reads, "Don't move. Call 911." Upon learning of his situation, the 911 operator asks him to slowly and carefully check for a tube protruding out of his lower back. There was. The operator replies, "Sir, don't panic, but one of your kidneys has been harvested. There's a ring of organ thieves operating in this city, and they got to you. Paramedics are on their way. Don't move until they arrive" (p. 4).

Sean Hall (2012) explains urban legends exist for a purpose: to communicate some type of moral to others in a simple, transferable, and memorable form. As critical consumers of communication, we need to be wary and not be taken in by urban legends, nor misled by fiction instead of fact. And as creators of ethical communication, we need to be wary of using false stories to appeal to people's vulnerabilities.

As evidenced with these examples and likely your own experiences, storytelling – or narratives – are *rhetorical*; rhetoric being the art of communicating influence (Gronbeck, 1998). The next section explains an important theory on how narratives are constructed and how they work.

Narrative Paradigm Theory

A foundational way of understanding communication was developed in the 1970s by sociologist and philosopher Walter Fisher. He conceived the narrative paradigm theory (NPT) as a broad communication theory that views human communication through a narrative lens. NPT has five assumptions (Table 6.1) which can be summed up in this statement: *We engage in the world through storytelling and we have a natural capacity to both logically evaluate and symbolically interpret these stories.*

To further explain, NPT argues that all human communication is narrative, that no human communication is purely descriptive, and that it is embedded with both rational elements and values. Thus, humans use both logical reasons as well as value – laden reasons to evaluate communication. Fisher termed this cooperative state **narrative rationality**, a capacity that humans inherently possess, allowing them to tell good from bad stories, moral from immoral stories, and acceptable from unacceptable stories (Cragan and Shields, 1998).

Table 6.1 The five assumptions of narrative paradigm theory (NPT) (Fisher, 1973). © John Wiley & Sons, Inc.

NPT has five assumptions
• All humans are storytellers
• All human communication is best viewed as a story
• Through communication, humans use "good reasons," supported by values, for believing or acting
• Humans naturally possess a narrative logic (or rationality) that they use to judge communication
• Humans create and recreate reality through the telling and retelling of stories

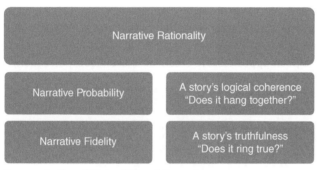

Source: Author. © John Wiley & Sons, Inc.

A person arrives at narrative rationality through two main avenues of evaluation. Fisher calls these evaluative concepts **narrative probability**, concerning a story's logical coherence, and **narrative fidelity**, concerning the story's truthfulness.

To review, NPT says human communication is narrative, rhetorical, and thus persuasive in nature. It's important to understand how it is *rhetorical* and how that affects our understanding. Rhetoric concerns the force or power delivered by a communicative object, symbol or performance: the ways in which it affects the beliefs, attitudes, values, perceptual orientations, and behaviors of its consumers. As defined earlier, rhetoric's nature is to influence.

Fisher's recognition of narrative's rhetorical force is important in the analysis of visual communication. It is common in narrative criticism that **form** – *how* content is presented – is the dominant rhetorical feature. Burke suggested that meaning-making is grounded in audience-oriented form rather than subject-oriented content (Gronbeck, 1997, p. 361). The rhetorical critic must explore not just words, but all the properties of pictures, to unearth how communication is influential (Gronbeck, 1998, p. 126; Mitchell, 1994).

Myths and Archetypes

Fisher stressed that "human communication in all of its forms is imbued with myth . . . arising in metaphor, values, gestures" (Fisher, 1987, p. 19). Myths with archetypal elements, along with symbolic imagery, metaphors, and other tropes, factor into how stories make sense to us.

Myths

Myths are public dreams.

(Campbell, 1988)

Myths are recurring stories containing beliefs and values that are significant, long-lasting, and widely accepted as being true within a culture (Figure 6.2). Our values do not come ready-made, but rather are cultivated through history and experience (Mumford, 1946). Value-laden myths function to provide meaning, identity, and a comprehensive understandable image of the world (Fisher, 1973, p. 161). Myths also provide a constant source of speculation and motivation to seek and achieve the ideal, for example, that a life of moral virtue will bring rewards. Yet in reality, we live our lives somewhere between two polar opposites. We dream of unattainable perfection, but we have

Figure 6.2 This map, by social realist artist William Gropper, was created to showcase the diversity of national myths and folk lore and was distributed abroad by the US Department of State starting in 1946 (Onion, 2013). *Source:* Library of Congress, Prints & Photographs Division. Reproduction number LC-DIG-ppm-sca-58859 (digital file from original item), LC-DIG-ppmsca-61134 (digital file from original item), LC-DIG-ppmsca-61135 (digital files from original booklet).

nightmares of complete failure. Myth is a projection of a vision of human fulfillment – an ideal – along with the obstacles to it (White, 1978, p. 175).

As myths are told and retold (or shown and reshown), they become naturalized and powerful (Nachbar and Lause, 1992; Storey, 1993). Barthes (1977) labeled the symbolic codes represented in myths as ideologies; they are mythic in the sense of having the appearance of being "natural" or "common sense" so that they are not questioned. "A given culture is only as strong as its power to convince its least dedicated member that its fictions are truths," writes White (1978, p. 153), which means a culture that embraces its myths is dynamic, not stagnant.

Through his research, Fisher discovered that deep structure myths run through *any* story. That is, each story is set in the context of larger, more encompassing stories. In fact, Fisher contends that all stories in American culture flow from two value-laden master myths: the idealistic/moralistic and the materialistic (Fisher, 1987, pp. 148–149), which Fisher labels the story's **master analogue**:

- The **idealistic/moralistic myth** is one of brotherhood. It values human equality, tolerance, charity, trustworthiness, community celebration, love, justice, and compassion.

- The **materialistic myth** is one of individual success. It values entitlement, individualism, heroic achievement, persistence, initiative, self-reliance, pleasure, the entrepreneurial spirit, and success.

This structuralist approach to narrative echoes the writings of semiotician Roland Barthes, who found common myths in the deep structure of stories, often with binary oppositions. In the West, the oppositions of culture/nature are transformed into indoors/outdoors, order/unruliness, attractive/unattractive, and us/them (Fiske, 1987). Within this dichotomy, the purpose of myths is to magically resolve the world's problems and contradictions. Lévi-Strauss (1974) observed that mythical thought always progresses from the awareness of oppositions toward their resolution. Mythic stories abound in popular culture film, television, and advertising, for example, myths of rags-to-riches, civilization against savage wilderness, and love conquers all. These familiar themes attempt to pacify us within the reality of an uncertain world. In fact, the characteristics of myths are at times dynamic, constantly changing and updating themselves.

FOCUS: Storytelling with Color

To use color strategically, storytellers must evaluate the impact colors have on specific audiences and within specific situations. Consider color schemes chosen by popular brands with known target markets. McDonald's uses high-energy colors like red and yellow, appealing to children yet also creating a sense of urgency. Starbucks's primary color is green, promoting a sense of relaxation in its stores and an eco-friendly mission in its sourcing and packaging. A Shutterstock (2015) analysis

(Continued)

shows how eight of the most basic colors have different meanings in the United States and beyond:

- *Blue* is considered the safest color choice anywhere, since it has many positive associations. In North America and Europe, blue represents trust, security, and authority, and is considered to be soothing and peaceful. But it can also represent depression, loneliness, and sadness (hence having "the blues").

- *Purple* is often associated with royalty, wealth, spirituality, and nobility. It is also symbolic of piety and faith, and sometimes mourning.

- *Green* represents luck, nature, freshness, spring, environmental awareness, wealth, inexperience, and jealousy (the "green-eyed monster") in Western countries. In the Middle East green represents fertility, luck, and wealth, and it's considered the traditional color of Islam.

- *Red* symbolizes excitement, energy, passion, action, love, and danger in Western cultures. In Asian cultures red is a very important color – it symbolizes good luck, joy, prosperity, celebration, happiness, and a long life.

- *Orange* represents autumn, warmth, and visibility in Western cultures. In Eastern cultures it symbolizes love, happiness, humility; Buddhist monks' robes are often orange.

- *Yellow* is associated with happiness, cheeriness, optimism, warmth (as the color of sunlight), joy, and hope in Western cultures. It also can signify caution and cowardice.

- *White* symbolizes purity, elegance, peace, and cleanliness in Western cultures; of course, brides traditionally wear white dresses at their weddings. But in China, Korea, and some other Asian countries, white represents death, mourning, and bad luck, and is traditionally worn at funerals.

- *Black,* in many cultures, symbolizes sophistication and formality, but it also represents death, evil, mourning, magic, fierceness, illness, bad luck, and mystery.

Source: Symbolism of colors and color meanings around the world. Retrieved from: https://www.shutterstock.com/blog/color-symbolism-and-meanings-around-the-world. Shutterstock, Inc.

Archetypes

The word **archetype** has its roots in the ancient Greek words "arhein" meaning original or old, and "typos" meaning pattern, model, or type. Thus, archetype means original pattern. Psychologist Carl Gustav Jung used the concept of archetype in his theory of the human psyche. He believed that universal mythic characters – archetypes – reside within the collective unconscious of people all over the world. Archetypes represent fundamental human motifs of our experience as we evolved. Consequently, they are recognized, identified with, and evoke deep emotions.

Archetypes are more than just characters; they are recurring images, story patterns, character types, ideas, or symbols found in myths. They evoke strong associations to the reader/observer. An archetype may be a culturally shared idea or a constant and universal idea. Archetypal elements and myths are the basic building blocks of stories that their creators use to create a world to which audiences can escape.

There are three types of archetypes: situational, symbolic, and character. Situational archetypes include a given experience that a hero or character must endure to move from one place in life to the next. Actions and events help create this plot. Symbolic archetypes serve as a representation of a specific person, act, deed, place, or conflict. Character archetypes have their own set of values, meanings, and personality types. Brands can be understood via the archetypes they embody. Marketing research firm Vision One (n.d.) and The Hartford (n.d.) offer some insights:

FOCUS: Character Archetypes

- *Innocent.* **Faithful and optimistic. Other words for innocent would be utopian, traditionalist, naïve, moral, romantic, loyal, and dreamer, but may risk being a little too naïve. The innocent strives to do the right thing and pursues happiness. Brand and business examples: The Honest Company, Annie's Homegrown, Coca-Cola, Dove.**

- *Everyperson.* **Solid citizen, good neighbor, honest, hardworking. The everyperson is empathetic, unpretentious, and down-to-earth. They strive to connect with others and seek a sense of belonging, but may risk losing self in efforts to blend in. Brand and business examples: Habitat for Humanity, Folgers, Craigslist, TOMS Shoes.**

- *Hero.* **Warrior, crusader, rescuer, soldier, winner. The hero is strong, competent, and courageous. The hero seeks to improve the world while at the same time proving their own worth, and may become arrogant and obsessive. Brand and business examples: US Army, Nike, Mothers Against Drunk Driving, Duracell.**

- *Caregiver.* **Saint, humanitarian, parent, helper, supporter. The caregiver is compassionate and generous and strives to protect and care for others, although may risk being exploited. Brand and business examples: Amnesty International, Dove, Allstate Insurance, Heinz.**

(Continued)

- *Explorer.* Seeker, wanderer, individualist, pilgrim. The explorer is true to their soul: seeking out and experiencing new things. May be at risk of aimless wandering and some inner emptiness. The explorer wants to have a more authentic, fulfilling life. Brand and business examples: Starbucks, National Geographic, Jeep, North Face, Red Bull.

- *Rebel.* Revolutionary, outlaw, misfit, subversive. The rebel can be a little outrageous but always linked to freedom with strategies of disrupting, destroying, or shocking ultimately to overturn what isn't working. Sometimes the path may turn dark and even become criminal. Brand and business examples: Greenpeace, People for the Ethical Treatment of Animals (PETA), Uber, Netflix, Virgin, Harley-Davidson.

- *Lover.* Partner, friend, intimate, enthusiast, team-builder. The lover celebrates physical joys and is passionate, appreciative, committed to people, work, or surroundings. However, pleasing others may risk loss of identity. Brand and business examples: Godiva Chocolate, Haagen-Dazs, Hallmark.

- *Creator.* Artist, imaginative, innovator, dreamer. The creator is driven to develop skill, express a vision, and create things of enduring value. May be too much of a perfectionist. Brand and business examples: Adobe, LEGO, Pinterest, Crayola.

- *Jester.* Fool, trickster, joker. The joker enjoys the moment, seeks to lighten up the world, and is averse to boredom. May be considered frivolous and a time-waster. Brand and business examples: GEICO, Ben & Jerry's, Southwest Airlines, Skittles (Figure 6.3), IKEA.

Figure 6.3 Skittles TV Commercial: Bleachers "Contract the rainbow, taste the rainbow." *Source:* Youtube.

- *Sage.* **Expert, scholar, detective, thinker, adviser, professional, planner. The sage seeks the truth through self-reflection and analysis of the world. Fears being misled. Detail obsession may delay or prevent action. Brand and business examples: PBS, Smithsonian, Google, Harvard, Audi.**
- *Magician.* **Visionary, catalyst, inventor, healer, charismatic leader. The magician offers win–win solutions through knowledge of universal laws; however, may become manipulative. Brand and business examples: Disney, Polaroid, Apple.**
- *Ruler.* **Boss, leader, royalty, politician, role model, manager. The ruler has a talent for responsibility, enjoys control, and exercises power to create prosperity and success. May become authoritarian or fail to delegate. Brand and business examples: Mercedes-Benz, Microsoft, Moody's, Rolex.**

For a descriptive list of more than 70 character archetypes compiled by *New York Times* best-selling author Caroline Myss, search for "Caroline Myss A Gallery of Archetypes."

THE ART AND SCIENCE OF VISUALS

LO2 Recognize how visuals construct narratives.

Seeing comes before words

(John Berger)

Art critic John Berger's reminder that seeing comes before words (1972, p. 33) tells us the world surrounds us with images, speaking their own language freely, uncontained by spoken words.

This chapter focuses on visual narratives as rhetorical (influential). Visuals have a long history of persuasion. As early as the eighth century CE, St. John of Damascus (675–749) defined "image" as a likeness that serves not only as a remembrance of what has taken place, but also as an expression of the future, a foreshadowing.

Descriptive Content and Literal Form

A visual narrative is a series of pictorial representations that make up a plot. These representations are constructed through their descriptive content – *what* a story says through characters, actions, and settings – and through their literal form – *how* the story is told. For example, the content might feature a middle-aged female shopper dressed in a sweat suit, buying a bouquet of flowers from a street vendor. But *how* she is depicted through form – for instance, from a distant or close perspective – also suggests meaning and helps guide how viewers should think about her. Setting entails both time and place of action, and not only physical location but atmosphere, tone, feeling, and conditions surrounding characters.

Content: Characters, Actions, and Settings

In the simplest structure, key characters are typically a protagonist (one who solves problems of conflict) and an antagonist (who stands in the way of the protagonist).

Elements of plot include:

- *Exposition or introduction*: What we need to know initially to understand the story
- *Rising action*: Series of events that develop conflict
- *Climax*: Turning point when characters try to resolve conflict
- *Falling action*: Ending becomes inevitable with events leading to story's closure
- *Resolution*: Unknotting of the conflict

In *Made to Stick,* the Heath brothers explained various "sticky" elements that make stories engaging and memorable. We can learn how to be better visual communicators by understanding some of the elements pictorially.

- *Be unexpected*. Be mysterious, ask curious questions, tease your audience. What's happening in Figure 6.4? Who are these people and what are they doing? We also want to know what happened, and what's going to happen? We want to know the answer to unanswered questions. Mystery makes a story interesting and engaging. This should remind us of the gestalt principle of closure – something missing more deeply engages an audience – moving them to anticipate the completion of the story.
- *Be credible*. Trust in the believability of communication has become a near worldwide issue for businesses, media, governments, and even nonprofits, for

Figure 6.4 Pictures with mysteries – what's happened? – make visual stories more interesting.

our visual messages to have credible authority. One way is to use graphics in a simple and clear way. Narrative theory tells us that believable stories are ones that people can relate to through past experiences, common values, and their resonance with stories known to be true.

- *Be emotional.* Emotion makes people care; it makes them feel something. Characters that evoke empathy, plots that tell emotional stories, facial expressions, gestures, color, lighting, movement, and spatial elements all can contribute to emotion of a narrative. The more concrete the appeal is, the stronger the emotional reaction. Think of images warning against drunken driving and smoking.

FOCUS: Storytelling with Graphics and Typography

Infographics. Visualizations or infographics in the news have become increasingly popular as an alternative way of storytelling. But how do news consumers use and appreciate them?

To answer this question, researchers first conducted an eye-tracking study to measure consumers' use by tracking their direct attention to visualizations on three different news platforms (print newspaper, e-newspaper on tablet, and news website). The researchers' second study conducted focus groups and a survey among readers of these news media to examine the extent to which news consumers actually value the inclusion of visualizations in the news. Results showed that news consumers do indeed read news visualizations, regardless of the platform on which the visual is published. And, visualizations are appreciated, but only if they are coherently integrated into a news story and thus fulfill a function that can be easily understood (MDG, 2018).

Typography. The right font and spacing can improve not only readability but your credibility. For example, a study at Massachusetts Institute of Technology (MIT) showed one group of people an article with a clear font and good spacing. Another group was shown the same article with a hard-to-read font and poor spacing. The results? No surprise: Good typography, shown to group one, makes readers more engaged. People found the text easier to read and felt more in control while reading it. It put readers in a better mood, giving people a positive reaction (MDG 2018).

So, what does good typography entail? The Nielsen Norman Group has been studying consumer behavior for decades. Key recommendations based on usability research are:

- *Font size.* **Small fonts may look nice on designers' monitors, but they challenge the end reader. As the size of type increases, readers tend to exhibit faster reading speeds.**

- *Contrast.* **People want words to stand out so avoid busy or textured backgrounds. Due to aging, a 40-year-old's retina receives half as much light as that of a 20-year-old.**

(Continued)

- *Spacing.* **Text is easier to read with good spacing between words, characters, and lines. Reading speed and comprehension improve when extra line spacing is added.**
- *Font type.* **While novelty fonts may be fun, they're often frustrating to readers. In fact, people find fonts that emulate handwriting or gothic style harder to read. Again, no surprise. For screen reading, try Gill Sans or Helvetica to increase legibility. For print, use a traditional serif font like Times New Roman or Palatino.**

Form

The uncertainty of **visual syntax** (in other words, the lack of a recognizable compositional structure for sense-making) plays a central part in the processes of visual persuasion. While words have conventionally fixed meanings, rules of grammar and syntax, and a linear and logical structure (Audigier, 1991), images escape these controls and "stand in for a more complex reality," than words (Foss, 2005, p. 142). Often, visuals invite the viewer to participate in meaning construction through form: how the story is presented. When we talk about visual syntax, we are talking about form.

Form helps to structure meaning in pictorial representations through spatial and temporal juxtapositions, and color and lighting.

Spatial juxtapositions may include:

- Distance relationships between characters to establish consensus or alienation.
- Wide, distance shots to establish setting and context.
- Close-ups that privilege detail as significant to understanding the narrative.
- Low angles looking upward to make the subject look strong and powerful.
- High angles looking downward to make the subject seem vulnerable or powerless.
- Centered, straight on perspectives to suggest agency and authenticity.
- Marginalized perspectives to diminish importance of the subject.

Temporal juxtapositions may include:

- Long shots to establish authority, value, or to guide the narrative.
- Temporal compression though montage or movements within and between frames, including jump cuts, cross-cuts, and fast motion proposing passage of time and possibly dismissive or marginalizing.
- In static shots, the perception of time can be created through various techniques found in Photoshop and other software.

Lakoff and Johnson (1980) advise us that the meaning-making role of pictorial form directs how the content is presented and often imbues it with subtexts of deeper meanings. Figure 6.5 helps to illustrate the two-part relationship of content and form. Try describing it. Is your focus on its descriptive content: two barren trees in a country

Figure 6.5 How content is formed (two barren trees photographed close-up from a low angle) provides subtexts of deeper meaning. *Source:* Johannes Plenio/ Shutterstock.com.

landscape? Or is your focus on the literal form due to its spatial relations: a close-up of two trees from a low angle, and a narrow field of view. Either describes it correctly, but neither does it completely. Considering sense-making from both the descriptive and the literal structure of the image helps us more fully understand images as pictorial narratives (Barbatsis, 2005).

Figurative Imagery

Both symbols and **tropes** help to construct meaning in visual narratives. You read about symbols in Chapter 4 as semiotic signs that evoke associations. Symbols generously infuse our everyday culture, for example, the facial profile on a US quarter is an iconic sign for George Washington, an empty rocking chair may be an indexical sign for an absent relative, and a rainbow flag carries symbolic meaning for the LGBTQ+ community. Symbols require cultural knowledge for interpretation.

Tropes

Tropes are commonly recurring motifs in creative works. Pictorial tropes, specifically two of the master tropes, metaphor and irony, work to render the unfamiliar familiar (Barbatsis, 2005, p. 337; White, 1978).

- *Metaphor* is one of the classic tropes: meaning motifs created by words or expressions that function figuratively (non-literally). To review visual metaphor, detailed in Chapter 5, it is a pictorial representation that transfers meaning from one concept to another. For example, the verbal metaphor "the car is a cheetah" brings two seemingly separate ideas together to create a new idea, suggesting a fast and sleek vehicle. Pictorially, the car would be juxtaposed with the image of a cheetah – or it may be converged with some cheetah imagery (spots on its hood?) – or a cheetah may be visually suggested without showing the animal. Analyzing metaphors entails (i) determining its two terms (subject and frame of reference) and (ii) naming which features are imposed from one onto the other.

- *Irony* is an expression that signifies an oppositional meaning: often, but not always, implying sarcasm or seen as insulting. See Chapter 5 to review two types of irony: hyperbole (use of extreme exaggeration to emphasize a characteristic or to imply criticism) and litotes (use of diminishment and negativity to gain positive attention). Another example of litotes is the statement "you won't be sorry" carrying the meaning "you'll be happy." Advertising often uses hyperbole as an exaggeration of a selling point (a promise or an experience) as this ad for Extra Big hamburgers does (Figure 6.6). "Dramatic irony" is different; a visual foreshadowing, it alerts the viewer to plot developments before the character(s) experience them.

Other tropes include metonymy and synecdoche.

- *Metonymy* suggests meaning by using a close association with a concept and not a physical part of it. For example, pharmaceutical ads that don't feature the drug but rather the active person who consumes it. Or billboards for Marlboro cigarettes that don't feature smoking but flashy images of young people partying.

Figure 6.6 **Example of visual hyperbole: extreme exaggeration emphasizes a characteristic.** *Source:* afahc.ro.

- *Synecdoche* is when an object or concept is represented by a part of it, or conversely, a part of an object or concept is represented by the whole. For example, a tire stands for a vehicle, or conversely, a map image of France stands for the study abroad trip to Paris.

NARRATIVE CRITICISM

LO3 – Learn how to analyze and create visual narratives for professional communication.

Learning and practicing how to analyze visual narratives will improve your ability to create and use them well in your professional career. Narrative criticism will help you identify what makes a story hang together and ring true. Since NPT sees all human narration as story, you may think that critiquing and creating stories should come naturally, without theoretical knowledge. That's sufficient when you have little stake in how the story is received. But if you are a strategic visual communicator, you'll need to have a firm understanding of how pictures structure thought: of how images tell a reliable story that is believable and acceptable to your intended audience.

FOCUS: Ethical Implications of Storytelling Through Immersive Journalism

Many journalism organizations have enthusiastically embraced **augmented reality (AR)**, **virtual reality (VR)**, and **360° video** to tell stories that are more humane and more emotionally compelling. However, some critics state the vivid content that arouses emotions is not only memorable but often inaccurate as it causes individuals to make moral judgments.

The story sharing capabilities of these virtual technologies are powerful. AR layers visual and auditory information onto the physical environment: common uses are in games such as Pokémon Go and in social media phenomena such as Snapchat filters. VR is more immersive in that individuals wear headsets equipped with smartphones or even more sophisticated devices and become part of a virtual world. They may move around it, manipulate items, or virtually decorate a home using apps such as Home Depot Project Color. In journalism, an individual can participate in what appears to be the actual scene where events occurred. A 360° video (often labeled VR) provides camera footage that the user can manipulate, usually on a smartphone, allowing users to move their gazes in every direction.

In a well-regarded *New York Times* 360° video entitled "Visiting Dad in Prison" (*New York Times*, 2017), viewers rode with two little girls on a long bus trip to Florida's Charlotte Correctional Institution, accompanied them through security

---

(Continued)

and being reunited with their father, and then rode home with them. An analysis of this 360° (Duffy and Page, 2019) found that gaps in a recognizable story sequence and the lack of a reliable narrator raised ethical questions. Media critic Douglas Rushkoff warns:

> I think immersive media has a really limited purpose, certainly in terms of journalism and informing people. I guess you can make people feel certain ways by immersing them in certain kinds of worlds. But in most of these experiences you are just watching people who can't see you, so in some ways it exacerbates the sense of power that privileged people can feel over less privileged people.
>
> (*cited in Paura*, **2018, p. 4**).

Analyzing Narratives

Follow these steps to analyze and evaluate visual narratives. Depending on the image or images you choose, not all steps will be relevant.

1. **Descriptive content**. Identify what Fisher calls structural concepts: characters, plot, and setting.

2. **Narrative probability**. Ask if the content is logically consistent: if it "hangs together." Accomplish this with the following:
   a. Characters.
      i. Which characters received more emphasis?
      ii. Are the characters behaving characteristically?
      iii. Are there inconsistencies in character behavior?
   b. Plot. (Stories have a beginning, middle, and end, with these sequential elements: introduction or exposition, rising action/conflict, climax, falling action, resolution.)
      i. Did any plot elements receive more emphasis?
      ii. Are any missing?
      iii. Is there any illogical progression?
   c. Setting.
      i. Is the physical environment appropriate to the story and to where the storytelling occurred?
      ii. How do atmosphere, tone, feeling, and conditions surrounding characters establish setting?
   d. Identify any "deep structure" myths or any archetypal elements.
   e. Consider how form (temporal and spatial orientations; color and lighting) impacts the consistency of the content.
   f. Consider how figurative imagery is used and how it contributes to meaning.

3. **Narrative fidelity**. Ask if the content "rings true" with personal experiences of the real or ideal viewer: if it resonates with stories known to be true.
   a. Assess the soundness of its rational reasoning.
      i. Are the story's facts accurately presented?
      ii. Do any facts seem to be missing?
      iii. Does the story's reasoning flow logically?
   b. Assess the soundness of its value-laden reasoning.
      i. What values are reflected and are they relevant and undistorted for the topic of the story?
      ii. Are the values consistent with those of the ideal/real audience?
      iii. Are the values consistent with those of any identified myths?
      iv. Does the story have a moralistic or materialistic master analog?
   c. Consider how form impacts the rationality and values of the content.

Example Analysis

Home & Garden Television (HGTV) is part reality and part fantasy, part drama and part entertainment, part oppressive and part liberating, and maybe more. Consistent with recurring themes on entertainment television, HGTV routinely features homes with problems, people with frustrations, a hero or two, honest hard work, and happy endings. Its logo emphasizes the original "home and garden" focus of the network first launched in 1994; however, now its programming focuses mainly on the home.

Source: Shaw Satellite G.P.

For a critic conducting narrative analysis of TV programming, audience demographics provide a good understanding of its real audience. HGTV's viewers are predominantly female homeowners, median age of 41, who have attended some college and earn above-average salaries (National Media Spots, n.d.). Viewers are entertained by peeking inside other people's homes and experiencing the transformations. In 2020, HGTV continued to hold its place as the fourth most-watched cable network after Fox News, CNN, and MSNBC (American Target Network, 2020).

A narrative analysis (Page, 2004) of three episodes of *Decorating Cents* found the plots involve a problem needing solving. In one episode, *characters* include the HGTV host Joan who functions as "storyteller" and laborer; Rebecca, a young female artist serving as the troubled "victim" of a problematic situation; and Cy, a designer/artist and "protagonist" who as creative visionary solves the conflict and gets the most emphasis. This emphasis, and the behaviors of all characters, are consistent with known roles in HGTV stories.

The narrative hangs together (*narrative probability*). The *setting* is appropriate to the story: a home in its before, during, and after stages. (The likely at-home setting of viewers is also appropriate to the storytelling where the transformation transpires symbolically). At first Joan is alone in Rebecca's loft, providing a linguistic and visual exposition as she walks through it, giving viewers a full look inside Rebecca's very personal space.

The *plot* is revealed as the action rises and viewers learn of the conflict. The setting is the problem: Rebecca's loft apartment combines living area with workspace *and* gallery. As she gets more successful and has more showings, her space needs to look more like a gallery. She needs help with both hiding clutter and exposing art. The atmosphere, tone, and feeling in the setting is at first one of confusion, created by a connect-the-dots visual puzzle of tools, materials, and artworks. With the arrival of Cy, reimagining begins. Content and form are alternatively amplified and compressed to illuminate the conflict and build to a climax. The transformation is a collaborative effort, bringing a new aura of order and reverence, and the action falls toward a resolution. The transformation occupies the longest time in this story, which is appropriate to the genre and audience expectations.

The narrative doesn't ring quite true (*narrative fidelity)* as the show's production constraints of a 22-minute time slot impact its rational reasoning. A habitual viewer would likely accept missing facts (fast forwards) as reliable for the genre; a new viewer may question it. Values are imbued with the camera's respectful eye on Rebecca's art, Cy's workmanship, and Joan's labor, helping to let the story serve a higher purpose than an ordinary room redo.

The deep structure *myth* is woven into the plot, as viewers participate in a ritual: the elevation of living space to a sacred place through incorporation of works of art. Here again, a habitual viewer with home transformation interests or aspirations, would likely share the values of simplifying, beautifying, and purifying.

Form similarities appeared in all the HGTV stories studied: lengthy time sequences and close perspectives of the characters communicate the value of work, especially handiwork, and the collaborative process of making. The important transformation stage in each story employs temporal compression (fast forwards and flashbacks) and amplification (long or frequent close-ups) to advance the plot and its meaning. Often hard labor is fast-forwarded, conventionally signifying passage of time but symbolically proposing insignificance. Those moments that linger on the touch of the human hand involve the viewer more personally.

The episodes make rich use of *figurative imagery*. Sometimes the audience's viewing position is that of the host's, and whenever she gets a brainstorm or "looks into" the future (we're shown images), we experience the dramatic irony of knowing what the other characters do not yet know. This descriptive foreshadowing involves us in anticipation and as accomplices; seeing is knowing. The stories are also rich in visual *metaphor*. In the first story featuring an art studio, we see the subject Rebecca through the context of her labor, her art. The guest expert's service is not for Rebecca but for her art. Her art is his muse, positing a connection between "high" art and "popular" art. And her artwork is both the catalyst for change and the obstacle to change in this story, suggesting that art can be both inspirational and provocative. As an orientational visual metaphor, the upward movement and high position when making the "art-friendly" yellow walls, and the making of the elevated light fixtures, suggest uplifting qualities, and the elevation of the ordinary to the virtuous.

The *myths* of ritual and transformation guide the storyline, which has consistent values. *Archetypal* characters include a magician (a visionary and creator of sacred space). The narrative has a moralistic/idealist *master analogue*.

Applying NPT and Visual Narrative Analysis in Your Work

This section calls on you to build your analytic and creative skills. You will choose a visual narrative that interests you, analyze it, and then create your own visual narrative. While you won't be expected to conduct complex research and analysis, these projects allow you to sample and experience these processes.

Challenge: Research –Evaluate – Create (REC)

Step One: Research

Select a visual image, series of images, or short video. For your first venture into narrative analysis, a single image offers a good exercise. Choose an advertisement, a magazine cover or illustration, an editorial cartoon, a meme, a news photograph, a book jacket cover, a movie poster, or the like.

Next, conduct some general research on the image's subject matter, which should help you understand the nature of the source and the characteristics of the real or ideal audience. Write a brief summary of your findings.

Step Two: Evaluate

Analyze your visual narrative using the process of visual narrative criticism introduced in this chapter.

1. Identify the descriptive content.
2. Assess the image for narrative probability. Does it logically hang together?
3. Assess the image for narrative fidelity. Does it ring true?
4. Consider how form impacts content.

5. Consider how figurative imagery is used and how it contributes to meaning.

6. Identify any deep structure myths and any archetypal elements.

7. Does the story have a moralistic or materialistic master analogue?

Step Three: Create

Plan and create a concept rough: a 6- to 8-frame storyboard using PowerPoint (or similar software), telling a positive personal story. It could be of a vacation episode, an adventure, one day on campus, a sports event, and so on. This will be the foundation of a short video to be produced and uploaded to your university website for the purposes of new student recruitment.

Produce two deliverables:

1. **Written plan**. This explains what will guide your concept rough.
   - Identify the characters
   - Describe the plot
   - Describe the setting(s)
   - Suggest spatial and temporal treatments
   - Choose one type of figurative imagery and specify its use
   - Suggest a mythical story that aligns with your story
   - Suggest an archetypal character for your story

2. **Executed tactic**. Now follow your plan to create the concept rough, using your own photographs or illustrations, or images downloaded from the Creative Commons or a similar copyright-free source. If you choose to use copyrighted images, remember they may only be used for classroom assignments and may not be publicly published (including posting/sharing online).

PRACTICE ACTIVITIES

1. **Step one: preparation**. The Heider-Simmel experiment, of Heider and Simmel, 1944 and replicated by others, showed people simple objects moving in an animated film. The goal of researchers was to understand how people developed impressions about behavior and its causes. They purposely used "faceless" objects to focus on people's perceptions of movement. Michotte (1950) in a similar study noted that participants didn't simply describe what they observed (such as "object A is pushing object B") but instead talked about them in human or animal terms. That is, they assigned personality traits, intentions, motivations, relationships, and threats. Subjects would describe a triangle as being a bully, the little shapes as being sneaky, and one object as wanting to date another one. They would even predict what action would take place next and why. The goals of these studies were generally not to discuss how narrative works in visuals, but we think it again underscores our human need to

understand the world through stories even from the movement of triangles, circles, and rectangles.

2. **Step two: evaluate**. Search for "Heider-Simmel experiment" to watch the original animation and make your own interpretations.

3. **Step three: create**. Now conceive of your own story and produce a concept rough using faceless shapes. It can simply be an 8- to 10-frame storyboard, using animated PowerPoint slides that are then exported to video. Share your video with classmates to discover how they interpret it.

CHAPTER SUMMARY

This chapter illustrated how narratives run throughout human communication and revealed what makes narrative (story) believable and accepted, or not. It concentrated on the visual aspects of narrative, providing examples in editorial cartoons, book covers, illustrations, infographics, commercials, slides, personal photographs, social media images, and TV programs. Guided by Fisher's NPT, you learned of a narrative's components and how to conduct an analysis to evaluate its consistency and believability, and you applied that knowledge in your own work.

KEY TERMS

Narrative rationality   A capacity that humans inherently possess allowing them to tell good from bad stories, moral from immoral stories, and acceptable from unacceptable stories.

Narrative probability   The story's logical coherence.

Narrative fidelity   The story's truthfulness.

Form   *How* content is presented in spatial and temporal juxtapositions, and color and lighting.

Content   *What* a story says through characters, actions, and settings.

Myths   Recurring stories containing beliefs and values that are significant, long-lasting, and widely accepted as being true within a culture.

Master analog   A story's deep structure myth, whether idealistic/moralistic or materialistic.

Idealistic/moralistic myth   One of brotherhood, valuing human equality, tolerance, charity, trustworthiness, community celebration, love, justice, and compassion.

Materialistic myth   One of individual success, valuing entitlement, individualism, heroic achievement, persistence, initiative, self-reliance, pleasure, the entrepreneurial spirit, and success.

Archetype   Original pattern; the basic building blocks of stories found in characters, situations, and symbols.

Visual syntax   form (see definition of form).

Tropes   Commonly recurring motifs in creative works.

Augmented reality (AR)   Layers visual and auditory information onto the physical environment.

Virtual reality (VR)   Requires individuals to wear headsets equipped with smartphones or even more sophisticated devices and become part of a virtual world.

360° video (often labeled VR)   Provides camera footage that the user can manipulate, allowing users to move their gazes in every direction.

REFERENCES

American Target Network. (2020). Top 10 Cable Networks (Total Day Viewers). http://
americantargetnetwork.com/industry-landscape/ (accessed October 4, 2020).

Audigier, J. (1991). *Connections*. New York, NY: Lanham.

Barbatsis, G. (2005). Narrative theory. In: *Handbook of Visual Communication* (eds. K.
Smith, S. Moriarty, G. Barbatsis and K. Kenney), 329–350. Mahwah, NJ: Earlbaum.

Barthes, R. (1977). *Image. Music. Text.* (trans. S. Heath). London: Fontana Press.

Berger, J. (1972). *Ways of Seeing*. London, UK: Penguin Books.

Campbell, J. (1988). *The Power of Myth*. New York: Doubleday.

Cragan, J.F. and Shields, D.C. (1998). *Understanding Communication Theory: The Communicative Forces for Human Action*. New York: Pearson.

Duffy, M. and Page, J.T. (2019). Seeing is believing? Ethical implications for AR, VR, and
360° technologies in journalism. Paper presented at the Association for Education in
Journalism and Mass Communication conference, Toronto (August 2019).

Fisher, W.R. (1973). Reaffirmation and subversion of the American dream. Quarterly
Journal of Speech 59 (2): 160–167.

Fisher, W.R. (1987). *Human Communication as Narration: Toward a philosophy of reason,
value, and action. Columbia*. University of South Carolina Press.

Fiske, J. (1987). *Television Culture*. London, UK: Methuen.

Foss, S.K. (1994). A rhetorical schema for the evaluation of visual imagery. Communication Studies 45: 213–224.

Foss, S.K. (2005). Theory of visual rhetoric. In: *Handbook of Visual Communication* (eds. K.
Smith, S. Moriarty, G. Barbatsis and K. Kenney), 141–152. Mahwah, NJ: Earlbaum.

Gronbeck, B.E. (1997). Tradition and Technology in Local Newscasts: The social psychology of form. The Sociological Quarterly 38 (2): 361–374.

Gronbeck, B. (1998). Three rhetorics of the seen. Paper presented at the National Communication Association convention, New York (November 1998).

Hall, S. (2012). *This Means This, This Means That: A User's Guide to Semiotics*, 2e. London:
Laurence King Publishing.

Heath, C. and Heath, D. (2007). *Made to Stick: Why Some Ideas Survive and Others Die*.
New York, NY: Random House.

Heider, F. and Simmel, M. (1944). An experimental study of apparent behavior. American
Journal of Psychology 57: 243–259.

Lakoff, G. and Johnson, M. (1980). *Metaphors we live by*. Chicago: University of
Chicago Press.

Lévi-Strauss, C. (1974). *Structural Anthropology*. New York, NY: Basic Books.

MDG. (2018). Design matters: What marketers need to know about color and typography (infographic). https://www.mdgadvertising.com/marketing-insights/infographics/design-matters-what-marketers-need-to-know-about-color-and-typography-infographic (accessed September 22, 2020).

Melville, H. (1851). *Moby-Dick; or The Whale*. New York: Harper & Brothers.

Michotte, A.E. (1950). The emotions regarded as functional connections. In: *Feelings and Emotions* (ed. M.L. Reymert), 114–126. New York: McGraw-Hill.

Mitchell, W.J.T. (1994). *Picture Theory*. Chicago, IL: University of Chicago Press.

Mumford, L. (1946). *Values for Survival*. New York, NY: Harcourt Brace.

Nachbar, J. and Lause, K. (1992). *Popular Culture: An Introductory Text*. Bowling Green, OH: Popular Press.

National Media Spots. (n.d.). HGTV. https://www.nationalmediaspots.com/network-demographics/HGTV.pdf (accessed September 23, 2020).

New York Times. (2017). Visiting Dad in Prison. https://www.youtube.com/watch?v=ZDlToFjaCtI (accessed September 23, 2020).

Onion, R. (2013). A big, beautiful midcentury map celebrating American folklore. https://www.loc.gov/item/2011592193 (accessed October 4, 2020).

Page, J.T. (2004). Towards a theory of visual narrative analysis: What we see on HGTV. Unpublished doctoral dissertation. University of Missouri, Columbia. https://www.researchgate.net/publication/33694460_Towards_a_theory_of_visual_narrative_analysis_what_we_see_on_HGTV (accessed September 23, 2020).

Paura, A. (2018). Virtual reality creates ethical challenges for journalism. *IJNet*. https://ijnet.org/en/story/virtual-reality-creates-ethical-challenges-journalists (accessed March 27, 2020).

Shutterstock. (2015). Symbolism of colors and color meanings around the world. https://www.shutterstock.com/blog/color-symbolism-and-meanings-around-the-world (accessed September 23, 2020).

Storey, J. (1993). *An introductory guide to cultural theory and popular culture*. Athens, GA: University of Georgia Press.

The Hartford. (n.d.). The 12 brand archetypes. https://www.thehartford.com/business-playbook/in-depth/choosing-brand-archetype (accessed 23 September 2020).

Vision One. (n.d.). Brand archetypes. https://visionone.co.uk/brand-archetypes (accessed September 23, 2020).

White, X. (1978). *Tropics of Discourse: Essays in Cultural Criticism*. Baltimore: The Johns Hopkins University Press.

Chapter 7
Visual Voices
Fantasy Themes

Pictures *Can* Speak Louder than Words

College professors have never been known for their keen fashion sense, tending toward the tweedy, the frumpy, and the rumpled, though of course, there are numerous exceptions. Some would say that academics' presumed devotion to the life of the mind should supersede shallow impression management and superficial style (Meyers, 2012). But when a candidate for a professor's

Source: bonetta/iStock/Getty Images
bonetta/iStock/Getty Images.

Visual Communication: Insights and Strategies, First Edition. Janis Teruggi Page and Margaret Duffy.
© 2022 John Wiley & Sons, Inc. Published 2022 by John Wiley & Sons, Inc.

job went for an interview at a university wearing a bold plaid suit and polka-dot tie the hiring committee noticed, commented among themselves, and ultimately didn't offer the man a job (Schneider, 1998). You can imagine how such a conversation might have gone: "Was that suit stolen from a clown?" "Wearing a boxy plaid suit to an interview doesn't show a person with very good judgment." "It looks like he got dressed in the dark." And so on. As the committee talked, they might have begun to dramatize what they saw as the candidate's fashion faux pas, each building on others' comments and questions.

Sometimes such events and discussions might lead to inside jokes or symbolic cues. For instance, in the future, any fashion-challenged would-be professor might be called Mr. Boxy and everyone who'd been part of the committee or who had heard about it would understand the reference. You've no doubt had similar experiences where you and your friends and colleagues riffed on an individual or an event. This is the kind of communication that led Ernest Bormann to develop symbolic convergence theory (SCT) and its associated method of fantasy theme analysis (FTA) building on the ideas of psychologist Robert Bales.

Key Learning Objectives
1. Understand group communication as the symbolic convergence of imaginative ideas.
2. Recognize how visuals work in symbolic convergence.
3. Master concepts of symbolic convergence theory and fantasy theme analysis.
4. Appreciate visual symbolic convergence in the communication professions and apply this knowledge to understand consumers and other publics.
5. Learn how to analyze visual fantasies in communication and how to create compelling visual and textual messages.

Chapter Overview

In this chapter, we look at how participatory dramas unfold in media and in personal experiences. In today's world of emerging media, we have access to many perspectives in messages created, used, shared, and shaped and reshaped by users. All of these avenues can combine words with images, and often images are dominant. This chapter provides you with some tools to navigate our vastly expanding mediated world, analyze its visual communication, and understand and interpret collective visual expressions. SCT helps us understand how communication from people near and far can converge into unified messages. Its method, FTA, gives us the structure to analyze this communication in a systematic way and examine how it works to see previously unrecognized messages and characteristics. We begin by explaining how the theory developed and how it's been applied in communication. We then explain how to use the method to analyze visual symbols and how to apply it in professional work.

EVERYDAY DRAMATIZING: WE'RE ALL DRAMA QUEENS AND KINGS

LO1 Understand group communication as the symbolic convergence of imaginative ideas.

In the late 1940s, as social psychologist Robert Bales conducted research on interpersonal interactions in small groups, he noticed people tend to "dramatize" while working on decision-making tasks. This dramatizing showed up among group members as they discussed past or future scenarios and events. The conversation would speed up, group members would laugh, groan, joke, blush, and show signs of excitement and involvement.

Decades later, communication scholar Ernest Bormann extended Bales's observations, identifying the dynamic process of sharing group fantasies. In the 1970s, Bormann and a team of researchers developed SCT, inspired by their studies in small group dynamics. Bormann used the word **fantasies** to mean imaginative ideas. While the terms and concepts may sound strange, they have been shown to help us see the shared symbolic meanings groups develop that may spread out to entire communities of like-minded people.

Symbolic Convergence Theory: A Merging of Imaginations

SCT is a rhetorical theory, a way of explaining humans' use of symbols. In the language of rhetorical analysis, the symbols we collect and analyze are sometimes referred to as artifacts. In SCT, symbols are elements of communication that carry meaning: ideas either assigned or culturally learned. Symbols may be either verbal or nonverbal, and may be found in speeches, conversations, essays, comic books, websites, TV programs, films, art, music, advertisements, and even clothing (Foss, 2009, p. 5). The US flag is, in its simplest definition, a piece of cloth festooned with stars and stripes. But its symbolic meaning for patriotic citizens represents a proud history and a homeland, and acts such as burning a flag might be construed as treasonous.

SCT focuses on symbols that create meaning in social settings. These social settings cause us to adjust our approach to our experiences and perceptions. In this way, our reality is socially constructed through interpersonal and group conversations and the ideas and thoughts they inspire. Individuals' private imaginations, interpretations, and beliefs, which Bormann labeled "fantasies," converge through processes of communication. This term can be puzzling at first. If Bormann had chosen to use "imaginative idea" rather than fantasy, not much explanation would be needed. Think of rhetorical fantasies as a technical term, not psychological or subconscious phenomena (Bormann et al., 2003). Bormann offers this explanation:

> When we share a fantasy, we attribute events to human action and thus make sense out of what may have previously been a confusing state of affairs. We do so in common with others who share the fantasy with us. Thus, we come to symbolic convergence on the matter and we envision that part of our world in similar ways. We have created common villains and heroes and celebrated certain basic dramatic actions as laudable and pictured others as despicable. We have created some symbolic common ground and we can talk with one another about that shared interpretation with code words or brief allusions (1990, p. 106).

Convergence involves sharing of the same emotions and embracing the same values, going far beyond an intellectual agreement on rational meanings of symbols (Bormann, 1983, p. 102). As Bormann puts it, "they [group members] have developed the same attitudes and emotional responses to the personae of the drama; and they have interpreted some aspect of their experience in the same way" (Bormann, 1983, p. 104).

Key Assumptions

Key assumptions underpin SCT and contribute to its usefulness (Table 7.1). First, as suggested above, people's social reality and understandings of the world are created symbolically through communication and thus it "orders the world around them" (Cragan and Shields, 1995, p. 32).

Second, "meaning, emotion, and motive for action are in the manifest content of the message" (Cragan and Shields, 1995, p. 31). That is, the researcher can locate motives for actions and meanings people assign to events within messages. This understanding of messages – beyond logic and argumentation – provides "insights into the group's culture, motivation, emotional style, and cohesion" (Bormann, 1981, p. 16). Messages not only reveal motives but also, through involvement in dramatized events, people gain motivations and as a result may change their behaviors. Group members'

Table 7.1 Symbolic convergence theory (SCT) at a glance.

Belief	Usefulness	Terminology
Our social reality and understandings are created symbolically through fantasies communicated in social settings.	Communication helps to order the world that surrounds us.	*Symbols*: Carriers of meaning, i.e. words, pictures, etc.
		Fantasies: Creative or imaginative interpretations
Communication carries motives, meanings, values. Shared communication is influential.	When involved in dramatized communication, intentions, attitudes, and beliefs may chain out and converge with those of other participants.	*Dramatized*: Improvisational conversation
		Chain out: Build meaning off others' meaning
		Convergence: Coming together
Interactions may create a shared group consciousness.	This leads to a shared overall understanding, a rhetorical vision.	*Rhetorical vision*: Agreed-upon worldview or perspective; a common symbolic reality.

Source: © John Wiley & Sons, Inc.

attitudes and beliefs converge as they identify with characters, actions, and settings of messages and events in the process of dramatizing.

Third, when examining communication through the lens of SCT, the interactions of individuals create a group consciousness, shared meanings, and sometimes a collective, overall understanding called a **rhetorical vision** or worldview.

It's important to note that dramatized moments and symbolic convergence happen not only in a small group's shared meanings, but also among larger groups that hear a speech, see something online, or get caught up in a commercial. Moreover,

> the dramatizations that catch on and chain out in small groups are worked into public speeches and into the mass media and, in turn, spread out across larger publics and serve to sustain the members' sense of community, to impel them strongly to action (which raises the question of motivation), and to provide them with a social reality filled with heroes, villains, emotions, and attitudes (Bormann, 1981, p. 18).

SCT Lets You Look Under the Hood

While originally developed to understand how small groups came to construct a common reality, Bormann and others extended SCT's scope to include mass audiences, such as studying messages that arose and converged in national political campaigns.

Figure 7.1 A Mountain Dew commercial featured a stuntman hooked to a cable leaping from a platform and using his body to pierce a huge ball containing the soda and creating startling and dramatic images. *Source:* YouTube.

You might wonder why people don't take a "just the facts" approach to interpreting media messages or even activities they attend. Either an event happened or it didn't, right? But consider how people can come away with different and even polar opposite impressions of the same event or message.

Research on advertising ethics (Duffy and Gotcher, 1996; Duffy and Thorson, 2016) showed that some individuals found sexually charged advertisements to be exciting and appealing while others found them to be sexist and disgusting. People interpreted ads showing dangerous behavior (e.g. this ad for Mountain Dew, Figure 7.1) in much different ways as well. Some thought the ads were thrilling and wanted to emulate them while others thought they inspired people to take unnecessary risks. Each group applied its own dramatic interpretation of the messages and the values of the characters and their behaviors in the ads. Similarly, early in the Covid-19 epidemic in early 2020, wearing a face mask or refusing to wear a mask became polarizing visual symbols. For some political groups, masks were worn by smug liberals who wanted to suppress individual freedom. For those with different political views, those who refused face coverings were ignorant, reckless, and selfish (Lizza and Lippman, 2020). Similarly, when President Trump returned to the White House in early October after being hospitalized for the virus, his act of standing on the balcony and removing his mask provided a powerful visual representation of his beliefs and persona (Kolata and Rabin, 2020).

VISUAL IMAGES MAKE EMOTIONAL CONNECTIONS

LO2 Recognize how visuals work in symbolic convergence.

One way to interpret visual images in society, the stories they tell, and the values and motivations they carry is to view them as manifestations of a collective conversation. This visual language can be the tool of group dramatizations, or fantasies. SCT has been used to make sense of the visual content in mainstream and independent media texts, to identify rhetorical visions in advertising campaigns, editorial cartoons, news coverage, and late-night comedy sketches.

Puppy Love

For decades, Budweiser has used the Super Bowl to run emotional ads featuring their iconic and stately Clydesdale horses. In 2014, their "Puppy Love" ad included an adorable Labrador retriever puppy, up for adoption, who sneaks next door to the Clydesdale farm and nuzzles nose to nose with one of the horses. When the puppy is adopted, his horse friend, along with several others, break out from their stalls and run after the car. In the end, the puppy is back jumping and playing with the horse in the pasture.

No facts or logical arguments support the benefits of Budweiser and the spot does not even show the product. But Ernest Bormann gives us some insight into what's happening: "We are not necessarily persuaded by reason. We are often persuaded by suggestion that ties in with our dreams" (Bormann and Bormann, 1972, p. 171). The advertiser seeks to give you warm feelings in an engaging drama that you are likely to enjoy, connect with your attitudes about the brand, and possibly share. In addition, you're not likely to "argue" with an advertisement that is presented as a charming drama. In fact, although you know it's an ad, it doesn't "feel" like an ad or as if someone is trying to sell something.

Beyond advertising, dramatized events and symbolic realities are created in all types of communication. These dramatized explanations of events can never be neutral. They are always organized to present events from a certain perspective, and they invite others to share that perspective. Shared explanations provide the basis for argument in that they identify the "good reasons" and values from which argument can proceed. In addition, **fantasy themes** vary in their quality and artistry. Some fantasy themes may feature heroic characters and dramatic action while others may have little dramatic and persuasive power. More skillful and artistic dramas are going to be more effective in changing minds and behaviors.

True Believers

You may have heard politicians, conspiracy theorists, or religious figures express viewpoints that seem unhinged from reality, frightening, or silly. SCT helps explain how and why people who participate in a dramatized reality find their own viewpoints entirely realistic and logical. This symbolic communication imposes order and creates a shared reality from the flow of events and sensory impressions.

Figure 7.2 For fans of the Star Wars movie franchise, images and props help to assert their sense of community, as do logos representing their association. *Source:* Boston Globe/Getty Images.

You're probably a fan of a sports team, a movie franchise, a game, an author, a musical group, or a certain hobby. For instance, if you access a Star Wars community website such as http://www.starwars.com/community (Figure 7.2), you'll find a rich array of fan-produced films, blogs, inventions, clubs, and even the "Jedi News Network." Fans invest considerable energy and skill into producing and sharing with like-minded others. Many go to conventions, dress up as Star Wars characters, and compete for prizes. If you're not a fan, the prospect of hundreds of people gathering together and dressing up like Han Solo, Princess Leia, or Snoke seems silly and an absurd waste of time. But if you are a fan, you and fellow true believers celebrate and identify with these characters and participate in shared dramas.

Similarly, after a winning professional football game, passionate sports fans exult that "we won!" although the players are highly paid employees who will often go on to be recruited to other teams with equally passionate but rival fans.

Activism

In social media, email, texts, and even comments on news articles, we can see the power of shared symbolic worlds and how they chain out. Increasingly, they also feature images, often with a political or ideological purpose.

Significant human rights issues have historically produced iconic imagery that functioned to gain media attention, communicate a counter-narrative, and rally like-minded supporters. Typical examples include the controversial African American power salute from the 1968 Olympics with two African American athletes raising their arms as they received their medals. Another is the image of a lone protestor confronting a tank in Tiananmen Square in 1989, a day after the Chinese government violently put down student protests advocating democracy.

Protest images online now accelerate their influence as visual signification moves and morphs through culture. In 2014, socially mediated visuals included the prone bodies of protestors covering the ground: a recreation of the shooting of Oscar Grant III, a young African American man. He was shot in the back by a transit system police officer while he lay on the platform of a metro stop in Oakland, CA (Head, 2019). Earlier, in 2012, unarmed teenager Trayvon Martin was shot and killed by a man claiming to be a neighborhood watch volunteer. Images of Martin wearing a hoodie (Figure 7.3) rapidly circulated the Internet and became flashpoints for discussions of his death (Burch and Isensee, 2012). Others posted self-portraits with hoodies, or a hoodie without a face, or with calls to action. These visuals become collective iconic images, pushing issues into wider consciousness and public discourse. After the murder of George Floyd in Minneapolis, a centerpiece of the trial was a video of the crime recorded by a nearby teenager and observers thought it was a crucial element in the jury's decision finding the officer guilty (Eligon, et al., 2021).

Figure 7.3 Trayvon Martin, killed by neighborhood watch volunteer.
Source: Boston Globe/Getty Images.

MASTER THE BASIC CONCEPTS

LO3 Master concepts of SCT and FTA.

To analyze and create visual communication guided by SCT, you need familiarity with its method and basic concepts.

Fantasy Theme Analysis

FTA is the method of criticism that observes and critiques the following elements to understand the process of symbolic convergence.

Fantasy Theme

A fantasy theme is a dramatized message or conversation depicting characters engaged in actions that account for and explain human experience. It is a narrative description (story) that offers explanations for actions or events. It may be fictional or deal with fact; either way, it is an interpretation imbued with values. Bormann wrote, "The fantasizing is accompanied by emotional arousal; the dreams embodied in the fantasies drive participants toward actions and efforts to achieve them" (Bormann, 1985, p. 9). SCT explains the effect of the communicative force of fantasy chaining as it provides meaning, emotion, and motive for human action.

FOCUS: Hands Up, Don't Shoot: The Power of Visual Protests

On August 9, 2014, Michael Brown, an unarmed African American teenager, was fatally shot by a White police officer in Ferguson, Missouri. The shooting triggered intense public debate, civil unrest and massive social protests, resonating not only within the Black working-class suburb of St. Louis but both nationally and globally. One of the resonating reactions was the "Hands Up, Don't Shoot" (HUDS) protest gesture, adapted into multiple forms by diverse performers, and spreading through social media to influence a new movement against racial oppression.

Eyewitnesses reported Brown had no weapon and both hands were raised in submission when the last of a total of six shots were fired. Protestors in Ferguson responded by echoing this gesture: raising their hands high while gathered outside the police department. They also raised their hands later on the streets when confronted by police using tear gas and rubber and wooden bullets.

Photojournalists from major press syndicates documented these scenes, soon to be shared with a global audience. On August 13, approximately 300 students at Howard University, a historically African American university, posed for a photo with their hands raised.

(Continued)

Source: Cristina Salcedo/Shutterstock.com.

Posted to Twitter with the hashtag #DontShoot, it soon went viral. CNN reported that the photo inspired similar postings of HUDS crowds in New York's Times Square, and in New Orleans, San Diego, Columbus, Ohio, and Charlotte, NC (Yan, 2014). From then on, the hand-raising gesture became a widely repeated symbol in various contexts, evoking different meanings in the process including anger, frustration, empathy, innocence, and victimization.

Fantasy theme analysis was applied to 70 visual iterations of the HUDS image – as photos, drawings, and image macro memes – appearing during an 80-day period in 2014 and located on high visibility sites such as Twitter, Instagram, Storify, Etsy, Amazon, YouTube, news and personal blogs, and media websites. The findings are reported here, in order of importance:

Fantasy Type: "We Demand Justice" [27 images]
(rhetoric of empowerment)

Fantasy Themes

- **Setting**: Anger, disagreement, defiance. Visualizations: juxtapositions of opposing forces
- **Action**: Forceful accusations. Visualizations: "Don't Shoot" verbiage, use of satire
- **Character**: Empowerment and strength. Visualizations: close-ups facing camera, written claims, masculine bodies filling the image frame

Fantasy Type: "We are Michael Brown with our hands up" [16 images] (symbols of affinity)

Fantasy Themes

- **Character**: Celebrity publicity. Visualizations: recognized professional athletes and musicians
- **Character**: Symbolic Witnessing. Visualizations: individual portraits
- **Action:** Acts of Solidarity. Visualizations: mass gatherings off-site, street protests without obvious threat within frame

Fantasy Type: "Ferguson represents racism" [12 images] (symbol of reality for Black Americans)

Fantasy Themes

- **Setting:** Equality stops here. Visualizations: the iconic Gateway Arch broken apart
- **Character:** Targeted and victimized by oppressive forces. Visualizations: militarized local police, wording, Black citizens as targets

Fantasy Type "We are not a threat" [8 images] (subversion of dominant narrative)

Fantasy Themes

- **Character**: Innocent and harmless. Visualizations: children, distance
- **Setting**: Transparency. Visualizations: isolated groups in focus, gesture without apparent motive
- **Setting**: Spirituality. Visualizations: crucifix, body posture/eyes cast downward, funeral

Rhetorical Visions

- "We locate power and justice in our actions and voices."
- "Solidarity and empathy are under our control, shaping our community."
- "Equality remains elusive with discrimination a constant threat."

Sanctioning Agent: Solidarity, group cohesion
Master Analog: Righteous/social

Consider this everyday example: several students leave the classroom after learning they failed a group discussion assignment. As they gather in the break room, they try to make sense of the failing grade. One student admits she didn't do enough research. Another student concedes that going home for the weekend cut into his preparation time. A third encourages everyone to work harder to earn an "A" on the next assignments. They conclude, "There's little doubt that failing that assignment is the best thing that's happened to our small group." "Yeah, some good came out of our messing up – we realize we need to get better in the rest of the semester." "Yeah, it made us get our act together." Their resulting conclusions can be considered fantasy themes of redemption – a common theme of "fetching good out of evil." The students co-constructed a story to understand their reality and to plan future events.

Dramatis Personae

Dramatis personae are characters in real life, in a play, a movie, or any mediated product. Major characters portray human traits, sometimes positive and other times negative. There may be heroes and villains, fools, and victims. With visual rhetoric we quickly deduce meanings. For example, if a close-up of a political candidate's face presents a broad smile and direct gaze it suggests honesty and trustworthiness. Visual rhetoric also considers an image's function. A photograph of a political candidate as a toddler sitting on his father's shoulders and waving an American flag may give audiences the feeling of strong family bonds and patriotism.

Scene

A **scene** is the physical or symbolic location (setting) of the action. The drama may happen spontaneously in real time, it may be carefully staged, or a combination of the two. Many US political candidates carefully plan the backdrops for their events often using huge flags at rallies or photo shoots that show them as "regular citizens" – perhaps bowling, eating at a diner, or shooting baskets.

Plotline

The **plotline** is the underlying reason for the actions taken, or the conflicts faced, by the major character. This involves how conflict is resolved: such as "a triumphant love story," "a quest for justice," or "coming of age." In visual images, plotlines are often implied in the presentation. For example, a poster for the film *Batman v Superman: Dawn of Justice* shows the two main characters facing off in aggressive and powerful poses. The setting is a dark, rubble-strewn field with ruined buildings in the background and the air full of debris. Even if the viewer didn't know the premise or title of the movie, they would be able to deduce a major plot point of superhero conflict.

Symbolic Cue

A **symbolic cue is** a shorthand saying or image – recognized by participants – that stands for a more complete fantasy theme. For example, the clownish job applicant = Mr. Boxy; X = Malcolm X; "crying wolf" = lying; "Hope" = Barack Obama's 2008 presidential campaign; "We're loving it" = McDonald's. Visual symbolic cues: Pepe the Frog = White nationalists; a winged flying-W = Weezer.

Saga

A **saga** is an oft-repeated telling of the achievements in the life of a person, group, community, organization, or nation. The saga will often look like a fantasy theme; the difference is in the repeated nature of the telling and retelling and how it captures the preferred dramatization of a community and its leaders. In corporations, stories of founders are rife. They may be stories of Sam Walton's homespun personality as the catalyst for growing Walmart from a tiny store in Bentonville, Arkansas, to an international retail giant. They may be stories of eccentric genius such as Steve Jobs's obsession with aesthetics and detail as the impetus behind Apple's success. The researcher will likely find several different stories that form the saga. President Ronald Reagan distilled America's sense of itself as a model for all societies in his "Shining City on the Hill" speech. The phrase is drawn from the Bible's Sermon on the Mount and was used as early as 1630 by John Winthrop (1838), one of the early pioneers of what would become the United States, in urging his fellow shipmates toward a "model of Christian charity." President John F. Kennedy (1961) used the same phrase. This evokes the saga of "American exceptionalism" and the sense that the United States is different and better than all other societies.

Chaining

Chaining is when a story catches the attention of people in a group, they build on its meaning through their communication. The convergence creates social cohesion and often brings a sense of belonging and certainty with other members. This triggers a "chain reaction" producing increased and emotive conversation. As Bormann suggested, communities form not only due to individual interest or need but also based on the artistry of the message. Some messages such as advertising campaigns fail, not because the strategy and messaging were wrong, but the execution of the ads was inferior and unappealing to the target audience. Remember also that the artistry in message execution depends in great degree on the intended audience. Amateurish local car dealers often star in their own commercials and show a cringe-worthy lack of ability and professionalism. However, those clumsy executions may be effective and show "artistry" for their audience and goals.

Fantasy Type

A fantasy theme rarely appears alone. A **fantasy type** is a fantasy theme that recurs in group culture. It will feature a similar moral or theme, but different versions of the fantasy type will vary somewhat in characters featured, settings, and actions. For example, a frequent fantasy type in many organizations is that "the boss's assistant really runs things around here." Employees may express this in a variety of stories (fantasy themes) relating to how the assistant manages the boss, the assistant is the only one who gets things accomplished, and the like.

Rhetorical Vision

A composite of fantasy themes and types that provides a broader view; a symbolic reality embraced by a community of people, constructed by the stories they hear and the beliefs they hold. When a person arrives at a rhetorical vision, it can be very compelling.

Sanctioning Agent

The **sanctioning agent** is the bottom-line value that justifies the drama and legitimizes the rhetorical vision, or the course of action people take. It may be "the rich always cheat the poor" or "it's God's will."

Master Analogues

Usually a rhetorical vision can be categorized or labeled by a "master analogue" that integrates the fantasy themes. Groups with a shared rhetorical vision can constitute a rhetorical community: a community that sees the world in an essentially similar way. Overarching master analogues are:

- *Righteous*: The correct, proper, just, superior, right way
- *Social*: The trusting, caring, humane, social compact way
- *Pragmatic*: The efficient, cost-effective, expedient, practical way

Which College to Attend?

Most of us have debated which college to attend. Two professors assigned their research classes to study how high school students evaluate colleges (Cragan and Shields, 1995, pp. 46, 47). They discovered three warring dramas. One rhetorical vision valued college as a way to get a job quickly and inexpensively, supporting a "pragmatic" master analogue. Other students sought college to get away from home and share new experiences with new friends, supporting a "social" master analogue. A third group sought a challenging learning experience with a prestigious faculty, supporting a "righteous" master analog.

Some combinations of master analogs can also occur. Cragan and Shields (1995, p. 46) identify these as righteous/social, righteous/pragmatic, and social/pragmatic. A righteous/social vision might call on people's moral responsibility and duty to care for one another. A righteous/pragmatic vision suggest that doing what's right is also the most practical course of action such as a corporation's philanthropic program that both helps people and casts the firm in a positive light. A social/pragmatic vision would emphasize that by upholding the social contract and communities a practical outcome of stronger and more resilient towns and cities is more likely to occur.

In terms of product or service descriptions we can see the same categories emerge with somewhat different terminology (Cragan and Shields, 1995, p. 47):

- *Quality*: Competitive (*righteous*)
- *Service*: Engagement (*social*)
- *Price*: Utility (*pragmatic*)

Advertising campaigns tend to be driven by master analogs as well. Walmart promises to "Save Money. Live Better," a pragmatic approach. The upscale retailer Nordstrom promises "Service To The Customer Above All Else," a social approach. 3M Worldwide's slogan, "Innovation: Thou Shall Not Kill A New Product Idea," evokes a righteous approach. Consider other firms and their slogans or taglines: Nike's "Just Do It" (righteous), "Like a good neighbor, State Farm is there (social)," Apple's "Think different" (righteous) and "M&M's, melts in your mouth, not in your hands" (pragmatic).

APPLYING FTA TO VISUAL STRATEGIC COMMUNICATION

LO4 Appreciate visual symbolic convergence in the communication professions and apply this knowledge to understand consumers and other publics.

Up to this point, we have been considering the use of SCT and FTA in understanding the symbolic convergence in any rhetorical situation. Now, we turn to its usefulness in the communication professions, both as a research tool and a strategy for handling various challenges that may arise in your career.

Research

Imagine you've been asked to advise an organization on increasing employee morale, or how to successfully merge two companies' cultures. Perhaps you will work for a nonprofit needing to encourage healthy diets in teenagers, or as a consultant advising a municipality how to build community support for or against controversial housing developments. FTA analysis can be used as guidance in all of these situations.

For any audience research, it's important to gather and analyze data about a targeted segment of consumers. "Demographics" identifies the age, sex, education, income, location, and similar socioeconomic information. "Psychographics" refers to an identified audience's needs, interests, activities, attitudes, and values. "Sociographics" describes people's behaviors using a product or service. John F. Cragan added the concept of the "Symbographic™," applying SCT/FTA to determine the symbolic realities of audiences and pinpointing where they derive meaning, motive, emotion, and identity in their lives. SCT's analytic tools and vocabularies are helpful in interpreting actions and communication artifacts. For instance, a market researcher can use the same terms in analyzing and describing a focus group of consumers as they would for analyzing marketing messages. The symbographic process offers direction on how to position a brand, program, or organizational identity by answering these three questions (Cragan and Shields 1992, p. 208):

1. Is your brand symbolically unique?
2. Can you ground that identity in facts and reality?
3. Is it a profitable identity?

Apple's "Think different" slogan was symbolically unique in its positioning as a leader in innovation. The types of breakthrough products the company manufactures provide evidence for this positioning and its related claims. The successful marketing of products ranging from the introduction of the personal computer to the

Figure 7.4 Cristiano Ronaldo lends his athletic celebrity to the Jeep brand. Marketers believe that his public image is a good match emphasizing skill, adventure, and coolness. *Source:* Thananuwat Srirasant/Getty Images Sport/ Getty Images.

iPod, iPhone, iPad, and their iterations, speaks to profitability. Its righteous master analogue comports with the products' sleek designs, higher prices, and sheen of superiority over, say, some Android devices, many of which have equal or better functionality than some Apple products.

When soccer star Cristiano Ronaldo (Figure 7.4) signed with Italy's Juventus football club in 2018, Jeep expected to cash in as well as the Jeep logo is featured on team jerseys. Beyond Ronaldo's celebrity, marketers believed the brand's characteristics of freedom, adventure, and cool comported well with the footballer's style known to be fast, effective, and even predatory (Novy-Williams and Coppola, 2019).

Marketing Research Methods

Both still and moving images are becoming more important in marketing strategies, thus it's crucial for marketers to understand how people respond to and interact with messages and campaigns. SCT can be used in quantitative research, such as surveys, and qualitative research such as focus groups and in-depth interviews.

For instance, after showing campaign messages to a focus group, the researcher would gather and code the responses using SCT categories. Another option would be using an online survey that allows participants to view an ad and then write two to three sentences in response to an open-ended question: *Please write at least two sentences to describe thoughts and feelings that you had when you were watching the ad.* This methodology is based on cognitive interviewing: a technique often applied as pretesting for survey research (Blair and Brick, 2010). Again, the coding into fantasy themes, fantasy types, and eliciting the most powerful and persuasive rhetorical visions would offer findings to guide copywriters, creative directors, and media planners in creating high impact ads and campaigns.

SCT's Place Online

The Internet is an environment that challenges us to understand communication from multitudes of diverse people interacting from local to global locations. The words and images they use are symbols carrying meaning; a meaning that may develop resonance and influence as conversations build and expand. This exchange and performance may converge into shared meanings and even an agreement on overall meaning of a symbol (e.g. a collective understanding of the meaning of "justice"). For a professional visual communicator, knowing what is meaningful to your stakeholders and what symbols resonate with them – especially collectively – is a strategic advantage to guide message creation.

Public Relations: City Images and Political Campaigns

Macau is known as a casino city. Beyond this image, two researchers wanted to understand the cultural and historical representations of the city in both Chinese and English media. Using FTA, they studied the city's branding efforts evident in media reports, blog articles, and promotion materials, which were collected from three media types, namely earned media, shared media, and owned media. They found the symbolic pictures of Macau represented in various media types to be different, identifying 11 fantasy themes with nongaming elements. The study concludes that the rhetoric of the themes was weak and lacked any deep and enduring emotion for brand recognition (Mei and Ying, 2017). The results of this study diagnose a need for stronger branding.

Another category of public relations concerns political messaging. The US Republican presidential primary campaign in 2012 eventually yielded four competing candidates. A study asking, "what does credibility look like?" used visual coding and FTA to analyze images on the candidates' official Facebook and Twitter pages. It found that depictions of character traits such as trustworthiness and expertise varied widely and recommended more strategic political management of messaging strategies in online social media platforms (Page and Duffy, 2018).

FOCUS: Political Issue Advertising

In September 2013, many Internet users were startled by video ads set in doctors' examining rooms that used vivid visuals, audio, and body penetration imagery to discourage audiences from signing up for insurance exchanges mandated by the Affordable Care Act (Franke-Ruta, 2013). One spot featured a young woman expecting a pelvic examination by a physician. Instead, a figure with a grotesque Uncle Sam mask and costume emerges threateningly with speculum in hand. The other ad featured a young man expecting a proctology exam when the same startling character appears to the sound of a glove snapping.

Source: National Review.

The creators of the ad refer to the character as "Creepy Uncle Sam." On-screen verbiage discouraged young people from signing up for the Affordable Care Act (Obamacare) even though they would likely incur fines. Researchers used FTA to examine four anti- and pro-Obamacare video ads appearing in September 2013: two ads produced by tea party-backed political action committee (PAC) "Generation Opportunity" and two pro-Obamacare ads produced by the states of Minnesota and Oregon. The following is an excerpt of the analysis of the Generation Opportunity "Creepy Uncle Sam" ads.

The primary fantasy type, "Obamacare means omnipresent government surveillance and control over individual free will" is established in the opening frame of both ads: multiple old school television monitors suggest **panoptical** scrutiny. Viewers likely to be familiar with *The Matrix* movie series may identify this scene with a similar one in *The Matrix Reloaded*, where the protagonist meets the architect (of the matrix) face-to-face in a large room whose walls are covered with television monitors (revealing a system enacted to control humanity, placing human agency against determinism).

Other fantasy types are: "Young men and women who choose Obamacare are stupid, willing victims, and worthy of contempt;" "Obamacare will humiliate and emasculate young men and terrorize and molest young women;" and "The US government is a bully, a monster, and a torturer." The drama enacted by the two anti-Obamacare ads present the overall rhetorical vision that "Obamacare will turn healthcare into a horror show."

Public Affairs: Questioning News Sources

The Institute of Public Affairs (IPA) is an Australian think tank and high-profile news source that rejects the evidence of climate change and opposes mitigation strategies such as an Emissions Trading Scheme (ETS). Researchers used FTA to identify the anti-climate science fantasy themes developed by the IPA and traced the chaining out of these fantasy themes from the IPA into the news media. The rhetorical vision expressed by the IPA is one of hostility toward climate scientists and the scientific consensus on climate change, and the news media echoed that. Analysis showed the IPA used its access to the media as a news source to influence the public discussion on climate change in Australia (McKewon, 2012). The website dramatizes the organization's stance on what it considers excessive government regulation with a stock photo of bulging binders entitled "The 176 Billion Tax On Our Prosperity" (Figure 7.5).

The 176 Billion Tax On Our Prosperity

Figure 7.5 **The Australian Institute for Public Affairs (IPA) is a conservative think tank that supports several goals including reducing regulations governing business operations. This image appeared on its website relating to the "Red Tape Project."** *Source:* **Thomas Bethge/iStock/Getty Images.**

News Coverage: The Pope, a Nobel Prize, and a Nice Grown-Up

Pope Francis's 2015 visit to Cuba provided a unique opportunity for a comparative study of state-controlled and independent media systems. A study by Thomson et al. (2018) used FTA to explore how visuals created by US-based Associated Press (AP), UK-based Reuters, and Cuba-based Prensa Latina revealed the underlying rhetorical visions, ideologies, and priorities of each culture's media system. The study found that state-controlled and independent media depicted the Pope's visit differently in the degree of personalization shown, the social actors who were depicted, the purpose of the visit, how the Pope was shown in relation to others, and the location where the action occurred. Each media system highlighted its news values and priorities through these differences. Additionally, the images revealed two master narratives: Cuba as a model of Catholicism and the Pope as a model of hierarchy and conformity.

Another globally newsworthy event, Mo Yan's award of the Nobel Prize in literature provoked competing voices in the global Chinese media, ranging from official media to online citizen forums, and from Chinese mainland media to overseas Chinese Internet forums. Researchers used FTA to study the different media responses, finding opposing fantasy themes, for example, with Chinese official media = "Rise of China" and "Fame follows merits" and with overseas Chinese netizens in online forums = "Communist dictatorship" and "Oriental empire." Four rhetorical visions were shared among many of the media responses to Mo Yan's award, with varying sanctioning agents: nationalism, moralism, pragmatism, liberalism, and orientalism (Wu and Zhu, 2017). "Orientalism" is a concept holding that certain representations of Asians and Arabs tend to present stereotypes, overemphasize differences from the United States and Europe, and reinforce persistent colonialism.

An earlier research study using FTA found that, for three decades, newspaper and broadcast news coverage had framed American television personality Fred (Mr.) Rogers as a calming influence and treated him with deference and respect (Bishop, 2006). Journalists created a fantasy about Rogers that held him up as the embodiment of television's potential, potential that can be realized only by returning to quiet tolerance and the power of imagination: two elements at the heart of Mister Rogers' Neighborhood. To reporters in this interpretive community, Rogers offered hope for those struggling to raise children. A rhetorical vision of Rogers as "the world's nicest grown-up," was constructed out of the fantasy themes by journalists stepping outside their usual desired role as objective observers. Journalists who start off skeptical of Rogers and his approach find themselves captivated by his message, and they insert this experience into their coverage of Rogers, making it a key fantasy theme.

Magazines: Voices from, and for, Teens

A study exploring how *Teen Voices*, a magazine written and edited by teenage girls, found it created a rhetorical vision of empowerment through its text and photographs (Gerl, 2016). Using FTA, the researcher identified four fantasy types: (i) I am a survivor, (ii) I am a dreamer, (iii) I am an activist, and (iv) I can do anything. These were supported by sanctioning agents of individualism and personal strength.

Another study of the teen magazine *YM*, this time focusing on staff-produced content, yielded results quite opposite of those found with the teen-produced content in *Teen Voices*. In the process of appealing to female adolescents, *YM* featured articles asking provocative questions such as: Can a bra change our life? Are you a guy repellant? Are you a sucker for slime balls? Researchers examined both editorial and advertising images using FTA to discover the symbolic realities of adolescent life expressed in the magazine's rhetoric. This analysis revealed a social reality in which the only power available to young women is achieved through seduction, beauty, and fashion (Duffy and Gotcher, 1996). What would FTA analysis of a current magazine with the same target audience reveal today?

FOCUS: Where to Find Symbolic Convergence? Nonprofit Fundraising Campaigns

In the summer of 2014, two Boston College athletes started an online campaign called the Ice Bucket Challenge to raise money for a former teammate suffering from amyotrophic lateral sclerosis (ALS). The activity involved the dumping of a bucket of ice and water over a person's head.

Source: Boston Globe/Getty ImagesBoston Globe/Getty Images.

It started locally and grew globally via social media, raising $115 million for the ALS Association to fund its research budget. Its explosive growth was driven by

(Continued)

media interest, celebrity participation, social media posts, shares, and retweets. According to the *Boston Globe*, Facebook reported 1.2 million videos posted about the Ice Bucket Challenge, and more than 15 million people commented or "liked" the videos in less than two months.

While an FTA analysis has not been conducted on the campaign to the best of our knowledge, it is representative of the coalescing of causes, pictures, and people online, and would be a perfect candidate for any student wanting to test their new knowledge of SCT with visual messaging.

HOW TO ANALYZE AND CREATE VISUAL SYMBOLIC MESSAGES

LO5 Learn how to analyze visual fantasies in communication and how to create compelling visual and textual messages.

Most of us visit favorite websites, engage in social media expression, see political candidates' events, and consume advertising and other media without noticing the elements that create social reality for ourselves and others. SCT and FTA offer us the opportunity to see deeper structures and explain "what's going on."

Fantasy Theme Analysis

As we systematically record and synthesize the data, we can develop an understanding of why people interpret and respond to visuals as they do. We can discern the rhetorical strategies communicators use and see the elements that make messages persuasive and compelling to some degree, and their potential to chain out among audiences. Why would this be useful? Figuring out these strategies helps us home in on the motivations, fears, and aspirations of speakers and audiences. The ability to dissect the elements of a drama can heighten our abilities to question messaging that is manipulative or based on questionable premises. Knowing the processes behind dramatism can help us research and construct messaging that is more likely to be effective in reaching our target audiences whether you're doing a business presentation, creating a public service campaign, or even planning an event.

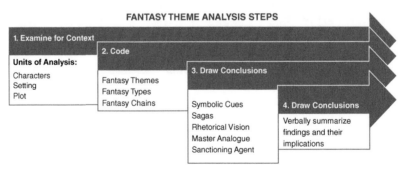

Source: Author. © John Wiley & Sons, Inc.

Example of a Simple FTA Analysis

This example uses a single image, an American Academy of Dermatology poster, and not images collected from multiple sources, to illustrate the FTA method. Usually, when we use SCT and the method of FTA, we're looking for evidence that fantasy themes have chained out among publics and created rhetorical communities. It is unknown if this public service ad produced by the American Academy of Dermatology was widely viewed or shared. We selected it for its skill and artistry in conveying an emotional message. As a beginner, you are encouraged to also choose a single image to test and practice FTA. Once you become familiar with the process, choose and work with a group of images to see the real magic of SCT. You will then want to refer back to all of FTA's basic concepts detailed earlier in this chapter.

Choose an Image

Locate an image, set of images, video, or other subject for analysis and gain an overall impression of the characters, setting, plot, and messages/goals of the item you're analyzing. This example analyzes a poster from the American Academy of Dermatology warning of the risks of skin cancer.

Source: American Academy of Dermatology.

Step 1: Units of Analysis

Begin to evaluate and code the various elements into fantasy themes. Fantasy themes are the most basic unit of analysis that structure the overall impression that viewers may experience (Shields and Preston, 1985). You'll find fantasy themes for the characters, the plotline(s), and the setting or scene.

- *Character(s)*: The character is a vital, healthy-looking young woman, smiling fearlessly. She is fit and dressed like a professional climber. Notably, a significant percentage of her skin is exposed to the elements.

- *Action/plotline*: The *action* reveals the character clinging to a cliff face high above a valley and swinging toward her next handhold. A climbing rope furls below disappearing toward an unknown location.

- *Setting*: The *setting* is dramatic, beautiful, and harsh featuring sharp, rocky outcroppings, dangerous peaks, and a climbing surface that is vertical and pock-marked.

For most viewers of the image, the juxtaposition of the jagged rocks and the climber's vulnerable body is disconcerting and is likely to lead to acceptance of the claimed riskiness of the behavior.

Step 2: Coding

Fantasies: The viewer is likely to engage with the setting, immediately discerning the jeopardy that the young climber appears to face. The image invites us to warn her of the peril. For any effective drama, a tension between opposing forces is necessary. In this case, the headline jolts the reader into making an explicit connection between the obvious dangerous activity the character is willingly – even joyfully – engaging in and the not so obvious but extremely real danger of skin cancer. In this sense, the image offers a visual simile and draws a clear line between the outlandish risk shown in the image and skin cancer.

Step 3: Drawing Conclusions

- *Master analogue*: This public service announcement (PSA) calls on people to act in certain prescribed ways and to encourage others to adopt these attitudes and values. Again, notice that the PSA's strategy limits the viewers' ability to internally argue with the drama and its legitimizing sanctioning agent. While people may differently evaluate the dangers of skin cancer, this drama largely bypasses the scientific arguments.

- *Sanctioning agent*: Shields and Preston Jr. (1985) define the sanctioning agent as the justification for acceptance of the message or overarching idea. It could refer to a higher power (God, humanistic ethics), a threat (war, invasion, impending accident), an opportunity (safety, economic security, freedom from hunger). This image calls out an urgent threat.

- *Rhetorical vision*: Risking skin cancer is life-threatening.

Step 4: Summarizing

Report your findings: With more complex or multiple images and video, this step can be very extensive. For the purposes of the following exercise, limit your analysis to two to three pages.

Your First Fantasy Theme Analysis

Try a simple analysis to begin with. Using this image from Tobacco Free CA, analyze it following the four-step FTA process.

Source: Tobacco Free CA.

Applying Fantasy Theme Analysis

As in previous chapters, this section calls on you to build your analytic and creative skills. You'll have the opportunity to investigate artifacts that interest you, analyze them, and then create your own visual messages. While you won't be asked to conduct a large complex research project or analysis, these activities will let you experience these processes.

Challenge #1: Research – Evaluate – Create (REC)

Step One: Research

Select an image or artifact you find moving, interesting, or, of course *dramatic*. It could be an advertisement, a concert or movie poster, or a news photograph. Remember that the artifact you select could be serious, funny, overtly persuasive, or subtle. You could also use a short video, keeping in mind that with video you have even more elements for analysis.

Next, conduct some general research on the image's subject matter. This may include looking into the current economic state of an industry, societal matters, or political considerations. This background knowledge gives you a better understanding of the literal, primary subject itself and situational contexts. Write a short summary of your findings.

Step Two: Evaluate

Analyze an image using the four-step process, but also referring to all the FTA components (listed earlier in this chapter). You may find it easiest to go through the elements one by one, answering all the questions, and then go back and make some revisions. Once complete, combine your research findings and your evaluation into a short paper (two to three pages). Start with a statement of why you chose to analyze this image or set of images. Then describe your secondary research and what you learned about the issue, the image, its creators, and its likely goals and write up your findings. In your conclusion, state what insights you gained from your research. Do your findings and insights offer interesting perspectives on society? What behaviors are praiseworthy or wrong? What roles for men, women, children, moms or dads, the elderly, etc. can be seen? Is it possible or likely that the visual message might have unintended consequences such as stereotyping or demonizing certain behaviors?

Step Three: Create

Develop a dramatistic strategy for an ad, poster, or news photo *in the same subject category* of the one you analyzed. For instance, if you analyzed a perfume ad, create another ad for perfume. Describe how you would devise a strong appeal for the target audience using an image or images. Be sure to explain what dramatic elements you would emphasize to get the desired response from the audience.

Create the visual with your own photos, sketches, or images from the Creative Commons or similar. If you choose to use copyrighted images, remember they may only be used for classroom assignments and may not be publicly published (including posting/sharing online). If you analyzed a video such as a TV ad, you may want to make "storyboard:" a common tool we use in developing ads, films, and videos. There are several tutorials and tools available online such as http://www.wikihow.com/Create-a-Storyboard, as well as apps for iOS or Android platforms.

Note: you can also incorporate words, but the primary communication vehicle should be visual. Don't worry if you're not a skilled visual artist. What's most important is your thinking (strategy) underpinning your choices. The visuals you analyzed may, for example, have emphasized action and resulted in a pragmatic master analogue and rhetorical vision. You might decide that a character/actor emphasis would be a more effective persuader or that a focus on a social or righteous master analogue would be stronger. Once finished, be sure to explain the reasoning behind your decision-making.

Challenge #2: Research – Evaluate – Create (REC)

Step One: Research

On Instagram, choose *two* professional accounts. The accounts should have some like-minded purpose, for example, politicians running against each other (or elected but with differing platforms) or competing product brands (like United and American airlines). However, they don't have to be in opposition. You may choose two similar nonprofit organizations (like Save the Children and Children International), two college towns' tourism bureaus, or two insurance companies, and so on.

Next, conduct some general research on the accounts' subject matter. This may include looking into the current economic state of an industry, societal or cultural matters, or political considerations. This background knowledge gives you a better understanding of the literal, primary subject itself and situational contexts.

Then, conduct the four-step FTA process on a sample of images from each account. Perhaps your sample will be "one week's postings" or longer; just so you have about 8–10 images. Identify the rhetorical visions each one reveals.

Write a short summary of your findings.

Step Two: Evaluate

Based on your findings in the research step, describe how you would advise ONE of the accounts to alter its postings based on dramatistic criteria. Do this in a one-page memo to the account holder.

Step Three: Create

Produce a PowerPoint or Keynote with no more than five slides that you believe tell a strong, visually dramatic story for the holder of the account. Take your own photos or choose images from the Creative Commons or other sources to make your points. If you choose to use copyrighted images, remember they may only be used for classroom assignments and may not be publicly published (including posting/sharing online).

CHAPTER SUMMARY

In this chapter, we discussed how images may chain out among audiences and create shared understanding of events including shared emotions and attitudes. People cocreate their social realities through communication on a range of platforms and media including television, social networks, mobile devices, and the like. By systematically analyzing images through the lens of SCT, researchers can better interpret audiences' worldviews and detect motivations and ideas that may not be superficially obvious. As citizens, our awareness of how different messages may be shaped by emphasizing actors, plot, and scene helps us view messages more critically. Similarly, applying SCT helps communicators develop more interesting, persuasive, and more dramatic messages, campaigns, and information.

KEY TERMS

Fantasies   Imaginative ideas with symbolic meanings.

Convergence   Sharing of the same emotions and embracing the same values.

Rhetorical vision   A group consciousness; a collective, overall understanding; a worldview.

Fantasy themes   Shared imaginative ideas with symbolic meanings.

Dramatis personae   Characters in real life, in a play, a movie, or any mediated product.

Scene   Physical or symbolic location (setting) of the action.

Plotline   Underlying reason for the actions taken, or the conflicts faced, by the major characters.

Symbolic cue   Shorthand saying or image—recognized by participants—that stands for a more complete fantasy theme.

Saga   Oft-repeated telling of the achievements in the life of a person, group, community, organization, or nation.

Chaining   When a story catches the attention of people in a group, they build on its meaning through their communication.

Fantasy type   A recurring fantasy theme.

Sanctioning agent   Bottom-line value that justifies the drama and legitimizes the rhetorical vision, or the course of action people take.

Panoptical   All inclusive; everything visible in one view.

PRACTICE ACTIVITIES

1. Select a series of ads that are part of the same campaign and conduct a FTA analysis focusing primarily on the visual aspects of the campaign.

2. Visit the Newseum's digital archive of newspaper front pages at https://www.newseum.org/todaysfrontpages. At the top right-hand side of the day's front pages, select "Archived Pages." There you may choose a significant news day, such as the 2018 Students Walk Out Over Gun Violence, the 2017 Women's March, or the 2011 Osama bin Laden Killed, among many others. Next, view the newspaper front pages from across the United States, select a sample of them, and conduct a FTA of their dominant images. Note, you can browse the front pages and download the images to your desktop.

3. In a team, select a nonprofit or charitable organization and identify its goals. Conduct research on the organization's target audience, possibly interviewing its director and examining secondary research about organizations with similar goals. Create two to three ads that you believe are likely to have dramatic appeal.

REFERENCES

Bishop, R. (2006). The world's nicest grown-up: a fantasy themes analysis of news media coverage of Fred Rogers. *Journal of Communication* 53 (1): 16–31.

Blair, J. and Brick, P. (2010). Methods for the analysis of cognitive interviews. Abt Associations. https://www.amstat.org/sections/srms/Proceedings/y2010/Files/307865_59514.pdf (accessed September 28, 2014).

Bormann, E.G. (1981). Fantasy and rhetorical vision: the rhetorical criticism of social reality. In: *Applied Communication Research: A Dramatistic Approach* (eds. J.F. Cragan and D.C. Shields), 15–29. Prospect Heights, IL: Waveland Press.

Bormann, E. (1983). Symbolic convergence: organizational communication and culture. In: *Communication and Organizations: An Interpretive Approach* (eds. L.L. Putnam and M.E. Pacanowsky), 99–122. Beverly Hills, CA: Sage.

Bormann, E. (1985). *The Force of Fantasy: Restoring the American Dream*. Carbondale, IL: Southern Illinois University Press.

Bormann, E. and Bormann, N. (1972). *Speech Communication: A Basic Approach*. New York: Harper and Row.

Borman, E. (1990). *Small Group Communication: Theory and Practice*. New York, NY: Harper & Row.

Bormann, E., Cragan, J.F., and Shields, D. (2003). Defending Symbolic Convergence Theory from an Imaginary Gunn. *Quarterly Journal of Speech* 89 (4): 366–372.

Burch, A.D.S. and Isensee, L. (2012). Trayvon Martin: A typical teen who loved video games, looked forward to prom. https://www.miamiherald.com/news/state/florida/trayvon-martin/article1939761.html (accessed December 24, 2020).

Cragan, J.F. and Shields, D.C. (1992). The use of symbolic convergence theory in corporate strategic planning: a case study. *Journal of Applied Communication Research* 20 (2): 199–218.

Cragan, J.F. and Shields, D.C. (1995). *Symbolic Theories in Applied Communication Research: Bormann, Burke and Fisher*. New York, NY: Hampton Press.

Duffy, M.E. and Gotcher, J.M. (1996). Crucial advice on how to get the guy: The rhetorical vision of power and seduction in the teen magazine *YM*. *Journal of Communication Inquiry* 20 (1): 32–48.

Duffy, M.E. and Thorson, E. (2016). *Persuasion Ethics Today*. Routledge.

Eligon, J., Arango, T., Shaila Dewan, S. and Nicholas Bogel-Burroughs, N. (2021). Derek Chauvin verdict brings a rare rebuke of police conduct. New York Times, April 21. Retrieved May 7, 2021 from https://www.nytimes.com/2021/04/20/us/george-floyd-chauvin-verdict.html

Foss, S. (2009). *Rhetorical Criticism: Exploration and Practice*, 4e. Long Grove, IL: Waveland.

Franke-Ruta, G. (2013). Creepy anti-Obamacare ads suggest where Uncle Sam wants to stick it. https://www.theatlantic.com/politics/archive/2013/09/creepy-anti-obamacare-ads-suggest-where-uncle-sam-wants-to-stick-it/279825/ (accessed December 24, 2020).

Gerl, E. (2016). Survivors and dreamers: a rhetorical vision of *Teen Voices* magazine. *Journal of Magazine and New Media Research* 17 (1): 1–26.

Head, T. (2019). The Shooting Death of Oscar Grant. https://www.thoughtco.com/shooting-death-of-oscar-grant-721526 (accessed December 24, 2020).

Kennedy, J. F. (1961). John F. Kennedy Presidential Library and Museum. Historic Speeches. http://www.jfklibrary.org/Asset-Viewer/OYhUZE2Qo0-ogdV7ok900A.aspx (accessed 25 September 2020).

Kolata, G. and Rabin, C. R. (2020). "Don't be afraid of Covid," Trump says, undermining public health messages. https://www.nytimes.com/2020/10/05/health/trump-covid-public-health.html (accessed October 7, 2020).

Lizza, R. and Lippman, D. (2020). Wearing a mask is for smug liberals. Refusing to is for reckless Republicans. *Politico,* May 1. https://www.politico.com/news/2020/05/01/masks-politics-coronavirus-227765 (accessed October 7, 2020).

McKewon, E. (2012). Talking points ammo. *Journalism Studies* 13 (2): 277–297.

Mei, W. and Ying, Z. (2017). Symbolic repertoires for city branding beyond casinos: the case of Macau. *International Journal of Strategic Communication* 11 (5): 415–433.

Meyers, D.J. (2012). Faculty fashion. *Inside Higher Ed.* https://www.insidehighered.com/views/2012/07/13/essay-faculty-fashion (accessed March 28, 2020).

Novy-Williams, E. and Coppola, G. (2019). Cristiano Ronaldo's move to Italy a Big Score for Jeep. Private Wealth, October 28. https://www.fa-mag.com/news/cristiano-ronaldo-s-move-to-italy-a-big-score-for-jeep-39691.html (accessed December 24, 2020).

Page, J.T. and Duffy, M.E. (2018). What does credibility look like? Tweets and walls U.S. presidential candidates' visual storying. *Journal of Political Marketing* 17 (1): 3–31.

Schneider, A. (1998). Frumpy or Chic? Tweed or Kente? Sometimes clothes make the professor. The Chronicle of Higher Education, January 23 pp. A12–A14.

Shields, D.C. and Preston, C.T. Jr. (1985). Fantasy theme analysis in competitive rhetorical criticism. *National Forensic Journal.* https://www.researchgate.net/publication/265074219_Fantasy_Theme_Analysis_in_Competitive_Rhetorical_Criticism (accessed October 27, 2019).

Thomson, T.J., Perreault, G., and Duffy, M. (2018). Politicians, photographers, and a Pope. *Journalism Studies* 19 (9): 1313–1330.

Winthrop, J. (1838). John Winthrop. A modell of Christian charity (1630). *Collections of the Massachusetts Historical Society* 7: 31–48. http://history.hanover.edu/texts/winthmod.html (accessed September 25, 2020).

Wu, M. and Zhu, W.-b. (2017). Rise of China or Western conspiracy? A fantasy theme analysis. *China Media Research* 13 (2): 23–36.

Yan, H. (2014). Attorney: New audio reveals pause in gunfire when Michael Brown was shot. CNN. http://www.cnn.com/2014/08/26/us/michael-brown-ferguson-shooting/ (accessed December 24, 2020).

PART THREE

Using Visuals in Professional Communication

Chapter 8
Advertising

#FaceAnything

Source: Olay Eyes.

With taglines such as "you're too confident," "you're too emotional," and "you're too outspoken," Olay, a Proctor & Gamble skin care brand, released the "Face Anything" campaign in fall of 2018. Featuring celebrities such as Jillian Mercado, a Latina model who has muscular dystrophy and uses a wheelchair, the campaign encouraged women to be unapologetically strong, bold, and true to themselves (Lowe, 2018). The highly visible executions enlisted nine inspirational role models to be the faces of the campaign, including Mercado, NFL sportscaster Kay Adams, gold medal Olympian Aly Raisman, and comedian Lilly Singh.

The campaign broke with a 10-page ad spread in *Vogue*, then expanded with Times Square and Grand Central ambient (outdoor) ads, plus events and social media. In line with the empowerment theme, the campaign included messaging on the products' performance and science. For example, the campaign staged a "makeup-free" New York Fashion Week show, where women walked the runway without makeup after taking Olay's "28-Day Challenge," to showcase how their skin changes after four weeks of using the products.

Olay's campaign reflected similar body-positive campaigns aimed at women from other cosmetic brands. Dove, a Unilever brand, had released several viral campaigns in previous years, including "Real Beauty" and "Choose Beautiful," encouraging women to be themselves and love their bodies. Proctor & Gamble's award-winning "Like a Girl" campaign for Always feminine products highlighted incredible things girls can achieve, helping to break down stereotypes and instill female empowerment. In the 1990s, The Body Shop, a retailer of women's skin and bath products, launched the "Love your body" self-esteem campaign with the creation of a mascot doll, Ruby. Unlike the Barbie doll, Ruby had more realistic body proportions. The slogan: "There are 3 billion women who don't look like supermodels and only 8 who do."

Of course, these "body-positive" campaigns have their critics. Dove's parent company also owns Axe grooming products targeted at young men. Axe is known for edgy ads that aim for a humorous tone but feature sexual stereotypes and gender roles. Other critics see ads for body positivity as simply cynical sales tactics purporting to support women in socially responsible ways but serving to distract people from the real obstacles women face in today's world.

What are brands' responsibilities in deploying images? You'll consider this more closely later in this book when we move from advertising to public relations and read about corporations' shift to include social responsibility into their business models.

Key Learning Objectives
After engaging in this chapter, you'll be able to:
Understand the definition and history of strategic visual communication.
1. Recognize and critique visual rhetoric in advertising, especially the extensive use of metaphor.
2. Explore and assess contemporary uses of visual rhetoric in advertising.

Chapter Overview
As we turn to practice areas in visual communication, we begin with **advertising**. Think of an ad you've recently seen. Most likely, it has compelling visuals or video that draw your attention, showcase a product or service, and associate the brand with a particular lifestyle or outcome. Often, the ad encourages you to *see* the desirable outcome from using that product. At an even more basic level, the visuals in the advertising engage you because they may be surprising, entertaining, or fun, and thus you're more likely to pay attention.

Effective and emotionally compelling advertising without photography is almost unimaginable, so we begin with photography's influence in society and how that influence melded with advertising. We then turn to understanding advertising as *strategic* visual communication. Advertising is strategic in that marketers and advertisers conduct research on audiences, discover desirable target markets, find key insights, and shape messages likely to be persuasive for them.

In this chapter, you'll learn to look at ads differently, going beneath the surface to discover how visuals in advertising can draw attention to certain aspects of a product, associate that product with a desired lifestyle, and use symbolism to link it with deeper emotions. In addition, you'll see how some advertising appeals have questionable ethics. The chapter then covers visual rhetoric in advertising. Rhetoric, as we discuss it here, involves using language and images to persuade others. Visual metaphors are one of the most common and effective tools advertisers employ. It closes with examples of how ad visuals work in social media, e-mail marketing, outdoor and ambient areas, television, and finally product placement.

PHOTOGRAPHY IN SOCIETY

LO1 Understand the definition and history of strategic visual communication

The photographic image, with its power to move and influence perceptions, is the dominant form of visual imagery in **strategic communication**. Strategic communicators seek to maximize message effects by coordinating the optimal combination of media, social, digital, and interpersonal factors to accomplish organizational or marketing goals. This book focuses on how to identify strategic approaches in *visual* communication and understand it from rhetorical, critical, and cultural perspectives. You can apply your knowledge of strategic visual communication in many professional career paths including research, campaign strategy, art direction, graphic design, copywriting, photography, video storytelling, promotion planning, and more, all located within the broader fields of marketing, advertising, and public relations. In fact, everyone working in strategic communication should have a good knowledge of how visual content contributes to effective messaging, beginning with understanding its history.

A History of Photographic Influence

Photography's historical context, its reception, and its influence have changed over the years. The camera's arrival significantly impacted society because people now had the ability to capture and produce images of the "real." Photographic visuals reflect and influence society, and their power is magnified today in our digital and connected world.

The photograph's reflection of the "real" is what allows the photographic image to immediately attract our attention as viewers. The potency of the photographic visual as a frame of the "real" is quite an old story. Beginning with artists' sixteenth-century use of the camera obscura (see "The Early Image Makers" feature) and continuing through the nineteenth century stereoscope and first Kodak camera, art historian Jonathan Crary (1992) cites the developing technology's gradual imposition of a normative vision on viewers of photography. A normative vision is a particular *way* of seeing, one that a society or culture prefers, and one that may suppress other perspectives.

As technology developed in the twentieth century, scholars who studied the influence of visual images on society voiced concerns about the "dangers of a society saturated with **pseudo-images**," (Barnhurst et al., 2004). We can think of pseudo-images as made-up images without an original source, posing dangers of deceiving viewers with publicity and illusion. The concept of pseudo-images was developed by sociologist Jean Baudrillard (1970/1983), who warned of a "postmodern condition" in contemporary Western society; a condition characterized by uncertainty and questioning of tradition.

Baudrillard coined the term *simulacrum* to describe this new type of reality, a "hyperreality." It contains artificial images that no longer refer to what's "real" but exist only in relation to one another. Consider, for example, how **memes** and other digital content have effortlessly moved into our lives, evoking engagement and merging into our conversations with others. We're able to understand the meaning of such memes because we recognize other images that they refer to.

In a 2016–2017 study of the most popular memes on the Internet, one of the most common memes on Twitter was Evil Kermit (Sonnad, 2018): a screenshot of Kermit the Frog, the well-known Muppet character, standing next to a Sith version of himself (borrowed from the *Star Wars* films). Its caption read, "me: sees a fluffy dog/me to me: steal him" (Figure 8.1). Within 10 days after its first upload, thousands of retweets and likes catapulted it into popular variations. In less than two weeks, pop culture and news sites Pop Sugar, Cheezburger, and Buzzfeed broadcast the trending images. This triggered variations with Miss Piggy, further reported and promoted by more pop culture news sites and blogs. As Baudrillard predicted much earlier, the *virtual*

Figure 8.1 Popular Twitter meme "Evil Kermit." *Source:* Lifewire.

representation – manipulated, opinionated, persuasive imagery – became celebrated as *experience* and representations of the "real" had become rooted in everyday life.

Consider the photographic image and advertising. When historian James Truslow Adams coined the phrase "American Dream" in his 1931 book, *The Epic of America*, it had more to do with idealism for wide-open opportunities than what it came to mean: materialism and a pursuit of the "good life:" constant themes in the history of advertising. A useful way to get an understanding of how advertising's influence has progressed is to look at the current state of the industry in the contexts of social media/mobile, e-mail marketing, ambient, TV, and product placement and how the power of the visual image has evolved.

FOCUS: Culture Jamming Creates a Visual Battlefield

As an example of culture jamming, communication student Yuritzi Castell parodied the familiar "Dummies" book cover to make a statement on a popular assumption that visual communication is easy to understand.

Culture jamming attacked Paris during the shopping extravaganza after Thanksgiving Day, known in the U.S. as Black Friday and celebrated in France as "Vendredi Noir." In 2015, it coincided with the United Nations Climate Change

Conference (**COP21**) in Paris, attended by world leaders from 196 different countries. Throughout the night, small groups of climate change activists in Paris employed creative disruption tactics due to a state of emergency ban on protests. The activists replaced more than 600 ad panels at bus stops around the city with original artwork posters that mocked corporate sponsors of the talks. The action was a project sponsored by Brandalism, a UK organization that uses culture jamming to connect corporations' complicity with critical societal issues. Culture jamming uses "consumer culture as a viable path to social change" (Carducci, 2006, p. 130). Using the posters as a strategy of creative activism to subvert public advertising, Brandalism sought to connect corporate culture, the dominance of advertising in public spaces, and its promotion of everyday consumption to environmental sustainability.

Brandalism, a cross between "brand" and "vandalism," positions itself as "a revolt against corporate control of the visual realm," wrote Adweek (Natividad, 2015). It launched in 2012 with the goal of seizing public space back from advertisers. Advertisements, when seen as narratives about consuming commodities, have traditionally provoked concern from critics. The arguments are that ads discursively construct the world, subdue inequality, promote a normative vision, and reflect the logic of capitalism and the society of the spectacle – a society that values appearances over the genuine (Goldman and Papson, 2000). Culture jamming turns them into a "field of contestation" (Sandlin and Milam, 2008, p. 332).

The visual rhetoric of the Brandalism posters mimicked, or appropriated, the look and feel of the targeted advertisements with the goal of directly linking the advertising industry to climate change. The action attacked many of the corporate sponsors of COP21, including BMW, the Coca-Cola Company, Air France, Moody's Corporation, and Dow Chemicals (Climate Action, 2015). Eighty-two artists from 19 countries helped to create the posters and Brandalism activists placed the artworks in advertising spaces owned by JC Decaux, reportedly one of the world's largest outdoor advertising firms and an official sponsor of the COP21 climate talks (Kirkpatrick, 2015). To see the culture-jammed ads, image search for "Brandalism UK climate change 2015." (The website of the Vancouver-based magazine Adbusters, adbusters.org, is another good source to view examples of culture jamming.)

The posters, through visual subversion, appropriation, and augmentation of imagery in the sponsors' traditional advertising, resulted in messages of corporate greed, inadequate politicians, consumer saturation, Earth in mourning, and public commitment to the environment (Lekakis, 2017). In a Mobil "subvertisement," rhetorical interventions featured an image of offshore oil drilling and the statement (translated from French) "we know about the impact of fossil fuels but publicly denied it" (Lekakis, 2017, p. 321). The Mobil corporate logo was juxtaposed with hashtags of protest events, e.g. #ClimateGames. In another poster, Apple's iPhone is crowned but bleeding from the top, with accompanying text, "the king is dead" and "designed to become obsolete within two years" (Lekakis, 2017, p. 322). The street art also appeared on Brandalism's website, social media channels, and was reproduced extensively through global media coverage.

Strategic Visual Communication

Strategic communication is goal oriented, aiming to inform as well as persuade on behalf of a client or an organization. Hallahan et al. define it as "communicating purposefully to advance (the organization's) mission" (Hallahan et al., 2007, p. 4). It provides particular information, influences desired attitudes, and encourages specific behaviors.

Visuals dominate today's communication, providing the fields of advertising, public relations, and marketing powerful tools to influence or persuade audiences and to mobilize support for a cause – commercial, political, or social (Kohrs, 2018). Understanding how visual language works in an age of all-pervasive image-making enables strategic communicators to effectively manage perceptions and relationships between brands and audiences, organizations and stakeholders.

The Internet, together with the rise of digital media technology, has driven exponential growth in visual communication through the creation and sharing of images of all kinds. By 2022, online videos will make up more than 82% of all consumer internet traffic – 15 times higher than it was in 2017 (Cisco, 2020). Three hundred million people use Facebook Stories daily; 500 million use Instagram Stories every day (Zephoria, 2020). By 2023, Snapchat is projected to have an estimated 356 million users (eMarketer, 2019).

THE POWER OF VISUALS IN ADVERTISING

LO2 Recognize and critique visual rhetoric in advertising, especially the extensive use of metaphor.

Advertising needs to first attract our attention before engaging us in a persuasive effort. When encountering ad messages that we don't purposefully seek out, we may overlook them or just skim them. Thus, the visual image's rhetorical properties must make the advertising message arresting and memorable at a glance; it must call out "hey, you!" It's well-established that advertisements with visuals that provide emphasis or evoke curiosity attract more attention than those without them (Burnkrant and Howard, 1984; Huhmann and Albinsson, 2012; Mothersbaugh et al., 2002; Petty et al., 1981).

Historical Snapshots

Controversy and advertising are old, familiar partners. Ethically questionable images and cultural symbols of femininity, masculinity, racial minority stratification and exclusion, sexual orientation, and multiculturalism have either intentionally or unintentionally been reflected in advertising (Cortese, 2015). Looking back at the twentieth century, here are a few examples.

In women's magazines, a popular media form in the 1900s, advertisements called out to the reader to sell goods by portrayals of women. In newsstand magazines of the 1930s and 1940s, Lifebuoy ads and its ongoing comic book ad stories depicted women as naïve and embarrassed about their bodies. Consider the visual rhetoric in one of the ads for Lifebuoy soap. It depicts a woman and man dancing closely together, with the caption, "A good dancer – but 'B.O.' spoiled it all!" and "Lifebuoy stops Body Odor" (the soap's manufacturer, Lever Brothers, coined the term B.O. for body odor). Viewed from over a hundred years later, the ad seems laughable. The image of a well-dressed and seemingly middle- or upper-class couple has no clear relationship with the claimed features of the product. However, for the intended audience of women, it may well have stirred anxiety on the part of what Berger calls the "spectator-buyer." (1972, p. 134). Someone who saw herself as attractive and desirable now may think that in reality she is unpleasant. The ad attempts to have female viewers see themselves through the eyes of a male, see themselves as lacking, and envision that a purchase can fix a social problem. Find the ad with an image search for "vintage Lifebuoy ad A good dancer."

FOCUS: The Early Image Makers

Behold the "camera obscura," the first camera, invented in box form in the seventeenth century. The term is Latin for "dark room." The device consists of a closed box with a small hole on one side that lets in light. On the opposite side of the box, the light projects an upside down and reversed view of the external world outside the hole, with color and perspective preserved. Art historians believe that seventeenth-century Dutch painter, Johannes Vermeer, may have made use of a camera obscura to help him conceive, and even trace, the complex composition for his 1666 masterpiece, *The Art of Painting*.

In the nineteenth century, the "stereoscope" arrived. It was a device that looked like binoculars and used two photographic images to present a 3D image. It was

Source: Kunsthistorisches Museum, Vienna.

(Continued)

a kind of early augmented reality and various versions of the technology were very popular through the early twentieth century. A great source of entertainment, the stereoscope was often used to depict rail travel, a transportation mode that was rapidly developing at the same time and was an object of fascination for many people (Collectors Weekly, n.d.).

With the invention of the stereoscope, and subsequently other optical devices, people experienced a new sense of power in using, producing, and interacting with images. By the mid-nineteenth century, a culture of the "visual" began to emerge as visual images were becoming drivers of life's everyday experience. Society began to prefer the image to the thing and a copy to the original, writes Crary (1992), *and was aware of this*. He was inspired by a growing cultural acceptance of the visual image to satisfy the absence of the real thing; an acceptable substitution for firsthand experience.

Think about how vacation photographs can be more meaningful to you, and perhaps suggest more enjoyment, than the actual experience. Or how a picture of an exotic destination can stimulate you, without you ever having gone there. With the early photographic tools, a chief activity of society became producing and consuming images for a satisfying and exhilarating participation in the visual culture of the day.

If you look at contemporary ads, you'll find they often also use similar strategies connecting images and pointing viewers to an interpretation that something is lacking in their lives. Research reveals that when many women see visual content showing thin and sexy models, it can contribute to or reinforce body shame, appearance anxiety, or internalization of the thin ideal. While many ad approaches are based on objective facts, logic, and reasoning, most use appeals such as humor, fear, scarcity, desire, and of course sex – especially for consumer products. From makeup to liquor to cars, brands have used sex to sell.

In their book, *Sex in Advertising,* Tom Reichert and Jacqueline Lambiase report that a fifth of all ads use sex (2003). In early twentieth-century ads, sexy images promoted Listerine Mouthwash, and later women in sexually provocative situations, poses, and attire appeared in mainstream publication ads. Victoria's Secret ads presented skinny models wearing bras and underwear in sensual poses. Carl's Jr. sexualized hamburgers through the sensual appeal of Paris Hilton and Kim Kardashian, and Burger King used images of women in bikinis. In 1998, the perfume Chanel No. 5 asked consumers to "share the fantasy" in a sexy and surreal ad based on the fairy tale, Little Red Riding Hood.

Analyzing the narratives and storytelling of ads can reveal initially unseen meanings. In the 1990s, Calvin Klein introduced sexualized and provocative ads and Benetton was notorious for its innovative yet sometimes offensive ads addressing cultural and political moments. The commercial use of a photograph taken from a *Life* magazine article on the AIDS crisis picturing grieving parents with their dying son – evoked great concern (image search for "Benetton AIDS ad.") Two researchers used the lens of narrative (storytelling) in evaluating the ethics of some of the controversial or innovative ad campaigns in the early 1990s (Bush and Bush, 1994). Because of complaints from special interest groups, competitors, and broadcasters, certain advertising campaigns had been pulled from the media. Bush and Bush identified inconsistencies between the ads and their intended or influential audiences. The researchers proposed that care be taken during the creative process – before production and release – to identify potentially unethical aspects that may have damaging effects.

Visual Rhetoric in Advertising

The first two decades of the twenty-first century generated a significant increase in research examining *pictures* as an ad's main persuasive elements. Before this recognition of visual rhetoric's leading role, an ad's potency was often attributed to the audience's emotional reactions/empathy or to its attractive or prestigious spokespeople. However, McQuarrie and Phillips (2005), among others, found that visuals, especially visual metaphors, were more effective than verbal claims. Beginning in the late twentieth century, scholars suggested that the artful deviations in ads containing rhetorical figures – nonliteral visuals that call attention and evoke curiosity – lead to readers' enjoyable engagement and varying interpretations: what Barthes labeled the "pleasure of the text" (Barthes, 1985).

Pictures are also easier to "read" because they generate *both* verbal and image recognition codes in the receiver, in contrast to words. Scholars have concluded that pictures are remembered and recalled better than words, and that they form stronger attitudes compared to verbal elements – a phenomenon called the picture superiority effect (Theodorakis et al., 2015). Researchers determined that "the visual element is understood to be an essential, intricate, meaningful, and culturally embedded characteristic of contemporary marketing communication" (McQuarrie and Mick, 1999, p. 51).

However, not all visual rhetoric in ads may achieve desirable outcomes in certain situations. Visuals accompanying controversial themes can be objectionable, for example, in ads dealing with topics such as eroticism, violence, racism, and death (Theodorakis et al., 2015). Careless choice of visuals may result in unfavorable emotional response and diminishment of the ad's and the brand's credibility.

Visual Metaphors

Many advertisements deliberately deploy visual metaphors, as Table 8.1 illustrates. Sometimes they link a product or service with socially desirable and meaningful traits, or more pointedly with another product that carries special and unexpected qualities.

Meaning becomes more obvious when both terms (literal and figurative) of a pictorial metaphor are used, as is the case with many ads. They are more straightforward and often found in lifestyle brands like beer, wine, jewelry, or perfume. For example, an ad for the fragrance Gucci Guilty conveys the metaphor "perfume is romantic" by showing both the perfume bottle (literal) and a passionate couple (figurative).

Table 8.1 Advertisement visual metaphor examples.

Primary subject	Secondary subject	Meaning/projected properties
Ketchup	Fire extinguisher	Exciting flavor
Ketchup	Sliced tomatoes	Fresh, grown, natural, single ingredient

Source: © John Wiley & Sons, Inc.

The Heinz ketchup ads play upon figurative representations that present desirable characteristics. In Figure 8.2 the visual builds on the insight that consumers want fresh and healthy foods that are grown, not manufactured. It visually links fresh tomatoes and the Heinz packaging. Presumably, this insight came from market research that identified the most important product qualities that target audiences desired.

In Figure 8.3, a strong visual metaphor invites the viewer to see Heinz ketchup as a fire extinguisher that will "extinguish the bland." The red color of the ketchup and the tag emphasize the relationship with a fire extinguisher and adds urgency to the persuasive message.

What Kinds of Visual Metaphors Work Best in Ads?

We know from substantial research that viewers prefer ads with metaphors over ads without metaphors. But what kinds of metaphors are most preferred? Metaphors of moderate complexity, called "unified" metaphors, according to recent research that evaluated three types of metaphors (van Mulken et al., 2014) (Figure 8.4 provides illustrations). The simplest type called "adjacent" metaphors (b) compare this *to* that, with two items placed next to each other. The moderately complex (and most preferred) "unified" type (c) blends together this *with* that, combining two images to propose meaning. The third type, "implied" metaphors (d), have the most complexity, omitting "this" completely and just picturing "that" with clues to an absent image. Refer to Chapter 6, Three Categories of Visual Metaphors, for example images. As you can see, the Heinz ads constitute unified metaphors.

Figure 8.2 This visual metaphor highlights the product's freshness.
Source: Kraft-Heinz, Inc.

Figure 8.3 A simple design for this ad draws emphasizes the red color under-scoring the metaphor of ketchup as fire extinguisher. *Source:* Mike Gaines.

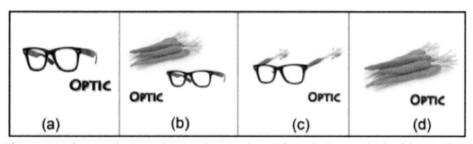

Figure 8.4 Viewers don't understand metaphors of modest complexity (c) as well as simple metaphors (b), but viewers prefer them more. And preference gets stronger still when viewers also understand the metaphor. *Source:* van Mulken et al. (2014).

The Takeaway

Among ads using visual metaphor, those of moderate complexity (unified) present original, unrealistic, and fantastic objects that make them most effective. Viewers prefer and appreciate them because of these surprising, unconventional aspects. The ads invite attention and engagement, and viewers enjoy the process of figuring them out with some, but not too much, effort. Simpler juxtaposition (adjacent) metaphors don't require that level of engagement – and consequently aren't enjoyable. Replacement (implied) metaphors can lead to misunderstanding and low appreciation due to lack of context.

FOCUS: Color and Contrast

Chapter 4 introduced gestalt design theories (see the feature Perception = Interpretation), explaining that how we group visual elements leads to determining their meanings. Examining the roles of color and contrast provides additional insight into the ways design elements can be harnessed to improve the effectiveness of visual communications.

(Continued)

Source: Charles Eshelman/FilmMagic/Getty Images.

Consider the gestalt principle of "good figure" (also called the law of Prägnanz) meaning that when a figure is closed, appearing whole, it is easier to perceive. When confronted with complex images, we tend to seek paths for easier and swifter comprehension. This coincides with the gestalt law of simplicity: people will prefer things that are simple, clear, and ordered, taking less time to process.

This advertising poster for the film *Trance* uses a visually engaging image that's aesthetically appropriate to its target audience. It communicates clearly with its relative consistency of color choices, helping the viewer to perceive the face as a whole despite the intervening abstracted shapes (O'Connor, 2013, p. 88).

Illustrating the law of similarity, the use of contrast, along with color, can help the eye group together shapes that share some level of meaning. In the illustration below, color and contrast act as catalysts in redefining perceived groupings. Inspired by the popular song "She's Broken," stylized quotes appeared on Pinterest and on T-shirts, mugs, wall art, and other products. The example shown carries letters spelling "SHE'S BROKEN" reversed out on a black background, with the letters "HE's OK" amplified in red.

Source: Deviantart.

In a visually congested world, the effectiveness of visual communications requires both engaging desired viewers and meeting the communication objectives. The strategic use of color and contrast, along with gestalt principles, can support both aesthetics *and* function (O'Connor, 2013).

THE CONTEMPORARY
ADVERTISING LANDSCAPE

LO3 Explore and assess contemporary uses of visual rhetoric in advertising.

Advertising is ubiquitous today with all its iterations and means of transmission, from social media to product placements to ambient locations. When conducting rhetorical analyses of advertising, one has unlimited choices. The following examples from differing platforms and media modes are provided to illustrate some of the compelling visual strategies in advertising today to help guide your selection and analysis of ads.

Social Media/Mobile Visual Messaging

Viral advertising is messaging that's especially crafted to be passed along or spread by consumers. Studies have shown that emotion is an important component that encourages pass-on behavior. A positive emotional tone – happy, excited, satisfied – greatly influences forwarding intentions (Chu, 2011). However, ads that trigger other strong emotional reactions like astonishment, shock, envy, and genuine sympathy are also deeply engaging. Think of the amyotrophic lateral sclerosis (**ALS**) ice bucket challenge that inspired many, including Mark Zuckerberg, Oprah, and Justin Timberlake, to participate and share their own videos. Some research establishes that narrative transportation – what happens when the audience steps into the story – in viral ads gets stronger when senders and intended receivers have personal ties (Seo et al., 2018).

Memes can be an integral part of a social media marketing campaign. Seamless, an online food delivery service, "news-jacked" the 2014 Academic Award nominations with a campaign called "OscarNomNoms." The memes featured spoofed film posters, for example, bannering "Wolf of Waffle Street" above a powdered sugar-dusted waffle. It encouraged user involvement, turning suggestions from followers into new film poster spoofs (Gilliland, 2017).

Tourism used to be about experience seeking. Not so any more, according to Justin Francis, the CEO of Responsible Travel, a company that arranges sustainable travel for customers. He writes, "Now it's about using photography and social media to build a personal brand," (Manjoo, 2018). Columnist for the *New York Times*, Farhad Manjoo reports that throngs of tourists in popular European destinations each summer turn them into selfie-stick-clogged, "Disneyfied" towns. While this trend, called #MeTourism, can make personal experiences less authentic, it can benefit the destination or product. Tourism brands will contract with "influencer marketers" – celebrities or online opinion leaders – who then post favorable content. Nonpaid, organic advertising through social media selfies can also result from providing people compelling reasons to create content for a brand. One motivator could be a brand's existing ad campaign. For example, a Turkish Airlines advertising campaign with star athletes Lionel Messi and Kobe Bryant featured their selfies in a range of extreme locations.

E-mail Marketing with Visuals

E-mail has been used as a marketing tactic since the late 1970s. Since then, in spite of all the attention we give to social media, e-mail usage has skyrocketed. In 2017, a market research firm predicted that the total number of business and consumer e-mails sent and received per day would reach 269 billion – and that figure would rise to 319 billion by the end of 2021 (Olenski, 2018). A few years earlier, the Direct Marketing Association cosponsored a study revealing that e-mail had a media return-on-investment (ROI) of 122% that was significantly higher than the ROI for social media (Olenski, 2018). Adding video content into emails can not only help educate readers, but also increase click-through rates, conversions, and brand awareness (Hey, 2019).

One study (Scheinbaum et al., 2017) used real brands, Audi and Apple, and their authentic marketing verbiage and videos. In an experiment, participants were randomly assigned to the e-mail with wording only or to the e-mail that also included video. When compared to the wording-only marketing e-mails, researchers found that audiovisual messages heighten informativeness, product interest, perceived prestige, intentions to spread e-word-of-mouth for a brand, and willingness to pass along the e-mail to friends and family – thus converting the recipients to brand advocates.

On the other hand, e-mail senders targeting recipients *not* familiar with the sender or without much awareness of the brand, may *not* be so engaged with visual elements. A study in the *Journal of Marketing Channels* suggests "while fancy e-mails full of graphics and photos may be visually appealing, they are also not the best choice for an initial contact e-mail" (Dapko, 2014). Feedback from participants who received highly visual e-mails reported they looked like automated messages, not personal. The conclusion: a "less is more" policy should be a general guideline when deciding how much visual appeal to include; with one exception. Including a company logo may signal credibility and thus should be used in situations where perceived credibility may be especially low. The strategically designed logo carries not only type but semiotic elements that communicate a company's brand attributes.

Outdoor and Ambient Visuals

Outdoor signage and billboards, using moving or still text and images – think Times Square in New York City or downtown Tokyo, Japan – are usually placed along routes of transit, designed to target the identified passerby. Ambient ads, however, can be found in unusual places where ads don't normally appear. Not necessarily outside, they can be found on pizza boxes, concert tickets, and even bowling balls. All the ads are ideally masterpieces of simplicity: text + image = rhetorical message.

By thinking of the outdoor ad as a single frame cartoon, you can see how they quickly engage viewers to identify meaning and offer some pleasure in "getting it."

Figure 8.5 Pakistani cinema billboard invites passersby to participate in its interpretation. *Source:* Rupert Sagar-Musgrave/Alamy Stock Photo.

When erected in specific urban neighborhoods, however, billboards can be controversial. They have advertised fast foods, e-cigarettes, and alcohol in places with high exposure to children and teens. Campaigns with cultural insensitivities have also offended residents. In Washington, DC's Chinatown, a billboard advertising the gentrification of the neighborhood carried an objectional narrative. Lou (2010) claimed it de-ethnicized the neighborhood and promoted gentrification of Chinatown as a positive transformation driven by a corporation. This perspective reminds us that there can be diverse audiences and multiple points of view in response to the storytelling in ads.

Not all outdoor signage has simple design elements. Such signs can be elaborate, as illustrated by Pakistani cinema's "Lollywood billboards" (Figure 8.5). Their giant size, vibrant colors, and dramatic compositions articulate stories with a visual narrative that is allegorical (Ali, 2011). Allegory is a metaphor that implies a comparison, such as in a parable or story that delivers a broader message about the real world.

Taking the perspective of the viewer, Ali found that due to the billboards' diverse imagery, with sometimes conflicting stories, Pakistanis must furnish their own interpretations to understand them, and thus a billboard's story becomes an allegory for the viewer. While one purpose of the billboards is purely commercial, their visual rhetoric also allows the public viewer to engage in completing its "story." The story becomes allegorical through this complex, shared visual language inviting viewers to participate in interpretation. Ali's study illustrates the need, when critiquing (or creating) ads, to be aware of larger social and cultural contexts in which ads may be viewed and interpreted.

Televisual Ads

Television commercials use narrative strategies that are ideal for the critic new to visual analysis. They are typically stable and depict a relationship between the storyteller, customer, and the main character. Yet the main goal of the ads is to persuade customers to buy products and services. To effectively accomplish this, the narrative invites the prospective customer into the story as a possible buyer (Moraru, 2011). For example, a person viewing an ad may imagine themselves as a character perhaps driving a car, wearing a jacket, or experiencing a beach vacation. Narratives, as previously established, are stories with a beginning, a middle, and an end. They are a natural and enduring part of our life experiences, and they are essentially persuasive as they help people make sense of their lives, experiences, and identities. Think of the stories advertisers tell us about our holidays, our celebrations, our achievements and turning points. Of course, they also are intended to help consumers make sense of the role brands play in their lives.

Considerable research provides practical guides for advertisers suggesting that narrative structures are more effective than nonnarrative. Kim et al. (2017) found that the most effective approaches offer high emotional involvement, appear credible, are pleasurable for readers and viewers, and communicate how consumers could achieve their goals through a purchase. As discussed previously, visuals that create a compelling narrative are likely to produce better results.

Product Placement

Product placement advertising is generally defined as the inclusion of products and brands in media designed with a similar form and appearance to non-advertising content. Concave Brand Tracking reports the top brands found in 2018 movies (Concave Brand Tracking, 2019). Apple topped the list with over 3.5 hours of screen time in 52 movies featuring iPhones, laptops, and tablets. They appeared in *Jurassic World*, *A Simple Favor*, and *Ralph Breaks the Internet*. Dell was the runner-up with product appearances in 38 movies including *Ant-Man and the Wasp*, *Ready Player One*, and *Mission: Impossible – Fallout*. Ford appeared in 75 movies though it usually had less screen time: often a minute or less though most movie vehicles were Fords. Films included *Sicario: Day of the Soldado* and *Den of Thieves*.

A Grey Goose martini joined Will Smith and Eva Mendes as a character in the flirting sequence from the blockbuster 2005 movie *Hitch*. A semiotic analysis showed the importance of the role, identifying how it fitted into a narrative of desire, and leveraged uncertainty, surprise, and postponement. (Rossolatos, 2017). Although the product is minimally visible in the scene, it stands in for those human elements that we think of as flirting.

Product placement by nonprofits? Of course, although you may not have noticed. As nonprofits attempt to gain influence, membership, and funds in an increasingly crowded field, they are turning to popular culture as a way to spread both their brand and their message (Winston, 2017). Amnesty International was one of the first human

Figure 8.6 Product placement of Amnesty International poster in the TV series *Mean Girls*. *Source:* coveteur.com.

rights groups to use image branding through its distinctive candle-in-barbed-wire logo (Cmiel, 1999). Winston (2017) identified Amnesty International USA's use of product placement in popular film and television as a form of strategic communication.

Amnesty International posters have appeared in episodes of *The West Wing*, in the film *Friends with Benefits*, in high school hallways in *Mean Girls* (Figure 8.6), and on doctors' T-shirts in *ER* and *Scrubs*. Human rights issues of concern to Amnesty International have been purposely introduced in films such as *Lord of War* and *Blood Diamond* through a tactic known as product integration: different from product placement in that the product is integrated into the plot. Writers and producers work with Amnesty International to make sure their information is as accurate as possible. Winston (2017) concludes that Amnesty International's product placement and integration strategies are guided by three interrelated goals: brand management, issue advocacy, and social norms marketing.

PROFESSIONAL PROFILE: Jeff Hecker

Marketing Semiotics

Although I studied semiotics as part of my undergraduate degree, I never imagined that I would be applying it specifically as part of my work.

My career in marketing began in 2000 when I took my first advertising agency job. After about 12 years of working positions in ad agencies and in the advertising management groups of various "client" companies, I took the decision to refocus entirely on marketing research in 2013. Initially, my work consisted of traditional qualitative market research using methods such as focus groups, ethnography, and in-depth interviews. But it wasn't long before I discovered that marketing semiotics is an active – if niche – discipline in market research. And – after

---

(Continued)

undertaking some training on the use of semiotics in the market research context, I began offering this methodology to clients when appropriate.

There are many market research methods that seek to explore the emotional side of consumer decision-making: ethnographic observation, facial micro-expression analysis, neuromarketing, and of course the traditional methods like focus groups. But there is no one method that is the "silver bullet." Semiotics is one more "way in" to understanding how culture and brand cues shape brand choices.

Jeff Hecker is principal at Athena Brand Wisdom, a qualitative market research firm in Toronto.
Source: athenabrand.com.

Marketing semiotics looks deeply at the cues or "signs" related to a brand or product category, and their meanings in a culture. Because semiotics is focused on those symbolic elements of communication that people are less conscious of, it can be a great way to make sense of the relationship between consumers, brands, and the cultures they exist in.

Marketing semiotics explores questions like:

- **What impact will this color have?**
- **How might this image be interpreted?**
- **What associations does this wording evoke?**
- What is the underlying meaning of this consumer's response?

Often, my semiotics work is "desk research," using all of culture as its database. Advertising, packaging, fashion, pop culture; all are helpful in discerning the symbolic themes or "codes" that surround brands, and offer cues to which codes are tired and which are "emergent" – or new and fresh. Sometimes brands can position themselves on the leading edge of cultural change by leveraging emergent codes in their advertising, or by "refreshing" an older code for modern times.

We do a lot of semiotics work in the alcohol and pharmaceutical categories, where advertisers need to find symbolic ways to convey things that regulators won't permit them to say explicitly, and in mature product categories, where the lack of functional product differences necessitates more symbolic differentiation.

Semiotics is a difficult method to sell, because it strikes many potential clients as abstract or academic. But once clients get a taste for the power of semiotic analysis, they are often hooked. Longer-term, semiotics tends to be used in conjunction with other research methods, rather than strictly on its own, thus delivering on what market researchers call "bricolage" or triangulation; an additional perspective on a brand's particular complex dynamic.

CHAPTER SUMMARY

In this chapter, you explored the history of visuals in advertising and how professionals harness the power of visual persuasion. You also examined how practitioners use color and contrast in ad design and how activists appropriate outdoor advertising to make environmental issue statements. Additionally, the chapter took a closer look at the history of image-making and the emotional force of metaphors in ads through example analyses. Finally, you met Jeff Hecker, principal at Athena Brand Wisdom, who shared his personal story of getting into the business and how qualitative approaches such as semiotics can offer deep insights into consumers' interests and needs.

KEY TERMS

Advertising   Paid space or time purchased by brands and agencies to promote products, services, or ideas to target customer segments.

Strategic communication   A persuasive approach that seeks to maximize message effects by coordinating the optimal combination of media, social, digital, and interpersonal factors to accomplish organizational or marketing goals.

Pseudo-images   Photographic images that are not based on an original source but are created to appear as genuine photographs.

Memes   Ideas, visuals, or manipulated images that are shared in a culture, often on digital platforms.

Viral advertising   Persuasive messages created by brands in hopes that they will be broadly shared.

Product placement   The practice of placing products or persuasive messages in films and television programs as to gain exposure and awareness. Most product placements offer compensation to the film or television producers.

PRACTICE ACTIVITIES

1. Find a body-positive ad and use semiotic analysis (TEASA [technique, effect, audience, symbolize, alternative] or longer form: see Chapter 4) to discover how its visual rhetoric suggests meaning.
2. Find an ad (on any platform and format) that you feel is unethical and do a visual frame analysis (see Chapter 6).
3. Strategy focus: in a small group, brainstorm current lifestyle or entertainment events that could be "news-jacked" into a viral meme by a brand (as you read about in the Social Media/Mobile Visual Messaging section). Write a creative brief for the meme (or series of memes), explaining your strategy by referencing any of the theories introduced in this book.
4. Insurance companies are famous for creating humorous narratives in their video ads. Select one and apply principles from narrative paradigm theory (NPT) to evaluate its narrative coherence and fidelity (see Chapter 6).

5. Have fun with metaphors by selecting brand-generated (not citizen-generated) print ads from Absolut, Heinz, or other brands. Challenge yourself to find all three metaphor types: simple (adjacent), more complex (unified), very complex (implied). Refer to Chapter 5, Visual Metaphor Lessons from the Media, "Three Categories of Visual Metaphors."
6. Observe your surroundings and locate an intriguing outdoor or ambient ad. Photograph it and conduct a visual analysis by referencing any of the theories introduced in this book.
7. Be on the hunt for product placement or integration in the media you consume. Observe how it fits into the narrative and analyze its effectiveness from an NPT perspective (see Chapter 6).

REFERENCES

Ali, H. (2011). Visual reflections: Lollywood billboards, just a commercial medium or an ideological allegorical literacy? *Journal of Writing in Creative Practice* 4 (3): 401–426.

Aslam, S. (2018). Snapchat by the numbers: Stats, demographics & fun facts. Omnicore. https://www.omnicoreagency.com/snapchat-statistics (accessed September 29, 2020).

Barnhurst, K.G., Vari, M., and Rodriguez, I. (2004). Mapping Visual Studies in Communication. *Journal of Communication* 54 (4): 616–644.

Barthes, R. (1985). The rhetoric of the image. In: The Responsibility of Forms, 21–40. New York: Hill & Wang.

Baudrillard, J. (1983). The Consumer Society: Myths and Structures. London: Sage.

Berger, J. (1972). Ways of Seeing. London, UK: British Broadcasting Corporation and Penguin Books.

Burnkrant, R.E. and Howard, D.J. (1984). Effects of the use of introductory rhetorical questions versus statements on information processing. *Journal of Personality and Social Psychology* 47: 1218–1230.

Bush, A.J. and Bush, V.D. (1994). The narrative paradigm as a perspective for improving ethical evaluations of advertisements. *Journal of Advertising* 23 (3): 31–41.

Carducci, V. (2006). Culture jamming: a sociological perspective. *Journal of Consumer Culture* 6 (1): 116–138. https://doi.org/10.1177/1469540506062722.

Chu, S. (2011). Viral advertising in social media: participation in Facebook groups and responses among college-aged users. *Journal of Interactive Advertising* 12 (1): 30–43.

Cisco. (2020). Annual Internet Report (2018–2023) White Paper. https://www.cisco.com/c/en/us/solutions/collateral/executive-perspectives/annual-internet-report/white-paper-c11-741490.html (accessed December 24, 2020).

Climate Action. (2015). Sponsors. http://www.cop21paris.org/sponsors-and-partners/sponsors (accessed September 29, 2020).

Cmiel, K. (1999). The emergence of human rights politics in the United States. *Journal of American History* 86: 1231–1250.

Collectors Weekly. (n.d.) Antique and Vintage Stereoview Photographs. https://www.collectorsweekly.com/photographs/stereoviews (accessed December 24, 2020).

Concave Brand Tracking (2019). Top ten brands in 2018 movies – product placement, May 1. http://concavebt.com/top-10-brands-2018-movies-product-placement (accessed September 29, 2020).

Cortese, A.J. (2015). Provocateur: Images of Women and Minorities in Advertising, 4e. Lanham, MD: Rowman & Littlefield.

Crary, J. (1992). Techniques of the Observer. Cambridge, MA: MIT Press.

Dapko, J.L. (2014). Less is more: an exploratory analysis of optimal visual appeal and linguistic style combinations in a salesperson's initial-contact e-mail to millennial buyers within marketing channels. *Journal of Marketing Channels* 21 (4): 254–267.

eMarketer. (2019). Worldwide Snapchat Usage to Grow More than 14% This Year. https://www.emarketer.com/content/worldwide-snapchat-usage-to-grow-more-than-14-this-year (accessed December 24, 2020).

Gilliland, N. (2017. Econsultancy. https://www.econsultancy.com/blog/69519-memes-in-marketing-seven-memorable-examples-from-brands (accessed September 29, 2020).

Goldman, R. and Papson, S. (2000 [1996]). Advertising in the age of accelerated meaning. In: The Consumer Society Reader (eds. J.B. Schor and D.B. Holt), pp. 81–98. New York, NY: The New Press.

Hallahan, K., Holtzhausen, D.R., Van Ruler, B. et al. (2007). Defining strategic communication. *International Journal of Strategic Communication* 1 (1): 3–35.

Hey, R. (2019). How and why to use video in your email in 2019. https://www.abtasty.com/blog/video-email/ (accessed December 24, 2020).

Huhmann, B.A. and Albinsson, P.A. (2012). Does rhetoric impact advertising effectiveness with liking controlled? *European Journal of Marketing* 46 (11/12): 1476–1500.

Kim, E., Ratneshwar, S., and Thorson, E. (2017). Why narrative ads work: an integrated process explanation. *Journal of Advertising* 46 (2): 283–296.

Kirkpatrick, N. (2015). Activists flood Paris with ads mocking corporate sponsors of climate change talks. The Washington Post. December 2. https://www.washingtonpost.com/news/worldviews/wp/2015/12/02/activists-flood-paris-with-ads-mocking-corporate-sponsors-of-climate-change-talks/?utm_term=.a041a98b0cab (accessed September 29, 2020).

Kohrs, K. (2018). Public relations as visual meaning-making. In: Visual Public Relations: Strategic Communication Beyond Text (eds. S. Collister and S. Roberts-Bowman), 13–28. Routledge: London.

Lekakis, E. (2017). Culture jamming and brandalism for the environment: the logic of appropriation. *Popular Communication* 15 (4): 311–327.

Lou, J.J. (2010). *Chinatown* transformed: ideology, power, and resources in narrative place-making. *Discourse Studies* 12 (5): 625–647.

Lowe, L. (2018). Women will go makeup-free at New York Fashion Week as part of a new Olay campaign. https://www.today.com/series/love-your-body/aly-raisman-stars-olay-faceanything-campaign-t135572 (accessed September 29, 2020)

Manjoo, F. (2018). 'Overtourism' worries Europe. How much did technology help us get there? *New York Times*. https://www.nytimes.com/2018/08/29/technology/technology-overtourism-europe.html (accessed September 29, 2020).

McQuarrie, E.F. and Mick, D.G. (1999). Visual rhetoric in advertising: text-interpretive, experimental, and reader-response analyses. *Journal of Consumer Research* 26: 37–54.

McQuarrie, E.F. and Phillips, B.J. (2005). Indirect Persuasion in Advertising: How Consumers Process Metaphors Presented in Pictures and Words. *Journal of Advertising* 34 (2): 7–21.

Moraru, M. (2011). The narrating instances in advertising stories. *Journal of Media Research* 4 (1): 54–72.

Mothersbaugh, D.L., Huhmann, B.A., and Frank, G.R. (2002). Combinatory and separative effects of rhetorical figures on consumers' effort and focus in ad processing. *Journal of Consumer Research* 28 (4): 589–602.

Natividad, A. (2015). 600 fake outdoor ads in Paris blast corporate sponsors of the COP21 climate talks. Adweek. https://www.adweek.com/adfreak/600-fake-outdoor-ads-paris-blast-corporate-sponsors-cop21-climate-talks-168358 (accessed September 29, 2020).

O'Connor, Z. (2013). Colour, contrast, and gestalt theories of perception: the impact in contemporary visual communications design. *Color Research and Application* 40 (1): 85–92.

Olenski, S. (2018). Email marketing: threats and opportunities. *Forbes.* https://www.forbes.com/sites/steveolenski/2018/08/21/email-marketing-threats-and-opportunities/#8b7f47461b98 (accessed September 29, 2020).

Petty, R.E., Cacioppo, J.T., and Heesacker, M. (1981). The use of rhetorical questions in persuasion: a cognitive response analysis. *Journal of Personality and Social Psychology* 40 (3): 432–440.

Phillips, B.J. (2015). Introduction to the virtual special issue on visual rhetoric in advertising. *Journal of Advertising* 43 (4). http://explore.tandfonline.com/content/bes/ja_virtualissue2/phillips_jaintro.

Reichard, T. and Lambiase, J. (2003). Sex in Advertising: Perspectives on the Erotic Appeal. Routledge.

Rossolatos, G. (2017). A multimodal discourse analytic approach to the articulation of Martini's "desire" positioning in filmic product placement. *Social Semiotics* 27 (2): 211–226.

Sandlin, J.A. and Milam, J.L. (2008). "Mixing pop (culture) and politics:" cultural resistance, culture jamming, and anti-consumption activism as critical public pedagogy. *Curriculum Inquiry* 38 (3): 323–350. https://doi.org/10.1111/j.1467-873X.2008.00411.x.

Scheinbaum, A.C., Hampel, S., and Kang, M. (2017). Future developments in IMC: why e-mail with video trumps text-only e-mails for brands. *European Journal of Marketing* 51 (3): 627–645.

Seo, Y., Li, X., Cho, Y.K., and Yoon, S. (2018). Narrative transportation and paratextual features of social media in viral advertising. *Journal of Advertising* 47 (1): 83–95.

Smith, K. (2018). 41 incredible Instagram statistics. Brandwatch. https://www.brandwatch.com/blog/instagram-stats (accessed September 29, 2020).

Sonnad, K. (2018). Finally, a scientific list of the most popular memes on the internet. https://qz.com/1296094/most-popular-memes-finally-a-scientific-list-of-the-most-popular-memes-on-the-internet (accessed September 20, 2020).

Theodorakis, I.G., Koritos, C., and Stathakopoulos, V. (2015). Rhetorical maneuvers in a controversial tide: assessing the boundaries of advertising rhetoric. *Journal of Advertising* 44 (1): 14–24.

van Mulken, M., van Hooft, A., and Nederstigt, U. (2014). Finding the tipping point: visual metaphor and conceptual complexity in advertising. *Journal of Advertising* 43 (4): 333–343.

Winston, C. (2017). Nonprofit Product Placement: Human Rights Advocacy in Film and Television. *Atlantic Journal of Communication* 25 (1): 17–32.

Zephoria. (2020). The top 20 valuable Facebook statistics – updated August 2020. https://zephoria.com/top-15-valuable-facebook-statistics (accessed September 29, 2020).

Chapter 9
Public Relations

Fearless Girl

Source: Anadolu Agency/Getty Images.

On the eve of International Women's Day in 2017, State Street Corporation, a financial services company, introduced "SHE," a new ETF (exchange traded fund). The fund (with the ticker symbol SHE) invests in organizations with a

Visual Communication: Insights and Strategies, First Edition. Janis Teruggi Page and Margaret Duffy.
© 2022 John Wiley & Sons, Inc. Published 2022 by John Wiley & Sons, Inc.

high percentage of women in leadership. To draw attention to the fund – and the power of women in business – State Street commissioned a bronze statue, *Fearless Girl*, which has since become world famous.

The four-foot statue was installed in the dead of night in the heart of the financial district in New York City to be there when people began arriving to work on Wall Street the next morning. She was positioned to face Wall Street's iconic *Charging Bull* statue, as if staring it down. "Chin high, hands on hips, she stands for the power of women today and tomorrow," is how State Street described the statue.

The distinctive statue suggested the unique characteristics of the SHE fund, given that many companies don't have even a single woman on their boards despite multiple studies that demonstrate organizations with higher percentages of women in leadership roles outperform their competition.

The powerful visual image triggered viral sharing in a big way, leading to more than one billion Twitter impressions in the first 12 hours. The statue's appearance and placement also effected positive change. A year after the statue was installed, State Street reported that 152 organizations had added a woman to the board, and 34 others had committed to doing so. In spring 2018, the statue moved to a permanent space across the street from the New York Stock Exchange.

Source: Excerpted from https://www.prdaily.com/Awards/SpecialEdition/906.aspx © 2010 Ragan communications, Inc.

Key Learning Objectives

After engaging in this chapter, you'll be able to:

1. Understand public relations and its history from a visual perspective.
2. Recognize strategic use of visual rhetoric in public relations campaigns.
3. Critique visual rhetoric strategies in public relations campaigns.

Chapter Overview

This chapter explores public relations (PR) and the visual, beginning with PR spectacles in the era of publicity, later in images of PR practitioners in movies and television, and now the multiple visual strategies used by the profession in its modern era. To illustrate how PR supports an organization's interests, examples include emotionally charged topics like the environment, teen smoking, women's rights, and politics. You'll also see how rhetorical theories guide PR visual responses in cases involving corporate social responsibility (CSR), crisis and issues management, and city branding and tourism.

A BRIEF HISTORY OF PR: HOW VISUALS DEFINED IT

LO1 Understand PR and its history from a visual perspective

A simple way to differentiate advertising from PR is with the old saying, unattributable but widely quoted, "Advertising is what you pay for; PR is what you pray for." The ads we read, hear, and see are *paid* communication, purposely crafted and placed to convey an organization's informational or persuasive message. PR, on the other hand, crafts messages with the goal of sharing it – without paying for media placement – with various people (called "publics") to inform and influence. Nevertheless, PR is not free – it requires research, people, and planning, all of which often require substantial monetary investments.

Advertising, marketing, and PR often work together to address the same issues and needs for an organization. However, at its best, PR involves an information exchange between two or more people or "publics" with a goal of sharing information, creating trust, building reputation, impacting opinion, and influencing behaviors. Page and Parnell (2019) explain:

> Other key elements of PR that distinguish it from advertising include the need to master skills such as issues and crisis management, internal communications, and providing strategic communications advice. These and other related elements are unique to PR and are not found in advertising, sales, or marketing activity (pp. 3–4).

Looking back in its history, the role of PR in the United States was at first noble – building support for American independence in the late 1700s – but then took on some less ethical aspects often using exaggerated promotion and visual spectacles to attract attention and influence. While the practice later became a mature profession managing responsible communication for organizations, it's crucial to understand how its past use of stunts and hyperbole impacted the way PR is sometimes still viewed today.

The Golden Age of Press Agentry: Publicity Stunts

With a rapid expansion of newspapers needing content, along with a flurry of new businesses needing exposure, PR shifted into a more commercial focus in the 1800s. Visual appeals and attractions with extravagant deceptions figured prominently, as in the case of P.T. Barnum. Known as the "Great American Showman," Barnum promoted his namesake circus with posters making outrageous claims. For example, he publicized and exhibited an elderly African American woman and former slave, Joice Heth (Figure 9.1), as the 161-year-old former nursemaid to George Washington. In the poster's crude woodcut image, she is depicted with a wizened face and talon-like nails, luring onlookers to come and see this "curiosity" for themselves (The Lost Museum Archive, n.d.).

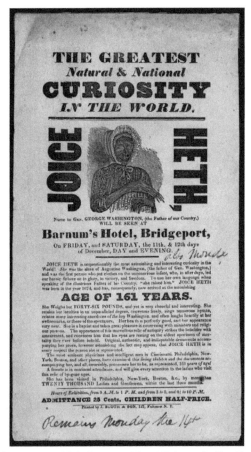

Figure 9.1 **Joice Heth poster, 1835.** *Source:* **The History Collection/Alamy Stock Photo.**

Barnum also originated what became a common sideshow attraction across the United States: the "Feejee Mermaid." It was promoted with woodcut posters and thousands of pamphlets, all depicting the mermaid with the body of a young beautiful woman to attract customers. Yet, when the creature was unveiled, it had the withered head and body of a monkey and the tail of a fish. Barnum created the hoax by using an associate to impersonate a doctor and member of the non-existent British Lyceum of Natural History, who arrived in New York to unveil the creature, and stating it had been caught near the Fiji Islands in the South Pacific (Mingren, 2016).

Barnum's contributions to visual PR went beyond eccentric exhibits and bombast. He conducted worldwide tours displaying "General Tom Thumb," a person of tiny stature (under two feet tall) who could sing, dance, and act. He promoted opera singer Jenny Lind, the "Swedish Nightingale" who performed in theaters throughout the United States to adoring crowds. Her image and name were exploited extensively with Jenny Lind cigar boxes, paper towels, and items of clothing. Kathleen Maher, curator of the Barnum Museum, suggests these visual wonders were early performances of what today we experience in reality television and musical contest shows (Page and Parnell, 2019).

Historical Snapshot: Popular Culture Images of the PR Practitioner

"Many public relations practitioners believe that the image of the publicist and the public relations professional is one of the most negative in history," says Joe Saltzman, director of the Image of the Journalist in Popular Culture project at the Norman Lear Center at the University of Southern California (USC) (Saltzman, 2012, p. 1). One way the image of the strategic communication professions emerges is through film and television depictions. The 1997 film *Wag the Dog* cast Robert DeNiro as a political "spin" doctor who manufactures a war for the US government to defocus from the president's sexual scandal. Interestingly, the film gained international popularity when the Clinton–Lewinsky scandal broke just a month after its release. In the long-running television show *Sex and the City*, a prominent character was Samantha Jones, a PR exec who threw parties for a living. In another well received TV program, *Scandal*, Olivia Pope was a crisis PR pro who defended or covered up political scandals.

In her pioneering study on PR in film and fiction, Professor Karen Miller stated, "fictitious characters . . . display very little understanding of PR or what practitioners do." She explained, "Sometimes, PR is magic," and other times, "it is almost embarrassingly easy" (Miller, 1999, pp. 22, 23). These representations should not be ignored or taken lightly, cautions Miller. While positive portrayals of accomplished PR professionals are available, they are far from prevalent.

Villains, Cheats, Magicians

Joe Saltzman, director of the Image of the Journalist in Popular Culture project, investigated portrayals of PR practitioners in more than 300 films and TV programs, dating from 1901 to 2011. He found that negative images range from press agents and their outrageous ballyhoo to publicity men and women who will do anything for their clients. Other characters are alcoholics and PR women who "charm" clients to get ahead in the profession, as well as true villains who are willing to lie, cheat, steal, and even commit murder to save reputations.

Yet, Saltzman found the PR practitioner's image in this media study was more positive than previously thought. Positive images ranged from those who will do anything within the law to get their clients publicity and protect them in crisis situations, to efficient and often likable press secretaries and military police public information officers. The PR professional as a hero who rebels against unethical practices and quits their job before doing something immoral is a frequent image, especially on television.

THE POWER OF VISUALS IN THE MODERN ERA OF PR

LO2 Recognize strategic use of visual rhetoric in PR campaigns.

The modern era of PR began in the early twentieth century. PR transformed to its current state as a communication management function for businesses, government agencies and politicians, nonprofit organizations, and grassroots groups. Consider the following examples of how visual images have been used strategically to support an organization's interests and concerns, particularly in emotionally charged issues involving the environment, teen smoking, women's rights, and politics.

Environmental Issues

The unfortunate truth is that our earth is facing a lot of environmental concerns, among them climate change, waste disposal, and some critically destructive events. They've triggered reactions with not only dramatic visual evidence but also artful parody.

Pacific Ocean Trash Island Becomes a Country

Environmentalists around the world became alarmed about a massive collection of plastic trash floating in the Pacific Ocean. The mountain of trash is the size of France and threatens aquatic life. The LadBible group, a media, news, and entertainment community aimed at young people, saw an opportunity to highlight the problem. It hired London-based AMV BBDO to create a campaign to raise awareness and spur activism in the youth demographic worldwide. The overarching goal was for individuals to contact the United Nations and ask them to take action (Griner, 2018). The AMV BBDO creative team developed a visual and tactile approach whose big idea was creating a new country: The Trash Isles. The Trash Isles had all of the elements of a real country: an official currency called "Debris," stamps, a flag, and even passports made of recycled products (Figure 9.2). Acclaimed actor Dame Judi Dench agreed to be Queen, Dwayne "the Rock" Johnson became Secretary of Defense, and former US vice president Al Gore was the first honorary citizen.

These highly visual materials raised interest and awareness and flowed through social media. In the first week after the launch, some 100 000 people signed up as citizens and ultimately the campaign reached half a billion people and spurred searches on Google for "plastic pollution."

Figure 9.2 Trash Island, the gigantic mountain of trash in the Pacific Ocean, had all of the elements of a real country. *Source:* Abbott Mead Vickers BBDO.

The Trash Isles won the top PR award for 2018 at the prestigious Cannes Lions International Festival of Creativity, held annually in Cannes, France. After their win, the AMV BBDO creative team, Dalatando Almeida and Michael Hughes and designer Mario Kerkstra, said of their win:

We wanted to put this country-sized problem under the noses of world leaders, literally, raising awareness of the crisis in our ocean and its impact. So to see the campaign getting recognition on a global stage is great as the more noise that is created around the issue, the harder it is to ignore. (Charles, 2018, Brooks et al., 2020).

Botched Response to Environmental Disaster

The 2010 BP Oil Company oil crisis in the Gulf of New Mexico was the biggest offshore oil spill in US history, killing 11 workers and releasing oil into the Gulf for 87 days. The subsequent corporate response has become a famous example of mismanagement – both in action and communication – and visual imagery played a big role. BP had closed its PR department in a budget-cutting move prior to the event, thus CEO Tony Haywood, ill-prepared for the international spotlight, made gaffes that stunned many. His appearances on the devastated beaches in a stiff white shirt provided negative optics as a visual sign of his lack of apparent empathy and compassion. These characteristics were also personified in his televised interview a little over one month after the explosion and spill. He stated, "There's no one who wants this over more than I do. I'd like my life back" (Lubin, 2010), evoking a huge backlash of public resentment and anger.

As oil continued to pump out of an uncapped pipe, spreading across the Gulf Coast, BP made its first effort of controlled messaging with an apology campaign. It proved an incorrect communications strategy can cause damage, and earn criticism and ridicule, particularly of the expense to create and run the TV, online, and print ads. According to the Associated Press, in the TV and online version of the ad, "Hayward then narrates over images of boom laid in clear water before uncontaminated marshes and healthy pelicans. Cleanup crews walk with trash bags on white sand beaches as he touts the oil giant's response efforts" (Associated Press, 2010). This imagery clashed with disturbing news photographs of beaches blackened by oil and pelicans coated in it, some immobilized by the gunk, others struggling with it dripping from their beaks and wings. Three years later BP launched a new website defending its response (Nola, 2013).

Nonprofit and Activist PR

Nonprofits are an extremely broad and expansive category of organizations with more than 1 million members in the United States. Digital and social media are an economical, accessible, and powerful communication tool for nonprofits because they are a smart and easy way for those with limited resources to use compelling visual imagery to get the word out, build relationships, and engage and activate communities.

Truth About Teen Smoking

Truth® Initiative is a nonprofit dedicated to ending teen smoking. In a wildly successful campaign, it used the social media dating app, Tinder, as a "star" in its videos. According to a study about smoking behavior on Tinder, profile pictures that include smoking get rejected with "left swipes" almost twice as often as those that do not (Truth Initiative, 2016).

Truth's strategy used prominent influencers – Internet stars and musical artists, including Frankie Grande (Figure 9.3) – to create an original song and music video called "Left Swipe Dat," using humor to frame tobacco as both unattractive and deadly. Leading up to the 2015 Grammys, the video stars started teasing the campaign in their social channels. A 60-second version premiered at the Grammys and a mobile YouTube takeover drove viewers to the full-length video. The campaign chained into teens' favorite TV shows, with MTV, Adult Swim, and ABC Family writing "Left Swipe Dat" into the scripts. Other YouTube artists created their own versions of "Left Swipe Dat" to encourage teens to do the same.

Figure 9.3 YouTube personality Frankie Grande joined other Internet stars and musical artists to ignite the Left Swipe Dat campaign to discourage teen smoking. *Source:* Slaven Vlasic/Getty Images Entertainment/Getty Images.

The Left Swipe Dat PR campaign, created and executed in collaboration with Ketchum PR, was named the Arts, Entertainment, Sports & Media Campaign of the Year, and the Nonprofit Campaign of the Year by *PR Week*. Judges called the campaign a brilliant, relevant, authentic, and creative approach to taking a "preachy message" and turning it into one embraced by teens (PR Week, 2016).

FOCUS: What Does Mental Health Look Like?

A mental health campaign produced a remarkable photography collection for public and media use to help reframe mental illness. Called the *Be Vocal* Collection, it was part of the Vocal: Speak Up For Mental Health campaign whose goal was to empower adults living with a mental health condition to speak up for themselves – and as a community – to advance mental health in America.

Behind the campaign was the fact that search engines often bring up disparaging imagery of mental health. The effort was conceived by a close partnership between Sunovion Pharmaceuticals, five leading mental health advocacy groups, singer and mental health advocate Demi Lovato, various creative professionals, and Getty Images.

(Continued)

An engaging documentary film and social media content also constituted the campaign, but its *Be Vocal* Collection of photos earned accolades, taking first place in the photography category of *PR Daily's* 2017 Video and Visual Awards.

Source: Shaul Schwarz/Getty Images News/Getty Images.

The collection offers the photos free for editorial use. It features 10 people living well with various mental health conditions (we include one example here), "showing what mental health can look like when people get the support they need – while also acknowledging the challenges of mental illness" (PR Daily n.d.; Be Vocal n.d.). The campaign website encouraged visitors to share the photos on social media to help reduce discrimination and create a more informed, accepting society.

Women's Activist and Grassroots Communication

In addition to social media, activist groups have made effective use of traditional PR tactics including media relations, thought leadership, staged events, and original research to promote their causes and create awareness and conversation.

The Women's March on Washington DC held January 21, 2017, the day after President Trump's inauguration, drew close to a million protesters to the nation's capital and to cities and towns on all seven continents. The protest movement began with a Facebook post by a concerned woman in Hawaii and grew through shares and likes by others who felt similarly about the 2016 election.

The Pussyhat Project was a nationwide effort, initiated by a screenwriter and an architect in Los Angeles, to create pink hats to be worn at the march for visual impact (Figure 9.4). In response to their call, crafters around the United States began making the hats using patterns provided on the project website for use with either a knitting method, crochet, and even sewing with fabrics. The project's goal was to have one million hats handed out at the Washington march. The hats used pink yarns or fabrics and were originally designed to be a unified, positive form of protest for Trump's inauguration, expressing solidarity in support of women's rights. The project launched

Figure 9.4 Sewn and knitted "pussyhats" being worn on a plane to the January 2017 Women's March in Washington DC. *Source:* Ted Eytan.

in November 2016 and quickly became popular on social media with over 100 000 downloads of the pattern to make the hat (McGough, 2017; The Pussyhat Project, n.d.).

The Pussyhat, with its top two corners in the shape of a cat's ears, meant to reframe the offensive use of the word "pussy" by Trump in his 2005 remarks that women would let him "grab them by the pussy" (Mathis-Lilley, 2016). Many of the hats worn by marchers in Washington, DC, were created by crafters who were unable to attend, but donated them to marchers as a symbolic way to be present. NPR's political reporter compared the hats to the "Make America Great Again" (MAGA) hats worn by Trump supporters: "it sends a very particular political message, one that is simultaneously unifying and antagonistic" (Kurtzleben, 2017).

Political Communication

Within this broad category are communication efforts by governments toward its citizens and other constituents; messaging by citizens, nonprofit organizations, and for-profit businesses toward the government or members of society; and communication by political office holders or seekers toward their constituents. **Public diplomacy** (**PD**), also considered a part of political PR, consists of governmental and mediated communication toward global citizens.

Image Maintenance

The application of PR tactics to politics is not new. According to the Institute for Public Relations, people like Alexander Hamilton and William Wilberforce, who led a movement to abolish the slave trade in Britain, have both been credited as founding figures in the application of image management to influence public opinion in order to achieve political ends (Arceneaux 2019).

For a contemporary example of political "good visuals," consider the image strategies of Louisiana's Governor John Bel Edwards during his bid for reelection. First, we must realize that the state of Louisiana is passionate about football. In fall 2019, Edwards held a press event at the New Orleans Saints' training facility not only to announce major funding for a renovation of their arena but to stage a **photo op** with Saints' quarterback Drew Brees and head coach Sean Payton. Edwards, a former high school quarterback, also ran athletic drills, competing with Brees. Thus, in this visual coup, Edwards positioned himself with two significant influencers in the state to make a not so tacit connection between the sports heroes and his campaign for reelection (Arceneaux 2019).

A New PR Tactic: Native Advertising as Public Diplomacy

Televised political action thrillers can both serve political PR purposes and benefit from PR visual communication tactics. Consider the international hit series *Fauda* (meaning "chaos") that was picked up by the streaming service Netflix. Created by Israelis to tell their story about the Israeli–Palestinian conflict, it can be viewed as mediated PD, communicating the Israeli perspective to a global audience. To further promote its narrative and viewership, the popular, yet controversial, program has used the strategy of "native advertising" a relatively new tactic in the PR toolkit.

Ad Age explains native advertising as a tactic in which ads are meant to mimic editorial content (Sebastian, 2014). In digital, the content appears within the feed of publication websites, fitting in with the editorial style and format but should be clearly labeled as advertising. In 2018, *Fauda* on Netflix paid for the creation and placement of an elaborate infographic, *A Land Divided*, appearing on the theatlantic.com website.

The infographic begins with the statement "The Israeli–Palestinian conflict represents one of the most fraught political issues in the Middle East, with no clear end in sight. Here's what the struggle looks like through the eyes of those who've lived it." It then graphically details its history while the user scrolls from 1948 to 2018. The infographic carries the disclaimer "Crafted by the *Atlantic*'s marketing team and paid for by Fauda on Netflix." (theatlantic.com n.d.). The Native Advertising Institute shortlisted *A Land Divided* for a Best Use of Infographic award in its 2018 competition.

Since 2011, "sponsored content" native advertising has been gaining momentum and even overtaking display advertising. The *New York Times'* T Brand Studio creates custom content for the newspaper. For example, they created a feature on incarcerated women sponsored by Netflix to promote the series *Orange Is The New Black*. The studio's website, www.tbrandstudio.com, is a good place to explore some of the best examples of native advertising.

FOCUS: The Art of Making a Political Ad Feel Like an Uplifting Movie

In 2018, a woman and former Air Force pilot, MJ Hegar, ran for US House District 31 in Texas. To differentiate herself from the eight-term incumbent, she created a campaign video that landed her in the national spotlight months before the election. "Doors," a three-and-a-half-minute short subject documentary of her life and character, went viral captivating online viewers and the media.

In the video, Hegar described a near-fatal helicopter incident in Afghanistan, her childhood with an abusive father, and her fight with the Pentagon to secure ground combat positions for women. The "doors" theme runs throughout, starting with a close-up of a door from the search and rescue helicopter she was piloting before she was shot, and it blew up: a door now hanging on the wall in her family's dining room. In the video, she's opening, pushing, kicking through doors that stood in her way.

Source: Cable News Network Inc. (CNN).

According to the *Washington Post*'s movie critic, the video was clearly inspired by the work of Martin Scorsese in that it was edited to resemble one continuous shot (Hornaday, 2018). The iconic Rolling Stones hit "Gimme Shelter" plays in the background. It's a prime example of how cinematic craft and production values are used to create contemporary political rhetoric, name notes, exemplifying visual storytelling at its most exquisite and economical.

VISUAL RHETORIC STRATEGIES IN PR CAMPAIGNS

LO3 Critique visual rhetoric strategies in public relations campaigns.

PR is an expansive field for many reasons, not the least are communication innovations that have allowed more voices to be heard. Because the communication universe has flattened with digital technologies and social platforms, anyone may initiate or control messaging. While there are now many more professional PR opportunities for both relationship and reputation building, the need for responding to issues, threats, and crises has also accelerated. Visual messaging plays a critical role in helping to communicate trustworthiness and expertise as well as empathy and emotion. The following examples draw on the PR practice areas of **corporate social responsibility** (**CSR**) – the corporate honoring of environmental, social, and economic concerns – crisis and issues management, as well as city branding and tourism promotion. They will help you see PR visual messages with a more informed and critical eye, as well as help you identify opportunities to analyze them.

Communicating CSR with Facts, Credibility, and Emotion

Corporations are now conscious of the kinds of impact they are having with all of their stakeholders, resulting in their engagement in "doing good" to benefit the environment and society as well as the financial health of the business. CSR engagement is taking many forms: philanthropy, paid employee volunteer efforts, funding a social cause, partnering with nonprofits, adopting environmentally sustainable practices, improving communities where the business is located or where it sources materials, and more. Ideally, companies integrate CSR into their business model so that in the normal course of business, they are operating in ways that enhance society and the environment, instead of contributing negatively to it. PR professionals often collaborate in the initiation and management of CSR engagement, but most significantly oversee communication strategies. A major challenge is to present the corporate "good works" as part of the company's ethos and not as just a marketing stunt.

Multimedia Microsites

Covering a broad category of CSR are the socially responsible business practices a company enacts or integrates into the way it does business. These are discretionary business practices that a business adopts and conducts to support social causes, to improve community well-being, and/or to protect the environment.

Coca-Cola replenishes water in locations from where it's taken to finish its beverages, and tells this story on its multimedia microsite *Water Stewardship and Replenishment Report* (Coca-Cola, n.d.). Classic elements of rhetoric guide its content. The site conveys credibility and trustworthiness through the transparency of its documentary visual content and the logos of its nongovernmental organization (**NGO**) partners. It

Figure 9.5 In a multimedia microsite, Patagonia shows how to conserve by buying used clothing. *Source:* Up-climbing.com.

communicates reasoning through facts, figures, and interactive infographics, and emotion through the site's design choices and its photographic and video storytelling.

Patagonia is a retailer of sustainable outdoor clothing and gear for what it calls the silent sports like climbing, surfing, skiing, snowboarding, and trail running. Its approach to CSR has been called revolutionary and has earned numerous awards from environmental organizations. As a result, the name Patagonia and its recognizable logo now carry the metaphorical meaning of quality products and environmental stewardship.

Consider this example of Patagonia's innovative CSR approach (Figure 9.5). After years of hosting pop-up swap meets where customers could find used clothing, in the fall of 2013 during New York's Fashion Week, Patagonia announced the addition of used clothing sections in its stores. Then in 2017 it went online with the launch of "Worn Wear," a permanent microsite promising to "celebrate the stories we wear" and inviting customers to trade, sell, and buy secondhand Patagonia products. The site also functions as a brand experience with video and still image storytelling – narratives that pass the test of reliability – plus invitations to events like regular Worn Wear Tours in the United States and Europe.

How "Bad" Can Do Good

With all the resources going into CSR, it's critical that a company effectively communicates these good works to all its stakeholders and audiences, including investors, consumers, employees, suppliers, community members, and of course, the media. Using emotional visuals in messaging about CSR can be one effective strategy to engage audiences. Interestingly, research suggests that *negative* emotional visuals are more successful than positive emotional visuals in increasing a viewer's memory of the company and its CSR initiative (Lee and Chung, 2018). These negative emotional visuals are ones that show the existing "bad" instead of the resulting "good."

For example, a research experiment (Lee and Chung, 2018) used fictional Facebook-format visual CSR messages on hunger in Africa, water shortage in Africa, and water pollution. Some contained positive images of desirable outcomes in a community or environment where a CSR issue had already been resolved. Others contained negative images portraying a current at risk state of a community or the environment, where a CSR issue was unresolved. The findings: negative images worked better. For example, a distressful image of a child suffering from malnutrition triggered recall of both the company and its CSR initiative. Why do you think that is? Much research has documented that when stronger emotions, such as compassion, care, distress, and so forth, are aroused in viewers, they are more motivated to remember aspects about the message and even take action.

Visual Persuasion in Risk, Issue, and Crisis Management

Risk avoidance communication aims to prevent people from getting sick or hurt. It encourages behaviors to avoid harm from alcohol or tobacco use, distracted driving, lack of physical activity, poor diet, unsafe sexual practices, disease exposure, and many other threats. Issue management communication seeks to keep potential problems from becoming real ones, for example, messages teach children how to be safe in the streets and even in their own backyards. Crisis communication arises often at unexpected times of damage to people, place, or business; sometimes all three. Visual messaging in this moment is essential to communicate honestly, credibly, and with care.

The Ugly Truth Works

While negative emotional visuals are memorable when connecting companies with their engagement in societal issues, visual fear appeals are working when the targeted viewers are themselves at risk. Human papillomavirus (HPV) is the most common sexually transmitted disease, with alarming global disparities between cervical cancer and use of the HPV vaccination. Although the need to increase HPV diagnosis and treatment are critical, barriers exist including high vaccine costs, competing health priorities, limited public acceptance, and lack of awareness of screening opportunities (Graham and Mishra, 2011).

Research offers one solution to encourage vaccine use: studies show the use of fear appeals in health, crisis, and risk PR campaigns may encourage the target audience to adopt safeguarding behaviors. To better understand the HPV-prevention messaging used by the Centers for Disease Control and Prevention (CDC), researchers analyzed three of its flyers and used eye-tracking methods with participants to learn how the flyers' visual images could affect attitudes, memory, and behavior intentions (Avery and Park, 2018). **Eye-tracking** measures eye positions and eye movement.

The "fear" visual flyer included pictures of the HPV virus and warts, while the "non-fear" visual flyer had a picture of a young patient consulting with a specialist wearing a lab coat on an exam table. The third sample, a text-only flyer, included the same text as the first two but no image. The results: (i) flyers with both visual types were more effective in all areas than the text-only flyer, (ii) viewers' attention to and recall of the message was weak on the "non-fear" flyer, and (iii) viewers' attention predicted intent to vaccinate *only* when a fear visual was used.

Visual Storytelling Keeps Children Safe

Children's safety is one of the top priorities for parents. Products that address this issue need to craft marketing messages that prioritize the goal they serve, and Verizon chose to do this in a very positive way. The telecommunications company's GizmoPal 2 is a wrist-wearable device that enables children to stay in touch with their parents. A video merely mentioning the device won first place as a PR video in *PR Daily's* 2017 Video and Visual Awards (find it at: fivemarysfarms.com/our-story).

It's an example of a reliable narrative with a story that hangs together and rings true. Verizon reached out to a credible "influencer," Mary Heffernan, a restaurateur from Silicon Valley who needed a better source for quality meats. To solve this problem, her family moved a six-hour drive away into northern California to start their own business, Five Marys Farms. She narrates the award-winning video through telling her own (and her family's) story with short cuts of life on the farm. One vignette dealt with connectivity. This is crucially important on the 1,800-acre property not only for learning how to deliver piglets from a YouTube video, but also for tracking down her four daughters and knowing their whereabouts and their safety with Verizon's GizmoPal 2 (the video's one fleeting mention of the product).

Verizon posted the video to YouTube and spotlighted the story during a 30-day period. Compared to the same time period the previous year, it helped achieve a 90% increase in sales of the GizmoPal 2 and led to a second video, this one produced in 360°.

Crisis, Issue, and Risk Communications Go 360°

PR communicators are creating more immersive storytelling with 360° video, augmented reality, and virtual reality. Used frequently in tourism, hospitality, and real estate promotion, immersive storytelling is reshaping the way many PR stories are told. Recent research on this technology reveals that during a crisis, immersive technologies increase people's attention, understanding, and attitudes toward the content by increasing empathy, provoking emotional reactions, and moving people to action in relationship to the crisis (Faustino et al., 2018). When managing an issue or communicating risk, disease awareness through immersive storytelling can create breakthrough empathy for stigmatized or misunderstood conditions. It also enables people to grasp their own risk status more effectively than does traditional messaging, for instance, regarding conditions of prediabetes (Weinrebe, 2017).

City Branding and Destination Image-Making

Tourism is one of the fastest-growing economic sectors in the world, meaning more destinations are competing for a larger share of this market. People want to go places, see things they've never seen, and do things they've never done, and the industry must turn that basic, but undirected, desire into action (Page and Parnell, 2019). Whether it's a nation promoting its heritage or a city promoting an annual festival, tourism has one major goal: attract people to come and stay for a while. Communications help them get there and help shape their experience once they arrive. For certain travelers, one strong attraction is magnificent architecture.

Architecture as Symbol

Architecture has long been featured in city marketing as both a destination image and experience. Chicago features iconic buildings, among them Willis Tower which lures visitors up to its 103rd-floor sky deck as well as the much smaller-scale Chicago Water Tower built in 1869 and now a Chicago Office of Tourism art gallery. These buildings, along with Navy Pier's 15-story Ferris wheel, the beaux arts-style of the Art Institute of Chicago designed for the 1893 World's Columbian Exposition, and the city's many stately buildings by architectural pioneers Daniel Burnham, Louis Sullivan, Mies van der Rohe, and Frank Lloyd Wright among others, all contribute to the city's reputation for architectural innovation. The Chicago Architecture Center website showcases the experiences offered to visitors – nearly 7,000 tours each year including boat, walking, bus, "L" train, and bike. Do a Google image search for Chicago and you're likely to find the mirroring "Bean" (formally known as Cloud Gate), a beautiful visual curiosity anchored in Millennium Park.

Appeal of the Dark Side

A city's history can also be told through architectural remnants from its past, as they embody the zeitgeist of the time. Some travel writers and cities find a tourism appeal in architecture signifying such darker times. For example, Transylvania's Dracula tourism highlights Bran castle, once home to the notorious Vlad the Impaler. Other former Soviet bloc countries are home to functionalist and modernist architecture left over from the Soviet era (1948–1989). Built under totalitarian societies, the buildings – with their uniform design and commanding presence – serve as symbols of a past oppressive society (Paletta, 2012).

Many of these monumental Communist buildings are seen today as monstrosities and some have been demolished for this reason as well as the ideology they represented. However, there are some architectural outliers: buildings with an otherworldly design aesthetic that still exist, such as the honeycombed exterior of the Chemnitz Stadhalle, now a culture and convention center in eastern Germany. Soviet era sanatoriums remain the most innovative and often the most ornamental buildings of their time, writes Maryam Omidi (2017) in *Holidays in Soviet Sanatoriums*. Many of them remain popular tourist destinations today. For example, the Druzhba sanatorium overlooking the Black Sea in Yalta, Ukraine (Figure 9.6), still draws health and medical tourists. It's been compared to a supervillain's lair and a huge planetary gear set from the sky. When it was built

Figure 9.6 Once suspected to be a military weapon, the Druzhba sanatorium overlooks the Black Sea in Yalta, Ukraine. *Source:* Thomas Peter/Reuters/Newscom.

in 1985 Turkish spies thought it was another dangerous military object built to support the Cold War effort (Vasilevsky, 2018).

Given the stories embedded in architectural relics, some sociologists propose that cities in former Soviet bloc countries should use significant leftover buildings as part of a city's visual brand identity to attract tourists of history and heritage (Ochkovskaya and Gerasimenko, 2018). For example, in Warsaw, Poland, the former headquarters of the Polish Communist Party might appeal to tourists identifying some connection with it: Russians and Americans of Polish heritage, as well as tourists from throughout Poland.

Tourism Messaging: Online and In Hand

Brochures, leaflets, printed guidebooks, and maps all remain promotional staples at major tourist destinations. However, before visitors arrive, decision-making rests in online resources – mostly visual – and their capacity to influence. Promotional videos on YouTube play an important role. Semiotics, the science of analyzing the meanings of signs and symbols, can help guide how to create and communicate identity and image in these audiovisual messages. Tourists relate to destinations through certain framing symbols, mostly those already prominent in the media (Jakopović, 2015). Similarly, markers of location identity such as the sea or lakeshore, lighthouses or castles, are not only iconic signs, but symbols of character traits such as purity, courage, honor, and tranquility (Palmer, 1999). Tourists are seeking not only a physical destination but an experience of "Frenchness," English tradition, Italian romance, or American freedom, and knowing what cultural signs communicate these meanings is crucial to promotional texts.

PROFESSIONAL PROFILE: John Florek

Source: aejmc.us.

John Florek is VP Director of Creative Innovation at ARC Worldwide.

Before I started my career in advertising, my view of brands was that they were essentially metaphors defined by carefully selected images and words. And after graduating from the University of Missouri School of Journalism, I couldn't wait to get a job at a big agency as one of the lucky people responsible for those words. Unfortunately, at the time, the job market for entry-level creatives wasn't exactly booming. I didn't even get responses after sending my portfolio to most of the big-name agencies back home in Chicago. But, thankfully, eventually, a small promotions agency called "Frankel" needed a junior copywriter and took a chance on me.

In my first day on the job, I still couldn't articulate the difference between a *promotions* agency and a *traditional* agency, let alone predict that the difference would eventually define the way I structured the rest of my career. In college, I had envisioned spending my time writing clever headlines and taglines and commercial scripts. But at Frankel, I was spending more time coming up with contests, events, and *experiences*. It wasn't long before I realized that brands were not a combination of two ingredients, but three: images, words, and *actions*. In those first couple of years, I learned that I had a passion for brand activation. If advertising is where a brand talks the talk, activation is where it has to walk the walk and *prove its purpose*.

Take, for example, the Coke ad featured in Chapter 5. The two hands forming the outline of the iconic contour bottle is a passive statement that Coke bridges the gap, or acts as the common ground, to foster togetherness between two different cultures. It's a beautifully executed, powerful statement.

Clio Awards, LLC

But it's just a *statement*. For people to truly connect with a brand, it needs to take *action* and give people a way to *participate*. Coke did just that in 2013 with their "Small World Machines" in a remarkable way.

The high-tech vending machines were installed in two popular shopping malls in Lahore, Pakistan, and New Delhi, India: two cities that are close in proximity but seemingly worlds apart due to decades of political tension. In the spirit of global togetherness, the machines invited mall-goers to put aside their geography and share a moment as fellow humans over a Coke. Using embedded livestreaming cameras and touchscreen technology, people in each location could see one another projected onto the front panel of the vending machine and were encouraged to complete a friendly task together – wave, touch hands, trace a peace sign, or dance – before the machines would vend a Coca-Cola.

When you consider all the different ways a brand like Coke can communicate its purpose in the world, examples like this one demonstrate what has become a core guiding principle of my career: actions speak louder than ads.

Sources: https://www.fastcompany.com/1683001/how-coca-cola-used-vending-machines-to-try-and-unite-the-people-of-india-and-pakistan; https://www.coca-colacompany.com/stories/happiness-without-borders

CHAPTER SUMMARY

This chapter offered a full menu of PR efforts that used visual communication for strategic purposes, challenging you to find *how* the visuals worked to inform, shape attitudes, or persuade publics to take some action. You read how nonprofits encourage a healthy public image for mental illness and how businesses use multimedia engagement to encourage ethical consumption. You discovered the usefulness of photo ops in gaining widespread attention by political candidates. And you learned that sometimes it's the negative picture that's most memorable when an organization talks about its social responsibility projects.

KEY TERMS

Public diplomacy (PD)   Efforts of one nation to directly communicate with foreign publics.

Photo op   An arranged opportunity to take a photograph, with celebrities, politicians, or at events, for PR purposes.

Corporate social responsibility (CSR)   The corporate honoring of environmental, social, and economic concerns.

NGO   Nongovernmental organization; the typical reference to an international nonprofit that's independent of government.

Eye-tracking   Process to measure eye positions and eye movement.

PRACTICE ACTIVITIES

1. Explore how one of your favorite brands visually presents its social responsibility or sustainability work online. On the company's home page, scroll to the bottom to find "Responsibility" or a similar term. Once you select that, explore and choose one visual image, logo, infographic, or other visual to do an analysis using your choice of methods from this book.

2. Go to Coca-Cola's corporate website at https://www.coca-colacompany.com/home. Explore and choose an image for visual analysis using the method of your choice.

3. Using Pinterest, search for CSR Reports and browse some. Don't let the length of the reports scare you – many are filled with great imagery to analyze.

4. PR also takes the form of booths at local fairs, larger events, and even pop-ups at parks and on city streets. Experience one, take several photographs or videos, and conduct your analysis.

REFERENCES

Arceneaux, P. (2019). Political public relations at its finest: The news management function of electoral politics. https://instituteforpr.org/political-public-relations-at-its-finest-the-news-management-function-of-electoral-politics (accessed October 5, 2020).

Associated Press. (2010). Apologetic BP ads draw criticism. www.independent.co.uk/news/world/americas/apologetic-bp-ads-draw-criticism-1992907.html (accessed October 5, 2020).

Avery, E.J. and Park, S. (2018). HPV vaccination campaign fear visuals: an eye-tracking study exploring effects of visual attention and type on message informative value, recall, and behavioral intentions. Public Relations Review 44 (3): 321–330.

Be Vocal. (n.d.) The Be Vocal Collection – Changing Perceptions of Mental Health in America. http://www.bevocalspeakup.com/mental-health-stories-and-photos.html ().

Brooks, B.S., Horvit, B.J., and Moen, D.R. (2020). News Reporting and Writing. Boston: Bedford/St. Martin's.

Charles, G. (2018). AMV BBDO scoops design Grand Prix at Cannes for 'Trash Isles'. https://www.campaignlive.com/article/amv-bbdo-scoops-design-grand-prix-cannes-trash-isles/1485468 (accessed October 5, 2020). © 2018 Haymarket media group Ltd.

Coca-Cola. (n.d.) Water stewardship and replenishment report. https://www.coca-colacompany.com/water-stewardship-replenish-report (accessed October 5, 2020).

Faustino, J.D., Lee, J.Y., Lee, S.Y., and Ahn, H. (2018). Effects of 360° video on attitudes toward disaster communication: mediating and moderating roles of spatial presence and prior disaster media involvement. Public Relations Review 44 (3): 331–441.

Graham, J.E. and Mishra, A. (2011). Global challenges of implementing human papilloma-virus vaccines. International Journal for Equity in Health 10 (27).

Griner, D. (2018). Giant piles of garbage win big at Cannes. Adweek. https://www.adweek.com/creativity/giant-piles-of-garbage-win-big-at-cannes (accessed October 5, 2020).

Hornaday, A. (2018). Ocasio-Cortez, Hegar, and the art of making your political ad feel like an uplifting movie. https://www.washingtonpost.com/lifestyle/style/ocasio-cortez-hegar-and-the-art-of-making-your-political-ad-feel-like-an-uplifting-movie/2018/07/05/1d741a5a-8062-11e8-b0ef-fffcabeff946_story.html?utm_term=.ec53c92a5a1b (accessed October 5, 2020).

Jakopović, H. (2015). YouTube's role in destination image creation. Journal of Education, Culture and Society 1: 217–226.

Kurtzleben, D. (2017). With 'Pussyhats' at women's marches, headwear sends a defiant message. NPR. https://www.npr.org/2017/01/22/511048762/with-pussyhats-at-womens-marches-headwear-sends-a-defiant-message?t=1537802720404 (accessed October 5, 2020).

Lee, S.Y. and Chung, S. (2018). Effects of emotional visuals and company–cause fit on memory of CSR information. Public Relations Review 44 (3): 353–362.

Lubin, G. (2010). BP CEO Tony Hayward apologizes for his idiotic statement: "I'd like my life back." https://www.businessinsider.com/bp-ceo-tony-hayward-apologizes-for-saying-id-like-my-life-back-2010-6 (accessed October 5, 2020).

Mathis-Lilley, B. (2016). Trump was recorded in 2005 bragging about grabbing women "by the pussy". Slate.com. http://www.slate.com/blogs/the_slatest/2016/10/07/donald_trump_2005_tape_i_grab_women_by_the_pussy.html?via=gdpr-consent (accessed October 5, 2020).

McGough, A. (2017). The creators of the Pussyhat Project explain how craft projects are protest. Fast Company. https://www.fastcompany.com/3067204/the-creators-of-the-pussy-hat-phenomenon-explain-how-craft-projects-are-pr (accessed October 5, 2020).

Miller, K. (1999). Public relations in film and fiction: 1930 to 1995. Journal of Public Relations Research 11 (1): 3–28.

Mingren, W. (2016). The Fiji Mermaid: What was the abominable creature and why was it so popular? Ancient Origins. https://www.ancient-origins.net/unexplained-phenomena/

fiji-mermaid-what-was-abominable-creature-and-why-was-it-so-popular-005735 (accessed October 5, 2020).

Nola. (2013). BP launches new website defending the company's response to the Deep-water Horizon oil spill. https://www.business-humanrights.org/it/ultime-notizie/bp-launches-new-website-defending-the-companys-response-to-the-deepwater-horizon-oil-spill-usa/ (accessed October 5, 2020).

Ochkovskaya, M. and Gerasimenko, V. (2018). Buildings from the socialist past as part of a city's brand identity: the case of Warsaw. Bulletin of Geography. Socio-Economic Series 39 (39): 113–127.

Omidi, M. (2017). Holidays in Soviet sanatoriums. http://www.calvertjournal.com/features/show/9100/holidays-in-soviet-sanatoriums-ussr-tourism-photography (accessed October 5, 2020).

Page, J.T. and Parnell, L.J. (2019). Introduction to Strategic Public Relations: Digital, Global, and Socially Responsible Communication. Thousand Oaks, CA: Sage.

Paletta, A. (2012). The sublime sci-fi buildings that Communism built. The Awl. https://www.theawl.com/2012/12/the-sublime-sci-fi-buildings-that-communism-built/ (accessed October 5, 2020).

Palmer, C. (1999). Tourism and the symbols of identity. Tourism Management 20 (3): 313–322.

PR Daily (n.d.). Wide-ranging mental health campaign produces stunning photography collection. https://www.prdaily.com/Awards/SpecialEdition/891.aspx (accessed October 5, 2020). © 2010 Ragan communications, Inc.

PR Week. (2016). Arts, Entertainment, Sports & Media Campaign of the Year 2016. https://www.prweek.com/article/1386821/arts-entertainment-sports-media-campaign-year-2016 (accessed October 5, 2020).

Saltzman, J. (2012). The image of the public relations practitioner in movies and television 1901–2011. The IJPC Journal 3, Fall 2011 – Spring 2012 1–50. http://ijpc.uscannenberg.org/journal/index.php/ijpcjournal/article/view/25/50 (accessed October 5, 2020).

Sebastian, M. (2014). The Year in Native Ads. https://adage.com/article/media/year-content-marketing-native-ads/296436 (accessed December 24, 2020).

theatlantic.com. (n.d.). A land divided. https://www.theatlantic.com/sponsored/netflix-fauda-2018/a-land-divided/1853/ (accessed October 5, 2020).

The Lost Museum Archive. (n.d.). https://lostmuseum.cuny.edu/archive/joice-heth-poster-1835 (accessed October 5, 2020).

The Pussyhat Project. (n.d.) Our Story. https://www.pussyhatproject.com/our-story/ (accessed October 5, 2020).

Truth Initiative. (2016). Effort to get teens to "left swipe" tobacco earns 2 top awards from PR week. https://truthinitiative.org/research-resources/tobacco-prevention-efforts/effort-get-teens-left-swipe-tobacco-earns-2-top (accessed October 5, 2020).

Vasilevsky, I. (2018). Druzhba Sanatorium. http://architectuul.com/architecture/druzhba-sanatorium (accessed October 5, 2020).

Weinrebe, J. (2017). Transforming the patient experience with immersive technologies. MSL. https://mslgroup.com/blog/transforming-patient-experience-immersive-technologies (accessed October 5, 2020).

Chapter 10
Journalism

Refugee Border Crisis

Source: Kim Kyung Hoon/Reuters.

This photo of a migrant mother dragging her diaper-clad children away from tear gas fumes became the dominant image during Thanksgiving weekend in 2018 (Elfrink and Barbash, 2018). US border agents fired the tear gas after some people attempted to unlawfully breach the border fence between Tijuana, Mexico, and the United States. More than 5,000 migrants and refugees from Central American countries had walked toward the border attempting to pressure the US government to allow them to enter and apply for asylum, after having sheltered for about two weeks in a Tijuana stadium complex with capacity for only 3,000.

The jarring portrait was captured on camera by veteran Reuters photographer Kim Kyung-Hoon. Kim's photograph is the type of image that becomes iconic: Its emotion, drama, and intimacy have a universal appeal, explaining its appearance on online news sites and on the front pages of numerous newspapers, provoking worldwide outrage. Both children are wearing only T-shirts, and one appears to be wearing a pull-up diaper. One is barefoot, the other wears flip-flops. The woman who clutches their arms and drags them to safety is wearing a T-shirt featuring the happy cartoon faces of Anna and Elsa from the Disney movie *Frozen*.

In an interview with NBC News, Kim said, "I saw the woman and two children running away. One girl was barefoot from the beginning. The other was wearing beach sandals and lost them in the chaos" (Gutierrez and Siemaszko, 2018). Kim said he could hear the little girls coughing and crying and he immediately aimed his camera in their direction and started shooting.

News reports identified the woman as Maria Mesa, a 39-year-old mother who, with her five children, is fleeing violence in her home country, Honduras. They are trying to reach their father who lives in Louisiana. Her 13-year-old daughter is also caught in Kim's picture, running behind her mother. Her 3-year-old son, who does not appear in the picture, was with them and fainted after getting a lungful of gas (Gutierrez and Siemaszko, 2018; Law, 2018).

Kim is a South Korean, based in Tokyo, who has worked for Reuters for 16 years covering news events and tragedies, including plane crashes and the 2011 earthquake and tsunami that devastated Japan. When asked if he was rattled by what he witnessed and the heartbreaking sounds of children crying, he said "my job is to document what is happening. I try not to let my emotions get involved in my work" (Gutierrez and Siemaszko, 2018). He added that while he does not want to tell people how to feel about the photograph, he hopes that it will bring the situation at the border greater attention: "I just want to show what is happening here to another part of the world" (Law, 2018).

Key Learning Objectives

After engaging in this chapter, you'll be able to:
1. Understand journalism practices and history from a visual perspective.
2. Assess ethical issues in news imagery.
3. Recognize the use of visual rhetoric in contemporary journalistic media.
4. Critique the visual rhetoric of journalism.

Chapter Overview

This chapter reviews visual imagery of historical moments and eras in US journalism, revealing its role in documenting both the news and the culture. It includes a historical snapshot of **photojournalism**, concentrating on the twentieth century when the profession was at its height. Descriptions of significant moments in TV news coverage help to explain the dramatic visual impact moving images brought into American homes. The chapter also covers the persuasive quality of news visuals: how they may not only present news content in spectacular form, but also frame it from selective perspectives. You'll also read about ethical issues in visual practices such as digital manipulation, **fake news** images, **deepfakes**, online mugshot galleries, and misinformation that's packaged for virality. The positive benefits of social media platforms and their capacity for visual news dissemination are covered, as is news organizations' deep dive into video. Finally, you'll find examples of how to critique the visual rhetoric of various news products, inspected through the theoretical lenses introduced in earlier chapters.

PHOTOJOURNALISM

LO1 Understand journalism practices and history from a visual perspective.

Capturing visual images to tell news stories has traditionally been the responsibility of the photojournalist, educated and trained in the craft of still photography and the profession of journalism. For many Americans, iconic news images taken by photojournalists, many documenting historic turning points, are imprinted in our memories. For example, in the spring of 1970, a young photographer captured the moment a young woman kneels and cries out over a student slain by National Guardsmen: one of four students killed during a Kent State University demonstration against the Vietnam War. It stunned the nation and became a visual symbol of lost innocence. It was distributed on the Associated Press wire, appeared on the front page of the *New York Times,* and won a Pulitzer Prize for its creator, photojournalism student John Filo. It also inspired the song "Ohio" by Neil Young, "Tin soldiers and Nixon coming / We're finally on our own / This summer I hear the drumming / Four dead in Ohio."

Archived Visual Evidence

Throughout the history of print, video, and digital journalism, news images have brought to life the stories of the day from around the world. Some of the most honored and memorable appeared in the *New York Times*. In 2018, the newspaper worked with Google Cloud to digitize its photo archive of images featured once in the newspaper, or outtakes that were never used. The newly digitized trove includes "metadata." Metadata can include typed or handwritten captions or general information found with the photographs: notations beyond the actual photograph. The paper then created a regular feature called "Past Tense" taking readers on a visual journey to witness history through the eyes of professional photojournalism. Careers in photojournalism are waning because of shrinking news staffs and the rise of freelancers and amateur photography, especially with the ascendance of cell phone cameras.

One installment featured the *New York Time*'s coverage of California during the twentieth century: a destination pulsing with opportunity and energy. Its visual narrative told of the welcome the state gave to those escaping the segregationist South,

Figure 10.1 (Original caption) ENTHUSIASTIC GREETING: President Kennedy, relaxing yesterday on final day of Western tour, was surrounded by well-wishers when he went swimming in the Pacific near his brother-in-law's home in Santa Monica, Calif. Many in crowd waded in surf to get closer to the president. *Source:* Bettmann/Getty Images.

those seeking work and a better life for their families, and those who sought the freedom of its scenic roads and dramatic landscapes. An image by *Los Angeles Times* photographer Bill Beebe captures President John F. Kennedy's public magnetism *and* intimate accessibility (Figure 10.1).

Photojournalists and Popular Culture

Looking back in history, popular culture media in America have influenced the image of the photojournalist. In films of the 1930s and 1940s, photojournalists were often portrayed as bumbling, aggressive alcoholics and second-rate professionals: comic relief players in supporting roles (Brennen, 2004). Later, in the mid-twentieth century, films portrayed the photojournalist as young, Caucasian, male, and a loner. In one study of the 25-year period, 1954–1979, he was presented as someone obsessed with his work yet detached from the events he was covering (McDaniel, 2007). Beginning in about

Figure 10.2 Margaret Bourke-White, the first Western professional photographer accredited to enter the Soviet Union in the 1930s. *Source:* Alfred Eisenstaedt/The LIFE Picture Collection/Getty Images.

the 1980s, films idolized the heroic war photojournalists, experienced as reporters, yet either naïve or traumatized as roving cameramen negotiating foreign wars often in developing countries.

As newsrooms became more diverse in the later part of the century and beginning of the 2000s, female photojournalists were portrayed in leading or supporting roles in popular media; however, they were given less screen time than male photojournalists and often portrayed as romantics, whose helplessness and personal insecurities took priority over professional responsibilities (McDaniel, 2007).

However, one early female photojournalist defies popular culture depiction. New York City-born Margaret Bourke-White (Figure 10.2) was one of the most respected photojournalists in the country during the 1930s and 1940s. She joined *Fortune* magazine in 1929 and became the first foreign photographer to capture the Soviet Union's dramatic industrial rise while the Great Depression devastated the United States. She also documented the human aspects of the Dust Bowl in 1934, when a severe drought coupled with dust storms devastated America's Great Plains (ICP n.d.).

FOCUS: The Seven Sisters and their Influence

Seven women's magazines, collectively referred to as the "Seven Sisters," began publishing in the late nineteenth- and early twentieth-centuries with a focus on married women and the home. They included:

- *Ladies' Home Journal* (1873)
- *McCall's* (1873)
- *Good Housekeeping* (1885)
- *Redbook* (1903)
- *Better Homes and Gardens* (1922)
- *Family Circle* (1932)
- *Woman's Day* (1937)

The significance of the home is deeply rooted in these magazines and other early media. Desirable lifestyle fantasies arrived in hundreds of mail-order journals sent free to the working classes. The Seven Sisters brought similar content to middle-class women (Mott, 1957). The publications promoted products in both editorial stories and advertising, and by the 1920s, manufacturers began linking product consumption with social anxieties, self-image, and virtues (Wilson, 1983). This encouraged the transformation of the American family into consumers, a process well underway by the time television arrived in the early twentieth century. Critics of such journalism argued that the blurring of news and advertising violated journalistic principles.

Patriotic Shopping

In 1931, America was mired in the Great Depression, an economic disaster that left millions hungry and unemployed. Some economists believed that increased consumer spending and demand for goods could encourage the process of recovery. That year, public relations pioneer Edward Bernays pitched a plan to *Ladies Home Journal* (LJH) to do just that. A Bernays memo outlines his thinking (Marcellus, 2012, p. 394):

> The technique of propaganda applied in the World War by the United States to regiment the people of the nation to lay down their lives and give up their money, can be utilized with equal effectiveness in peacetime activities. In commercial life, propaganda . . . has won over the complete American public, and particularly American women, to entirely new habits of spending and living, notably – the refrigerator, the radio, the automobile.

The following year, LHJ ran an extensive campaign, orchestrated by Bernays, to persuade American *women* to end the Great Depression by going shopping. The February issue featured an illustration of a woman in fur-collared coat and fashionable hat, and "with a determined expression and a bundle of

(Continued)

packages leading a reluctant Uncle Sam by the arm" (Marcellus, 2012, p. 390). It also featured the slogan, "It's Up to the Women." The image and slogan were repeated in the magazine throughout 1932, and Macy's department store put the original painting in its New York City store window. It also appeared in pamphlets and newspaper ads. The campaign is historically significant, illustrating how public relations and *magazines* worked together to propose *women's* roles (Marcellus, 2012). While the campaign appeared unsuccessful in its goal to end the Great Depression, it nonetheless provides insights into how visual images connected patriotism, consumption, and our conceptions of the good life.

Source: Jane Marcellus (2012) "It's Up to the Women", Feminist Media Studies, 12:3, 389–405, DOI: 10.1080/14680777.2011.615631

Personal Health

As early as 1920, women's magazines began featuring both articles and advertisements on health, joining a trend toward "expert" knowledge of health issues. *Good Housekeeping* asserted itself as an authority not only on home life, but also on health advice for women. Unfortunately, the magazine's health articles were often misleading and factually wrong. The Scott Tissues ad warns readers that "at least 15 diseases can be caused or aggravated by improper tissue:" and women are particularly at risk (Chuppa-Cornell, 2005).

The Huffington Post (Www.huffingtonpost.com) The Huffington Post (Www.huffingtonpost.com)

Loss of Professional Photography

Technologies of the late twentieth century ushered in significant changes in visual journalism. Film became digital, print transferred to the web, and staff photographers lost jobs to independent freelancers. Visual journalists, both professionally trained and self-trained, began to produce video, audio, and slide shows. Technology continues to make it easy for professionals and amateurs to capture digital images and share them in many platforms including on social media.

What do newspapers lose when they use nonprofessional photography? The American Press Institute reports that researchers compared hundreds of published photos taken by nonprofessional photographers to photos taken by photojournalists, categorizing them as "informational," "graphically appealing," "emotional," or "intimate" (Stroud, 2018).

The nonprofessional photos were nearly twice as likely to be informational, but lacked emotion or creativity, as compared with the professional photos. Professional photos were also more likely to show action and depict conflict, two qualities known to increase audience attention, writes Stroud (2018). Many newspapers have cut back or even eliminated their photojournalism staffs in recent years.

Television

Television's arrival in the mid-twentieth century offered fast and often live moving visual evidence to supplement the news delivered in newspapers and radio broadcasts, as well as the advantage of relaying to audiences what words sometimes cannot. Significant moments in TV history brought engaging visual clarity to audiences:

1963 Assassination of President John F. Kennedy

This devastating event spotlighted television as a compelling and immediate way to process current affairs. "As the tragedy unfolded in front of the nation, it demonstrated how television could show the shooting and moment-to-moment action that neither newspapers nor the radio could" (New York Film Academy, 2015).

1966: The First Television War

While the Viet Nam War lasted from 1955 to 1975, the information in the US National Archives explains that by 1966, 93% of Americans owned TV sets, and networks competed for viewers with something unprecedented: *on-site* coverage of the war (Ward, 2018). Some have argued that graphic and emotional visual coverage of combat and both military and civilian injuries and deaths accelerated the United States' decision to withdraw from Viet Nam.

1979 Iranian Hostage Crisis

After 52 Americans from Tehran's US Embassy were taken hostage by Iranian militants, television news coverage needed to go beyond regular evening newscasts. In response, ABC created the late-night daily news program *Nightline*, featuring live coverage accessed via satellite technology and providing interviews and analysis on breaking stories.

1986 Explosion of NASA's Challenger

Americans, including many children, experienced the tragedy of live television when the shuttle exploded with teacher Christa McAuliffe onboard, video that was shown repeatedly to audiences.

1994 O.J. Simpson "Trial of the Century"

Extensive coverage of the celebrity and former professional football player began with live helicopter photos of him fleeing on Los Angeles freeways and continued through his 134-day murder trial that was fully televised by Court TV and partially by other networks.

2001 9/11 Terrorist Attacks

How the media covered the attacks signaled a change in how violent news is reported. ABC News chose not to repeatedly air video of the jets hitting the World Trade Center in New York City out of concern for viewers, especially children, a shift from the blanketed visual coverage of the Challenger explosion and Kennedy assassination.

2021: Capitol Hill Insurrection

Trump supporters' siege of the U.S. Capitol building on January 6, 2021 resulted in graphic journalist and citizen video, played repeatedly on broadcast and digital media. American and international audiences found themselves glued to their televisions, computers, and mobile phones. This video footage helped to move Congress to impeach President Donald Trump for an historic second time.

NEWS: VISUAL SOCIETY. VISUAL ANXIETY

LO2 Assess ethical issues in news imagery.

With the strong influence of television on news viewing beginning in the mid-twentieth century, visual culture scholar W.J.T. Mitchell cautioned that "a culture totally dominated by images has now become a real technical possibility on a global scale" (1994, p. 16). For example, Mitchell suggested, we can witness foreign wars on news programs as little more than spectacular televised melodramas, narratives of good triumphing over evil with little long-lasting public memory. He concluded that the need for critique and understanding of visual culture seems inescapable.

Scholars called for a better understanding of the stories that visuals tell, especially the "ambiguously 'transparent' film and video narrative" (Barbatis, 2005, p. 346), citing a compelling paradox. While the photographic quality of film and video *appears* to merely record and represent the "real," it's more important than ever to analyze and understand *how* photos and videos interpret raw experience as a **construction of reality**; in other words, we need to understand *how* they may structure our thinking and perceptions of reality.

The How and Why of News

Up until the late twentieth century, news reporting was studied for its gatekeeping and agenda-setting aspects: *how* it was selected and constructed, and how it influenced news consumers on what issues were important and what to think about them. Later, scholars began looking beyond the effects of news reporting, and at its narratives – *why* news stories were told in one way or another – interpreting the news as social construction. For example, sociologist Gaye Tuchman observed the process of news writing in major newsrooms and published a book that became a major turning point in our understanding of news, *Making News: A Study in the Construction of Reality* (Tuchman, 1978). She explained news-telling as news seen from specific windows on the world that differ depending on how the writer places their focus. These deliberate news choices then circulate and shape knowledge and beliefs. Other scholars, such as Lule (1988), Campbell (1995), and Lacy and Haspel (2006), have observed myth-making and cultural reproduction in news stories and the way the language of journalism established institutional authority and ideology.

FOCUS: Seeing the Refugee

News images influence how we understand local, national, and international phenomena. In the past, visual images of the immigrant have been provocative and antagonistic. In recent history, visual representations of the international female refugee have played a crucial role in shaping popular perceptions of the complex issue of asylum-seeking – as illustrated in this chapter's opening feature.

In a review of media images in the archive of the United Nations High Commissioner for Refugees (UNHCR) focusing on the female refugee, Johnson (2011) found the woman is framed through three different perspectives: radicalization, victimization, and feminization. These views serve to frame the issue as one of prevention, rather than integration. In contrast, in the 1950s, audiences frequently saw images of a graceful Russian dancer or a proud Polish family framed as refugees, and fleeing political persecution for freedom and democracy. Yet in more contemporary times, we're likely to see media images of children on the backs of exhausted mothers, bodies crammed into boats, and women mourning the loss of husbands and family (Johnson, 2011).

For example, this 2019 photo from UNHCR's "Refugee Media" depository documents a Syrian woman being comforted by a UNHCR staff member after arriving at Bardarash refugee camp in northwest Iraq.

Source: © UNHCR/Rasheed Hussein Rasheed.

Digital Manipulation

Since 1984, deliberate digital manipulation has become mainstream, not only in electronic cameras but in computer programs and smartphones that can easily manipulate images. Widely accessible photo-editing software along with the Internet provide easy opportunities for changing images and sending them out to friends or to everyone. The Bronx Documentary Center (n.d.) hosts an online exhibit of more than 40 photos in photojournalism and documentary photography that have been faked, posed, or manipulated: *Altered Images: 150 Years of Posed and Manipulated Documentary Photography.*

You can explore it at http://www.alteredimagesbdc.org. One, an August 1989 issue of *TV Guide,* carries a cover image with the head of Oprah Winfrey on the body of 1960s movie star Ann-Margret (see page 92, chapter 4). An example from 2003 helps explain why a staff photographer for the *Los Angeles Times* was fired for combining two of his Iraqi photographs into one to "improve" the composition. Not all manipulations are so radical, yet still are questionable. A 2012 photo of the funeral of two children, victims of Israeli bombing in Gaza, won photographer Paul Hansen a Pulitzer. However, due to the intense colors and lighting in the photo, Hansen was accused of over-manipulating the image with Photoshop to achieve an artificiality similar to a movie poster (Bronx Documentary Center, n.d.).

Fake News Images

It's too easy to fall for fake news on Facebook, according to Geoffrey Fowler, technology columnist for the *Washington Post.* "Even after decades of Photoshop and CG (computer-generated) films, most of us are still not very good about challenging the authenticity of images – or telling the real from the fake" (Fowler, 2018, para 14). Detecting what's fake in images and video is only getting harder. To get smarter about what we see online, Fowler recommends starting with increasing our skepticism of content that is shared by friends and family. He explains how he was tricked by a fake video that had earned 14 million views on Facebook (Figure 10.3). "When I saw the plane video, my suspicions weren't on high alert because it came from my friend, who I trust as a smart guy" (para 22).

Fake news producers use our friends to add to their credibility. Photorealism also plays an influential role. When shots of real news reports are appropriated into computer-generated graphics, they help to make the image appear somewhat credible. In the case of the faked flipped plane, the video's creator, a film director who plays around with computer graphics as a hobby, lifted an imaginative computer-generated video from YouTube. The photorealism in the faked video was enough to send it flying through the Internet.

According to Facebook's news feed manager, misinformation featuring manipulated photos and videos is among the most likely to go viral (Fowler, 2018). A doctored fake news image posted to Twitter in 2017 shows President Trump appearing to tour Houston after the disastrous flooding of Hurricane Florence (Figure 10.4). In the shot, he's leaning out of an inflated raft handing a red Make America Great Again (MAGA) cap to a victim clinging to a fence. However, the original image was taken two years earlier

Figure 10.3 A computer-generated video, falsely claiming to show a real plane doing a 360° flip while landing, was viewed nearly 14 million times on Facebook. *Source:* The Washington Post.

Figure 10.4 Fake photo of President Trump handing MAGA hat to Houston flood victim. *Source:* Tasnim News Agency.

during a flood in central Texas. Artist Jessica Savage Broer, a Trump critic, admitted she Photoshopped it to illustrate that people need to use more critical judgment. However, supporters of the president started sharing it on Facebook – more than 275,000 times – as evidence of the president's humanitarian work (Fowler, 2018). The *Washington Post* advises that if a photo seems Photoshopped or unrealistic, to drag and drop it into Google Images to learn the original source.

FOCUS: Deepfakes Challenge Our Trust in Reality

Culture today is largely structured around images as we engage with mobile phones, laptops, and other screened devices. We share memes, selfies, news of interest, and such. Some help to expose injustice, for example, police violence or sexual exploitation. For journalists, reliable visual evidence is critical for credibility, and open-source intelligence (OSINT) is commonly used to test the truth of images online.

Yet, significantly, it is becoming easier than ever to portray someone saying or doing something they never said or did, and it is getting harder to detect faked images from factual ones. These "deepfakes" are a form of synthetic media, which means they use artificial intelligence and machine learning to alter elements in a photo or video or recreate a person's face to look lifelike. Such recordings could be faked using tools available to almost anyone with a laptop and access to the Internet, resulting in content that's impossible to distinguish from the real thing. For example, University of Washington researchers (BBC News) used 14 hours of real footage of Obama (left image), allowing them to match any audio – Obama's words or even an impersonator's – with fake video (right image). To see for yourself, search YouTube for "Fake Obama created using AI video tool."

YoutubeYoutube

Even fact-checking resources and institutions are stretched to keep up with highly realistic fabrications as they get more sophisticated. Imagine a video showing an American diplomat in Afghanistan burning a Koran or a video showing foreign generals planning to assassinate their prime minister. The Center for Internet and Society at Stanford Law School suggests such recordings would be powerful provocations in a world already primed for violence (Chesney and Citron, 2018).

WITNESS, a human rights organization focused on using video and technology for good, has directed its Media Lab (https://lab.witness.org/) to research how to best test the veracity of images (Gregory, 2018). One way is to look for an image's provenance, tracing it back to its initial source and looking for any edits. This is ideal, but not always practical when covering news in risky

(Continued)

situations, trying to protect identities from harm, or excluding sources due to their lack of the latest technologies.

Not all deepfakes are malicious. They may be harmless creative content, satiric messaging, or just personal communication. Yet whether harmless or malicious, the news community and the general public need to better know how to assess visuals to avoid sharing misinformation or disinformation.

Ethical Dilemmas

Chapter 2 informed you of the ethical decision-making challenges in creating, observing, and using visuals. Beyond digital manipulation, we bring up two important issues: the publication and dissemination of individuals' photos to implicate them in crimes, and the strategy behind viral transmission of misinformation.

Mugshots

There are arguably valid public interest reasons for publishing mugshots. Mugshots are police booking photos of people arrested on suspicion of committing crimes but who have not yet been convicted. Standard tenets of the newspaper industry hold that jour-nalists should not change or hold back accurate information and that people have a right to know news about their community and the actions of their public servants. Informa-tion about the criminal justice system should be available and publishable. Mugshots are often public records and easy to obtain from local law enforcement.

But what once had the lifespan of the day's news in print is now forever visible on the Internet, and for some local newspapers' websites, their online mugshot galleries can be a web-traffic magnet and often their most popular feature (Hutchins, 2018). However, if the charges against those whose faces appeared are later dropped or judged untrue, those outcomes may not receive follow-up coverage and the mugshot subjects are preserved for readers as suspects. "Best practice would be to follow up on every single case," says Kelly McBride, a media ethics specialist at the Poynter Institute (Hutchins, 2018, para 7). However, the dilemma is that most newsrooms don't have the resources to do that.

Virality

The most effective misinformation is packaged for virality, advises the Poynter Institute for Media Studies that specializes in ethics and fact-checking. It's visual, adapted to mobile devices, easy to share, and easy to consume. The deceiving pieces can come in the form of images, videos, memes, and screenshots instead of URLs. Recognizing this, Spanish fact-checking outlet Maldito Bulo copied these formats during the Spanish election in December 2017, intending to make facts spread as easily as lies. It worked: one image discrediting an election-related hoax was shared thousands of times on Twitter, reached over 287,000 people on Facebook, and was reported by other media. Other debunking posts created by Maldito Bulo for social media saw similar results (Jimenez Cruz, 2018).

DIGITAL INNOVATIONS AND SOCIAL MEDIA

LO3 Recognize the use of visual rhetoric in contemporary journalism media.

With the introduction of social media and the rapid development of smartphones, consumers became able to instantly receive news articles as well as generate and disseminate their own news reporting. In 2018, social media was poised to soon overtake traditional media in American's news consumption. The Pew Research Center (2018) reported that 68% of Americans turn to social media for news. However, they also expect it to be inaccurate. By far, Facebook is the leading source. This growth goes together with news organizations, newspapers, and magazines, and individual journalists producing and posting content, especially visual content, in a wide variety of digital formats. Between the 2012 and 2017 publications of the Cision Global Social Journalism Study, there was a 12% increase in the number of journalists that said that they post content to social media platforms daily (Nicholson, 2017).

Instagram

Instagram originally launched as an app for "fast, beautiful photo sharing." Since its 2010 introduction, it has transformed visual communication online. Big brands, small businesses, influencers, personal posts, and news outlets use the platform to reach new audiences – especially younger ones – with visual representations. Instagram Stories lets publishers present a variety of news bites, slideshows, and video. And while journalists typically produce longer narrative articles, short-form news content is widely seen as in this creative infographic posted on Instagram by the *Guardian*'s US data editor (Figure 10.5).

Figure 10.5 News reporters and designers increasingly post creative graphics on Instagram. *Source:* Mona Chalabi.

The Economist, a UK political, literary, and general news journal, in print since 1843, now has broad content for an international readership and actively pursues new readers on digital platforms. More than 50% of its readers are North American. An example of the magazine's focus on the younger Instagram demographic concerns suicide, likely because it's the second leading cause of death in the United States of those aged 10–34 (NIMH, 2018). The magazine excerpted a longer article into an animated image addressing suicide prevention. Along with a mix of images and videos on its Instagram feed, it regularly asks followers to engage with its stories. "We want to find out what they think too – not just us telling them what to think, but to find out their opinion on really divisive issues," says Ria Jones, *The Economist*'s digital and social media picture editor (Scott, 2018).

Multimedia storytelling is now also possible on Instagram TV where media outlets such as the British Broadcasting Corporation (BBC), *Vice*, *Vogue*, *Esquire*, and *The Economist* can be seen. The BBC posts human interest stories with a UK focus, as they are best-performing (Southern, 2018).

Social Media as Launch Pad

In 2017, the *Washington Post* introduced a new publication for millennial women sharing it on Facebook, Instagram, and Twitter. Called *The Lily*, it used a title from a much earlier publication. Originally, *The Lily* was the first US newspaper for and by women, started in 1849 by Amelia Bloomer as part of the temperance movement. Eventually, the paper shifted focus, covering issues like the abolition of slavery and woman's right to vote and own property. Well-known suffragists Elizabeth Cady Stanton and Susan B. Anthony were part of *The Lily*.

The *Washington Post*'s *The Lily* (@thelilynews) successfully built its Instagram aesthetic – with every image one of a kind – created by a *Lily* designer and became a finalist in Digiday's Publishing Awards 2018 for Best Use of Instagram. In its first 12 months of existence, it grew an Instagram audience of 18,000 who followed its Stories: approximately 10 per day (Schmidt, 2018).

Video's Giant Wave

Some organizations that once presented news imagery in still photos, slide shows, and video reports are now using social media platforms to air longer-form news shows and documentaries.

BuzzFeed specializes in audiences under 50 and has a round-the-clock global newsroom. From fall 2017 through April 2020, BuzzFeed produced *AM to DM*, a live one-hour morning news show airing on Twitter with a viewership that was one-third international. On Facebook Watch, BuzzFeed launched *Future History: 1968* a documentary series that recaps major events of that year and *Profile*, a weekly interview show hosted by NPR's Audie Cornish.

Figure 10.6 Retro Report's documentary features the story of the mothers and grandmothers of the Plaza de Mayo in Argentina and their four decade long protests to learn the fate of babies taken during military rule. *Source:* YouTube.

In 2018, BuzzFeed launched a new website, BuzzFeed News, to cover big stories in a way that appeals to its younger demographic. Besides using social media, it has collaborated with Netflix on *Follow This*, a short-form video project which follows BuzzFeed News reporters on the job (Moses, 2018).

The nonprofit Retro Report, founded in 2014, publishes short-form documentaries on news topics shaped by investigative reporting and compelling storytelling. They offer insights into both current and historic high-profile events. The Emmy and Webby award-winning company has produced more than 175 short documentaries and video series. Its work is accessible through partner websites, broadcast networks, social media platforms, podcasts, and streaming services. Editorial partners include the *New York Times*, NBC News, *The New Yorker*, PBS, *Politico*, and *Quartz* (Retro Report, n.d., 2017).

Among Retro Report's documentaries are *Go or No Go: The Challenger Legacy*, focusing on how the space shuttle's disaster impacted the space industry; *The Black Athlete in America*, a collaboration with the *New Yorker*, examining the issues of race and sports; *Why Hasn't Sexual Harassment Disappeared?*, providing historical context to the Harvey Weinstein story and the #MeToo movement; and *Argentina's Stolen Babies and the Grandmothers Leading the Search*, created in partnership with Univision, detailing the search for disappeared babies during four decades under military rule (Figure 10.6).

Best Practices for News Sites

Here's what researchers Collier and Stroud (2018) at the Center for Media Engagement, University of Texas-Austin, found in a study of best practices in using links on seven mid-sized local broadcast news sites across the United States.

- To get more clicks, use an image with links rather than just text.

- To appeal to new subscribers in sponsored posts, use images (such as a journalist working or a picture of a top story) rather than show your logo.

- On Facebook, positive images and issue-focused headlines increase reactions and comments on political stories. Negative images increase clicks, but positive images increase reactions. This is important because Facebook's algorithm priortizes comments and reactions in addition to clicks. Focusing just on clicks misses the full potential of the platform.

CRITICAL ENGAGEMENT WITH NEWS VISUALS

LO4 Critique the visual rhetoric of journalism.

Visual theories provide insight into how news imagery proposes meaning and works persuasively. This section details examples of breaking news, opinion pieces, political commentary, and feature articles and suggests how a critic can analyze them.

Morality Metaphors in News Front Pages

Front page news is dramatic, covering wars, strikes, crises, accidents, natural disasters, and of course, politics. Within a dramatic news saga, the written and pictorial narratives often combine to reach beyond being newsworthy, becoming explanatory and even interpretive.

Government shutdowns certainly provide dramatic news: federal workers stop being paid, veterans lose their benefits, food safety programs cease to operate, nutritional programs are disrupted, small business loans and programs halt, and national parks close. The US government shut down in fall 2013 for 16 days when the Senate and House failed to agree on a budgeting resolution. It ended on October 17.

Researchers analyzed the headlines and accompanying shutdown-related photos and/or images on the October 17 front pages of the top 100 US dailies by circulation (for sources of newspaper selection see Newseum [n.d.] and Alliance for Audited Media [https://auditedmedia.com/]). Despite growing online readership, more than 80% of newspaper circulation at that time was the printed newspaper.

Using metaphor analysis, Duffy et al. (2014) found the newspapers' coverage of the shutdown's end clearly fell into the category of the conceptual morality metaphor, identifying the nation-as-family metaphor with a conservative "strict father" and liberal "nurturing parent" (Lakoff, 1996). The researchers identified metaphors of moral authority, moral strength, and moral order from either a conservative or liberal perspective, as well as metaphors of moral indignation and moral failure.

For example, in the *New York Times*, a large dominant photograph of an isolated Speaker John Boehner functions as target, followed by the headline as source, "Republicans Back Down, Ending Budget Crisis." Both elements work together, functioning as a metaphor to communicate a victory for moral authority: a challenger to defenders of public interest is defeated.

Visual Narratives in Editorial Cartoons

As you read in the beginning of Chapter 6 on narratives, humor can serve to help people navigate, understand, and get relief from a problematical situation. According to Ann Telnaes, past president of the American Association of Editorial Cartoonists and a cartoonist for the *Washington Post*, "The job of an editorial cartoonist is to expose the hypocrisies and abuses of power by the politicians and powerful institutions in society" (Donnelly, 2017). The editorial cartoon has used humor, satire, and parody to offer perspectives on important events, issues, and political figures. The drawings are usually guided by the cartoonist's opinions, functioning as critiques through exaggerations, distortions, and the use of known cultural frames of reference.

Benjamin Franklin drew the first known political cartoon in 1754, for publication in his paper, the *Pennsylvania Gazette*. This image of a snake separated into pieces (Figure 10.7), intended to persuade the colonies of the importance of unity while facing an imminent war between Britain and France.

Before digital started cannibalizing print, newspapers around the country had full-time editorial cartoonists on staff producing daily cartoons that reflected their independent views or the paper's political stance. A significant moment in political cartooning occurred when Garry Trudeau began his strip *Doonesbury* in 1970. Controversial and bold, Trudeau's work reflected American society and culture during highly divisive times. His cartoons about President Nixon's illegal behavior during Watergate earned him a Pulitzer Prize in 1975.

Figure 10.7 The first known political cartoon, created by Benjamin Franklin in 1754 for his newspaper, the *Pennsylvania Gazette. Source:* Library of Congress, Prints & Photographs Division, Reproduction number LC-USZC4-5315 (color film copy transparency) LC-USZ62-9701 (b&w film copy negative).

Figure 10.8 #MeToo movement is satirized by cartoonist Garry Trudeau in this December 3rd, 2017, cartoon. PAUL HÉBERT/Doonesbury/Andrews McMeel Syndication

Now in his fifth decade of cartooning, Trudeau's work appears daily in the *Washington Post*. His December 3rd, 2017 cartoon (Figure 10.8) addressed the #MeToo era, parodying the ignorance of men slowly realizing that times have changed, and no longer would they get away with sexist behavior toward women. His character, Duke, complains he can no longer gawk at his female employees. This use of satire identifies powerful men as the problem: that their beliefs about women and sex allow them to justify abhorrent conduct (Hébert, 2018).

Visual Rhetoric of Political Satire

Since running for and assuming office, President Donald Trump has been characterized and caricatured frequently on the covers of US and international magazines. One of this book's authors analyzed the visual rhetoric of these cover images and the metonymy of Trump as the "United States," seeking to discover what they suggested about Trump's reception on the world stage. Analysis of more than 450 covers of US and international magazines portraying Trump during the campaign and postelection found that dominant categories framed Trump as an insurgent and subversive, a traitor, and a tyrant.

For example, *Der Spiegel*, a center–left German magazine founded in 1947, is known for quality investigative journalism as well as controversial stories exposing scandals surrounding major political figures. Its covers often portray political figures in relation to other symbols. Its August 19, 2017, cover (Figure 10.9) addressed the neo-Nazi and White nationalist violence in Charlottesville, VA, on August 12–13, 2017.

Leading US and international magazines, such as *The Economist*, *TIME*, *The New Yorker*, and *Der Spiegel*, produced bold covers reacting to Trump's subsequent racist rhetoric and defense of the neo-Nazis and White supremacists. *The Economist*'s stark cover depiction

Figure 10.9 "The true face of Donald Trump" *Der Spiegel* cover by American artist Edel Rodriguez. *Source:* Spiegel Online.

of Trump is the creation of American artist Edel Rodriguez. "He deserves to be wearing that Klan hood," the artist told the *Huffington Post* (Frank, 2017). Rodriguez, a Cuban immigrant, felt compelled to warn his fellow citizens about the danger of electing a man like Trump, in whom Rodriguez recognized qualities of a dictator.

- *On the surface.* The dominant denotations are the stark white Klan hood with two small eyeholes, worn by a figure dressed not in the white Klan robe but a man's dark business suit, red tie, and white shirt. These images appear against a vacuum of solid black in the background. Of secondary importance is the cover logo in white type, *Der Spiegel*, and the magazine's signature red borderline frame. Of much lesser significance are the German cover lines, reversed out of the black in white type, which translate to "The true face of Donald Trump." They are positioned on the right side of the cover, in line with the hood's eyes.

- *Looking deeper.* Depicting the president of the United States wearing a Ku Klux Klan (KKK) hood transfers the known characteristics of racism and bigotry, evoking a specific event. The "Unite the Right" rally held that week by various far-right groups including neo-Nazis and white-robed KKK members resulted in violence. The rally was called to defend the Confederate flag, a symbol carrying various meanings for many Americans, and was met with peaceful protest. A few days after one protestor was hit and killed by a car driven by a White supremacist, Trump praised the far-right groups and the protestors as both "very fine people" who were equally guilty of encouraging violence.

Multiple contexts contribute to layers of meaning in this cover image: a Cuban-American artist who experienced the Castro dictatorship; a violent act in the United States that illustrated broiling sentiments of racism and bigotry; a despotic US president advocating tolerance for racism and bigotry; a German magazine whose first issue was born out of the defeat of Nazism; and the iconic symbol of the White supremacist KKK hood, evoking racial and ethnic intolerance and lynching.

- *Challenging hate.* Within the spectacles of the Trump era, the artist Rodriguez represents a challenge to spectators to talk back. He hopes his art might encourage others to stand up for what's right, even if it's uncomfortable or frightening. "Wow, that guy has some guts. Maybe I should get some, too" (Frank, 2017). *Der Spiegel* also sees meeting today's challenges and those of history and legacy as obligatory. The image of a hate group on a German magazine evokes the country's White supremacist past and its Nazi legacy and is likely a controversial choice.

Racist Visual Framing in *National Geographic*

The November 2018 cover of *National Geographic* drew criticism when it depicted a White American cowboy on horseback, calmly gazing into the Western landscape. The cover posed the question: Whose land is it anyway? On its Instagram page, the magazine's cover juxtaposed the cowboy and the words "Battle for the American West" with a Native American figure appearing animated in ceremonial tribal dress, positioned in front of a Utah state building (Figure 10.10).

This **visual framing** of the "civilized White hero versus the savage native" evokes both American history and myth. For decades, *National Geographic* also has been criticized for its colonialist approach to nonwhite cultures, specifically indigenous communities. It has been criticized for promoting visual tropes of "savage" or "uncivilized" Brown and Black people for decades (Amaria, 2018).

John Edwin Mason, a University of Virginia professor specializing in the history of photography and the history of Africa, has examined how *National Geographic* pushed readers toward racist stereotypes and tropes throughout its long history (it began publishing in 1888). Mason critiqued the November issue cover in an interview with Kainaz Amaria of Vox Media's *Vox*:

> The image of the White cowboy reproduces and romanticizes the mythic iconography of settler colonialism and white supremacy. After all, we know that most cowboys weren't heroic and that a very large number of them were Latino or black. We know that the land that the cowboy worked had been stolen from Native Americans. The myth was created to obscure all of that.
>
> The cover of the November issue tells us that it's about 'The Battle for the American West' and asks, "Whose Land Is It Anyway?" The photo of the cowboy, bathed in golden sunlight, while sitting on his horse and surveying the landscape, answers the question – implicitly but clearly. The American West is his. It's a White man's country.
>
> On Instagram, a photo of a Native American – dressed in tribal garb, mouth wide open – immediately follows the image of the handsome, stoic cowboy. The implied racial

Figure 10.10 Stereotypical images of the White heroic cowboy versus the Native American appear on the cover of *National Geographic*'s November 2018 issue. *Source:* National Geographic Image Collection.

hierarchy is clear. One is exotic and primitive; the other is, like the magazine's presumed readers, White and civilized. . . .

The cover photo also reminds me of the iconography of Afrikaner nationalism in South Africa. The man on a horse, wearing a wide-brimmed hat and commanding the landscape, was a recurring motif in Afrikaner nationalist imagery. As in the US, it grew out of a desire to naturalize and justify settler colonialism and the theft of lands owned by indigenous people. White Americans don't like to think of their country as a settler state, but, like apartheid South Africa, that's exactly what it is. . . .

The photographs in the online version of the cover story also create a racial hierarchy. Native people are seen only in traditional clothing. A photo of an ancient Pueblo dwelling and photos of petroglyphs and pictographs that are many centuries old represent their culture. Visually, they're associated only with the past. The article shows Whites, on the other hand, dressed in modern clothing and engaged in recognizably modern activities such as farming, mining, and outdoor recreation. They're surrounded by associated modern technologies of jeeps and trucks and mountain bikes. Whites, then, are depicted as progressive and dynamic, the opposite of Native Americans, who seem to be mired in the past.

FOCUS: Magazines, Women, and Sexuality

Cosmopolitan magazine began publishing in 1886 as a family magazine and eventually transformed into a women's magazine in the 1960s. For the next three decades, its cover, typically featuring a "Cosmo girl," was an icon for feminine sexuality. The cover model was often dressed in clothing signifying leisure and sexual availability, alongside cover lines offering love, success, sex, or money to the newsstand or supermarket reader. These provocative covers often promised a sexual fantasy to its readers, writes McMahon (1990), who suggested the sophisticated leisure attire of the cover models and the upscale tone of its ads appear to target a middle-income audience of single women. Later covers continue to present women as sexually provocative (Johnson and Sivek, 2009).

Source: The Advertising Archives/Alamy Stock Photo.

A different cultural expression of women's sexuality is found in photographs of women in US magazine cover stories and news articles from the 1970s and 1980s when the phrase "teenage pregnancy" began circulating as a cause for national concern. Visual representations of pregnant and teenage moms usually portrayed America's "problem" with teenage pregnancy (Vinson, 2012). Magazine cover stories featuring White female bodies and teenage pregnancy presented the issue as a problem that stemmed from women's seemingly irresponsible sexual behavior, according to Vinson, who adds that it downplays larger economic and social contributing factors.

Critics have noted that magazine stories, photographs, and advertising influence body and image ideals of young women. Research reveals that when many women see visual content showing thin and sexy models, it can contribute to or reinforce body shame, appearance anxiety, or internalization of the thin ideal. Through intentional and unintentional visual persuasion, readers are moved to want to lose weight, buy specific cosmetics, dress in certain fashions, and behave in certain ways to attract men.

Female athletes are stereotyped as well. For example, health and sport magazine covers reinforce gender stereotyping of female athletes, as in sexualized portrayals of Serena Williams on the cover of *Fitness* and *Sports Illustrated* magazines.

PROFESSIONAL PROFILE: James D. Kelly

Source: Tiantian Zhang, The Media School at Indiana University.

James D. Kelly is Associate Professor of Photojournalism at The Media School, Indiana University.

Some people *find* a job and others are *called* to a career (Yaden et al., 2015). My brother and I are just 18 months apart and both of us were called to our chosen professions by our early teens. He's a Catholic priest, and I'm a photojournalist. He was born to religious devotion and I was born to social responsibility. We were both called to service, and while our approaches are quite different, our goals are similar: help people be better people.

Not unlike the priesthood, journalism professes a belief in a power that binds us all together and results in great accomplishment. While not denying the supernatural, journalists profess a faith in the power of facts and the wisdom of truth. They believe that people have a right to know and that knowledge based on facts can empower a society to govern itself democratically without reliance on kings or other tyrants.

(Continued)

I was 16 when I got a part-time job developing film at my small-town newspaper before school. Soon I was making photos of high school sports and local events. My editor insisted I go on to college, so I studied journalism until I had a degree and could go back to work, first for a wire service and then for newspapers. Eventually I went back to college to become a professor of photojournalism. Professing is a similar calling.

Photojournalism is truth at 500th of a second. With it we hold time motionless and present it for inspection. The fan sitting in the best seats at mid-court cannot see what the photographer shows the crowd sitting at home. The guard flashing to the basket is a blur as the game progresses, but that same guard in the morning paper has a face filled with determination, muscles bulging with strength, and eyes fixed on the basket like lasers. It is often said that photojournalism shows folks what they would have seen had they been there. I say they show people what they *would not have seen* had they been there. And a great photojournalist can not only freeze a moment for inspection, they can find exactly the moment that contains all of the storytelling elements the reader needs to understand what happened in that moment.

There is great power in the magic of photography. Not only do we hold time still, but we decide which slice in the grand time continuum will represent the event. In modern photojournalism, that slice of time is selected from perhaps hundreds of images shot at 10 per second. It is made from just one of many perspectives according to myriad decisions about exposure, color, and composition. Like any story, what to include is a conscious decision.

The difference between most photos and those made by journalists is that faith I mentioned earlier. It is an obligation to facts, a promise to tell the truth: the same pledge that every journalist abides by. All photographs look factual because of their verisimilitude with actual experience. They look real. But like any story, they can be fictional or nonfictional. Truth is not of a camera's making any more than religious faith is made by a building called a church or temple or mosque. True stories are told by journalists called to help society understand itself by showing it a world that is right in front of it, in plain view.

CHAPTER SUMMARY

Beginning with the twentieth century, you read how significant advancements in technology greatly increased the visual impact of journalism, diminished the role of the professional photojournalist, and introduced serious ethical issues of photographic truth. The chapter also spotlighted how social media platforms, video products, and partnerships with production companies have extended news organizations' reach. Special features revealed the cultural influence of "soft" news products like general and special interest magazines. Features also covered how immigrants have been framed in news images and explained the dangers of "deepfakes."

KEY TERMS

Photojournalism   Communication of news and events primarily through photography, traditionally performed by professionally-trained photographers.

Fake news   A term that describes people's perceptions that some news stories are deliberately created or slanted to present inaccurate and misleading information about people and events.

Deepfakes   A form of synthetic media that utilizes digital tools to create images that are difficult to detect as inauthentic. Some are created with malicious intent, while others are created for humorous and satiric purposes.

Construction of reality   In the context of visuals, the concept that how certain images and ideas are presented can shape viewers' perceptions.

Multimedia storytelling   A form of narration about news and events that uses combinations of video, still images, photos, and text. Such stories often incorporate interactive elements.

Visual framing   The deliberate or inadvertent placement of visuals that may highlight or downplay certain aspects of an image or set of images, thus altering the meaning viewers may interpret.

PRACTICE ACTIVITIES

1. Take the "Fake or Foto?" quiz at https://area.autodesk.com/fakeorfoto.

2. *National Geographic* missed an opportunity to disrupt entrenched ways of seeing the West with its November 2018 cover. Consider better alternatives to the magazine's use of racially stereotypical images. How else could it portray a Native American? How else could it portray a White pioneer? Or, how else could it have portrayed a cowboy?

3. How would you solve the ethical dilemma of publishing mugshots, balancing the public's right to know with the accused's right to be forgotten?

4. Discover how the foreign press is visually framing news about American politics. Visit DW, BBC, Russia Today, China News, or Al Jazeera. Choose an image to analyze. Also compare how two of these sources visually handle the same news story.

5. Expand your news consumption by visiting the website of a news magazine and critiquing one (or more) of its covers.

6. Visit the Instagram or Facebook site of one of your regular news sources. How is it using the platform to present its brand of news? Choose one image to analyze.

7. Explore the Picture of the Year website https://poy.org and select a photo for visual analysis.

REFERENCES

Amaria, K. (2018). National Geographic's November cover falls back on a racist cliché. *Vox*. https://www.vox.com/identities/2018/11/1/18036682/national-geographic-november-cover-racist-cowboy-indian-cliche (accessed October 9, 2020).

Barbatsis, G. (2005). Narrative theory. In: *Handbook of Visual Communication* (eds. K. Smith, S. Moriarty, G. Barbatsis and K. Kenney), 329–350. Mahwah, NJ: Earlbaum.

BBC News. (2017). Fake Obama created using AI video tool. https://www.youtube.com /watch?time_continue=2&v=AmUC4m6w1wo (accessed October 9, 2020).

Brennen, B. (2004). From headline shooter to picture snatcher: the construction of photo-journalists in American film, 1928–39. *Journalism* 5 (4): 423–439.

Bronx Documentary Center. (n.d.). Altered Images. Gaza City, Palestinian Territories. http://www.alteredimagesbdc.org/#/hansen (accessed October 9, 2020).

Campbell, C.P. (1995). *Race, Myth, and the News*. Thousand Oaks, CA: Sage.

Chesney, R. and Citron, D. (2018). Deepfakes and the new disinformation war. The Center for Internet and Society. https://cyberlaw.stanford.edu/publications/deepfakes-and-new-disinformation-war (accessed October 9, 2020).

Chuppa-Cornell, K. (2005). Filling a vacuum: women's health information in *Good House-keeping*'s articles and advertisements, 1920–1965. The Historian 67 (3): 454–473.

Collier, J. and Stroud, N. J. (2018). Using links to keep readers on news sites. Center for Media Engagement. https://mediaengagement.org/research/links (accessed October 9, 2020).

Donnelly, L. (2017). Editorial cartooning, then and now. *Medium*. https://medium.com/@ lizadonnelly/editorial-cartooning-then-and-now-6c06fb10f25a (accessed October 9, 2020).

Duffy, M., Page, J.T., and Perrault, G. (2014). Journalists as moralists: social construction of news in U.S. Government shutdown coverage. International Communication Association, Seattle.

Elfrink, T. and Barbash, F. (2018). 'These children are barefoot. In diapers. Choking on tear gas.' https://www.washingtonpost.com/nation/2018/11/26/these-children-are-barefoot-diapers-choking-tear-gas/ (accessed January 9, 2021).

Fowler, G. (2018). I fell for Facebook fake news. Here's why millions of you did, too. https://www.washingtonpost.com/technology/2018/10/18/i-fell-facebook-fake-news-heres-why-millions-you-did-too/ (accessed January 9, 2021).

Frank, P. (2017). Anti-Trump illustrator is a Cuban immigrant who knows what a dictator looks like. *HuffPost US*. https://www.huffpost.com/entry/edel-rodriguez-art_n_589b8e9ae4b0c1284f2a7341 (accessed October 9, 2020).

Gregory, S. (2018). Heard about deepfakes? Don't panic. Prepare. https://www.weforum.org/agenda/2018/11/deepfakes-video-pragmatic-preparation-witness/ (accessed January 9, 2021).

Gutierrez, G. and Siemaszko, C. (2018). NBC News. Photographer reveals story behind iconic image of fleeing migrants at Mexico border. https://www.nbcnews.com/news/us-news/photographer-reveals-story-behind-iconic-photo-fleeing-migrants-mexico-border-n940271 (accessed October 9, 2020).

Hébert, P. (2018). This week in Doonesbury: a missed opportunity. Reading Doonesbury. https://readingdoonesbury.com/2018/01/18/this-week-in-doonesbury-a-missed-opportunity (accessed October 9, 2020).

Hutchins, C. (2018). Mugshot galleries might be a web-traffic magnet. Does that justify publishing them? Columbia Journalism Reviews. https://www.cjr.org/united_states_project/mugshots-ethics.php (accessed October 9, 2020).

ICP. (n.d.) International Center of Photography. Margaret Bourke-White. Para 2. https://www.icp.org/browse/archive/constituents/margaret-bourke-white?all/all/all/all/0 (accessed January 21, 2021).

Jimenez Cruz, C. (2018). How do you make fact-checking viral? Make it look like misinformation. Poynter. https://www.poynter.org/fact-checking/2018/how-do-you-make-fact-checking-viral-make-it-look-like-misinformation/?utm_source=API+Need+to+Know+newsletter&utm_campaign=10d212f72c-EMAIL_CAMPAIGN_2018_12_18_01_11&utm_medium=email&utm_term=0_e3bf78af04-10d212f72c-45835121 (accessed October 9, 2020).

Johnson, H.L. (2011). Click to donate: visual images, constructing victims and imagining the female refugee. *Third World Quarterly* 32 (6): 1015–1037.

Johnson, S. and Sivek, S.C. (2009). Framing sex, romance, and relationships in *Cosmopolitan* and Maxim. *Southwestern Mass Communication Journal* 24 (2): 1–16.

Lacy, M. & Haspel, K. (2006). Framing Black Shooters, Looters, and Brutes: An Analysis of Responses to Hurricane Katrina in Major News Coverage (Conference presentation). ICA 2006 Convention, Dresden, Germany. June 19–23.

Lakoff, G. (1996). *Moral Politics: What Conservatives Know That Liberals Don't*. Chicago: University of Chicago Press.

Law, T. (2018). The story behind the photo of a family running from tear gas at the U.S.-Mexico border. *Time*. http://time.com/5464560/caravan-mexico-border-iconic-photo/ (accessed October 9, 2020).

Lule, J. (1988). The myth of my widow: A dramatistic analysis of news portrayals of a terrorist victim. *Political Communication & Persuasion* 5 (2): 101–120.

Marcellus, J. (2012). "It's up to the women:" Edward Bernays, Eleanor Roosevelt, and feminist resistance to shopping for patriotism. *Feminist Media Studies* 12 (3): 389–405.

McDaniel, K.R. (2007). Reviewing the image of the photojournalist in film: how ethical dilemmas shape stereotypes of the on-screen press photographer in motion pictures from 1954 to 2006. Master thesis. University of Missouri. https://www.ijpc.org/uploads/files/Photojournalist%20Thesis.pdf (accessed January 9, 2021).

McMahon, K. (1990). The *Cosmopolitan* ideology and the management of desire. *The Journal of Sex Research* 27 (3): 381–396.

Mitchell, W.J.T. (1994). *Picture Theory*. Chicago, IL: University of Chicago Press.

Moses, L. (2018). Shani Hilton is driving BuzzFeed News' video gamble. DigidayUK. https://digiday.com/media/shani-hilton-is-driving-buzzfeed-news-video-gamble/ (accessed October 9, 2020).

Mott, F.L. (1957). *A History of American Magazines*. Cambridge: Harvard University Press.

New York Film Academy. (2015). A brief look at the history of broadcast journalism. https://www.nyfa.edu/student-resources/history-of-broadcast-journalism/ (accessed October 9, 2020).

Newseum. (n.d.) Today's front pages. Government Shutdown. http://www.newseum.org/todaysfrontpages/default_archive.asp?fpArchive=101713 (accessed October 9, 2020).

Nicholson, A. (2017). How successful journalists use social media. https://www.cision.com/us/blogs/2017/09/how-successful-journalists-use-social-media/ (accessed October 9, 2020).

NIMH. (2018). National Institute of Mental Health. Mental Health Information, Suicides. https://www.nimh.nih.gov/health/statistics/suicide.shtml.

Pew Research Center. (2018). News use across social media platforms 2018. https://www.nimh.nih.gov/health/statistics/suicide.shtml (accessed October 9, 2020).

Retro Report. (n.d.) About Us. https://www.retroreport.org/about/ (accessed October 9, 2020).

Retro Report. (2017) Annual Report 2017. https://www.retroreport.org/uploads/RetroReport_2017AnnualReport_Web.pdf (accessed October 9, 2020).

Schmidt, C. (2018). Nieman Lab. The *Washington Post*'s The Lily is building its Instagram aesthetic and sharing news with millennial women in the process. http://www.niemanlab.org/2018/06/the-washington-posts-the-lily-is-building-its-instagram-aesthetic-and-sharing-news-with-millennial-women-in-the-process/ (accessed October 9, 2020).

Scott, C. (2018). 'It's not just an audience, it's a community:' How *The Economist* is engaging with young people on Instagram. Journalism.co.uk. www.journalism.co.uk/news/-it-s-not-just-an-audience-it-s-a-community-how-the-economist-is-engage-with-young-people-on-instagram/s2/a725173/?utm_source=API%20Need%20to%20Know%20newsletter&utm_campaign=ceae9ee12b-EMAIL_CAMPAIGN_2018_07_25_12_16&utm_medium=email&utm_term=0_e3bf78af04-ceae9ee12b-45835121 (accessed October 9, 2020).

Southern, L. (2018). How BBC News has grown its Instagram following by posting less video. Digiday UK. https://digiday.com/media/bbc-news-grown-instagram-following-posting-less-video/ (accessed October 9, 2020).

Stroud, N. (2018). What do newspapers lose when they use non-professional photography? American Press Institute. https://www.americanpressinstitute.org/publications/research-review/what-do-newspapers-lose-when-they-use-non-professional-photography/. (accessed October 9, 2020).

Tuchman, G. (1978). *Making News: A Study in the Construction of Reality*. New York: The Free Press.

Vinson, J. (2012). Covering national concerns about teenage pregnancy: a visual rhetorical analysis of gender and race in images of the pregnant teenage body. Feminist Formations 24 (2): 140–162.

Ward, M. (2018). Vietnam: the first television war. US National Archives. https://prologue.blogs.archives.gov/2018/01/25/vietnam-the-first-television-war/ (accessed October 9, 2020).

Wilson, C. (1983). The rhetoric of consumption: mass-market magazines and the demise of the gentle reader, 1880-1920. In: *Culture of Consumption: Critical Essays in American History, 1880-1980* (eds. R.W. Fox and T.J. Jackson Lears), 39–64. New York: Pantheon Books.

Yaden, D.B., McCall, T.D., and Ellens, J.H. (2015). *Being Called: Scientific, Secular, and Sacred Perspectives*. Santa Barbara: Praeger.

Chapter 11
Organizations

1984

In 1984, Apple Computer deployed a one-minute Super Bowl ad that ran only once. It begins by showing a dark, dystopian scene shot mostly in gray tones with people dressed identically and marching in a single line. They are under surveillance from a large screen and ominous-looking guards. Suddenly, a young woman appears in full color wearing a red and white athletic uniform and carrying a large sledgehammer. She bursts into an auditorium where the people now sit in rows, gazes transfixed on a huge screen dominated by the face of a man who intones:

Today, we celebrate the first glorious anniversary of the Information Purification Directives. We have created, for the first time in all history, a garden of pure ideology, where each worker may bloom, secure from the

Visual Communication: Insights and Strategies, First Edition. Janis Teruggi Page and Margaret Duffy.
© 2022 John Wiley & Sons, Inc. Published 2022 by John Wiley & Sons, Inc.

Source: https://www.youtube.com/watch?v=VtvjbmoDx-I (2 screenshots)

pests purveying contradictory truths. Our Unification of Thoughts is more powerful a weapon than any fleet or army on earth. We are one people, with one will, one resolve, one cause. Our enemies shall talk themselves to death, and we will bury them with their own confusion. We shall prevail!

The young woman reaches the screen and, like an Olympic athlete, hurls the hammer into the screen, destroying it and alarming the audience. In the next scene, text scrolls reading "On January 24th, Apple Computer will introduce Macintosh. And you'll see why 1984 won't be like 1984."

Many of you are familiar with George Orwell's book *1984*, a novel that warned of a future dominated by a totalitarian regime and citizens controlled and manipulated by technology. What does this have to do with visual organizational communication? Some historical context will help. In the 1980s, many people believed that IBM, a dominant computer company, was poised to dominate the entire market and extend its ethos of efficiency and, some said, uniformity. Apple had its struggles and wanted to position IBM as the architect of a frightening future.

Not only did the ad build on a well-known novel and film, but it also employed numerous visual strategies to convey threats of thought police and a future where individuality is crushed, and divergent thinking is stamped out. The ad also used color, visuals, and movement to boldly highlight the differences its creators were attempting to show. We can think of this as an extended visual metaphor used by Apple to draw attention, to persuade and to communicate. It further served to underscore the concept that Apple was an innovative company willing to break through convention and liberate its users from the past.

You may not have thought about it, but organizations communicate; people inside organizations communicate to external and internal audiences, and publics observe and draw conclusions about the character of an organization and make judgments about whether they should do business with them or recommend them to others. Some go so far as to say that organizations themselves are created through communication and that it is the basis for organizational excellence and success. Or conversely, poor communication can be the root of dysfunction.

In addition, your ability to communicate effectively is a crucial element in your success, regardless of your role. This chapter will look at organizational communication from both inside and outside and focus particularly on the importance of visuals in contemporary firms. Increasingly, organizations are recognizing the importance of positive and effective corporate cultures and how to create and nurture them.

Key Learning Objectives
After engaging in this chapter, you'll be able to:
1. Develop visual and cultural literacy in organizational communication.
2. Assess organizations through analysis of visuals.
3. Recognize and critique when visuals misfire.
4. Apply visuals for influence.

Chapter Overview
In this chapter, you'll learn about how you can effectively "read" an organizational culture particularly from the standpoint of observing visual cues. As a skilled culture detective, you'll be able to assess the culture and even to consider whether it's a place where you see yourself being comfortable and positioned to move forward. In addition, you'll see how organizations use advertising, video, and visually oriented social media platforms to enhance brand reputations or as sales tools. You'll also see how to streamline employee communication and how to motivate workers with shared values. Brief "how-to" sections (Communicating Using Digital Medial and How To Put the Visual Edge in Presentations) will give you tips and resources on making your communication more effective by using visual elements. Such elements can help draw attention and make your presentations and discussions more engaging and memorable.

VISUAL MODES

LO1 Develop visual and cultural literacy in organizational communication

We're all immersed in images and photos every day, a factor that has grown exponentially because of technology and sharing capabilities and is usefully categorized in four major areas by Sibbet (2012). Because of this deep involvement, it's helpful to review and understand the major "visual modes" that guide us to experience and comprehend visuals.

Four Major Areas

The first major visual mode is **graphic design**: a huge category that includes artists, advertising creative directors, web designers, and many others working in a wide array of fields. Every ad you see, app you open, magazine you read, and website you access has designers behind it attempting to make the product more beautiful, arresting, functional, persuasive, and informative. Social media are increasingly visual as we see professional or amateur Instagrammers carefully crafting appealing visuals to attract followers and influence potential buyers.

A second important area is **data visualization**. This approach is often used to illustrate various types of information using data analytics that make information clearer and easier to grasp. News organizations enhance storytelling by creating graphic elements that quickly reveal relationships and changing conditions. For example, the *SF Chronicle* tracked the growth of Airbnb in San Francisco providing an interactive map showing residents the numbers and types of rentals in their neighborhoods. Bloomberg provided an illustration of the world's deadliest jobs in a graphic revealing that fishers, loggers, and trash collectors were in the most peril. Investigative news organization *ProPublica* presented "Disappearing Planet" showing how animal extinctions were taking place around the world with a scale to allow readers to investigate selected species. Once again, the graphic presentation powerfully revealed the rates of potential extinctions and engaged audiences in the issues. In each case, journalists gathered data about a phenomenon and then developed accurate and imaginative graphic elements to tell the story.

A third area is **cognitive visualization** wherein communicators use metaphors, symbols, evocative images, and other devices to increase understanding and engagement of audiences. Such tools help explain complex ideas and increase audiences' attention to the primary points communicators are emphasizing.

Finally, **visual facilitation** is the process designers and facilitators use in helping organizations in strategic planning. For example, some consulting firms offer "storymapping" in order to help strategists think creatively and more concretely about how an organization can move forward. See the "storymap" for the National Endowment for the Arts in Figure 11.1.

In this chapter, we'll talk mainly about cognitive visualization and how you can use research-tested ideas to enhance your abilities to understand organizations and improve your communication effectiveness.

In the following section, we examine how organizations communicate, intentionally or not, their "personalities" or cultures. As you read, think of this as similar to how people communicate about themselves through their clothing, hairstyles, and demeanors.

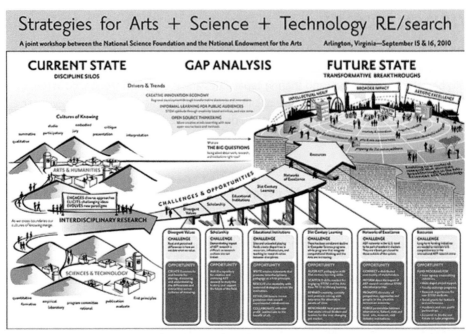

Figure 11.1 This "storymap" for the National Endowment for the Arts seeks to illustrate a new, collaborative, and cross-disciplinary approach to future projects that were formerly siloed. *Source:* The Grove Consultants International, https://www.thegrove.com/cs_NationalScienceFoundation.php.

Understanding Organizations as Cultures

Most of us don't think of organizations as having personalities, but like individuals, they do. Even a small group with a relatively brief shared history and experience will begin to develop preferred behaviors, inside jokes, and shared knowledge. This is the organization's culture.

We can understand **organizational cultures** by making various observations, suggests Schein (2017, p. 6): observing how people in a group interact, groups' rituals and ceremonies, the physical settings where people work and meet, and the taken for granted assumptions on how people should act or behave. A culture is "accumulated learning" resulting in patterns of behavior and systems of beliefs and values. Why does culture matter? Research shows that strong and positive cultures produce bottom-line results including employee retention, customer satisfaction, and success whether measured by profits or desired outcomes.

Organizational symbolism can also give us insights. Eisenberg and Goodall (1997) advise that we can interpret culture by attending to the stories, images, nonverbal exchanges, logos, and value statements. This may include websites, microsites, social media accounts, and brochures.

In previous chapters, you read about the concept of framing, or how we explain or present something to audiences, and how it influences their interpretations of the situation at hand. For example, if we frame an oil spill as an unavoidable accident, we then present a point of view that accidents just happen. If we frame it as an act resulting from incompetence or criminal behavior, people will draw different conclusions about the "goodness" or "badness" of the various individuals and organizations involved. Fairhurst (2011) cites the example of mining company CEO Robert Murray when one of the company's mines in Utah caved in, trapping six miners. He framed the event as caused by an earthquake, though critics insisted that it was the result of risky mining practices. Murray also framed his concern for the trapped miners by immediately going to the site and appearing in media. His visual appearance at the site was meant to communicate that concern.

Visual framing involves using photos, drawings, digital images, and nonverbal behaviors. As visuals tend to evoke more powerful responses than language, as Fairhurst (2011) points out, language can be used with greater precision. The late Apple CEO, Steve Jobs, was highly conscious of the staging and spectacle of his product announcements. His trademark black jeans and turtleneck, the high-tech backdrops, and sleek graphics all spoke to a culture of effortless cool.

Another aspect of visual modes is that they present information in a way that viewers or participants may not be consciously aware. As an individual enters into an environment, views an image, or sees another person, they may have an emotional reaction but may not identify the source of that feeling (Meyer et al., 2013). Thus, strategic communicators often seek to establish certain image atmospherics that set the stage for persuasion. Most audiences are more likely to attend to visual phenomena than they are to written material. Candidates for office in the United States literally stage speaking platforms with bunting and flags to underscore their patriotism.

The Mongols

If you have any doubts about the importance of visual symbols to *any* type of organization, consider the case of the Mongols motorcycle club, a group that has many chapters throughout the United States. Federal prosecutors tried for years to dissolve the Mongols, who are well known for their criminal activities including robbery, drug dealing, money laundering, murder, and kidnapping. The prosecutors finally seized upon the idea of taking away their logo or patch on the basis of a law that allows law enforcement officers to seize products used by people while committing crimes.

Like many other biker groups, the Mongols registered their trademark logo (Figure 11.2) with the United States Patent and Trademark Office and some legal experts consider it to be their intellectual property. Members wear jackets, T-shirts, and vests emblazoned with the logo and many have tattoos of the mark that features a Genghis Khan character on a chopper.

What does the mark mean to the members of the group? It represents an ethos of toughness, fearlessness, and belonging. According to gang expert and Professor William Dulaney, "the patch is like the American flag to these guys and speaks to the identity of the club, the individual, and the culture" (Kovaleski 2018, para. 11).

Prosecutors believed that seizing the patch would seriously erode the unity of the group, potentially leading to its demise. In a court filing, they stated, "the government will show that the marks served as a unifying symbols of an enterprise dedicated to intimidating and terrorizing everyone who is not a member, and assaulting

Figure 11.2 The logo of the Mongol's motorcycle gang. *Source:* AP Photo/ Ric Francis.

and killing those who have sworn their loyalty to other outlaw motorcycle gangs" (Kovaleski, 2018, para 21).

Mongols' members were worried that that the government's actions could, indeed, lead to the destruction of the club. "They take our patch," Mr. Santillan (Mongols president) said, "And then they can take all the clubs' patches" (Kovaleski, 2018, para. 36). In 2019, a federal judge ruled for the Mongols saying that taking away the Mongol's right to show the logo was a violation of the First Amendment (Rubin, 2019). Prosecutors said they would appeal.

Southwest Airlines

Southwest Airlines (SWA) is an example of a very different organizational culture that infuses almost every aspect of its operations with visual cues. The company pioneered low cost flights beginning in 1971 and has been consistently profitable: success it attributes to its focus on employees' well-being and a welcoming demeanor. "The mission of Southwest Airlines is dedication to the highest quality of customer service delivered with a sense of warmth, friendliness, individual pride, and company spirit" (Southwest Airlines n.d.).

Figure 11.3 Southwest Airlines (SWA) infuses its trademark bright colors into its aircraft, uniforms, bag tags, and even snack packaging. *Source:* Lippincott.

SWA's corporate offices send a "people-first" message with bright colors, open, welcoming spaces, and gathering places. The flight attendant uniforms hew to the palette of red, blue, and silver seen in the stylized SWA heart logo, the airplanes' color scheme, baggage tags, and even the peanut and pretzel snack packs (Figure 11.3). The emphasis on consistent visual branding continues on its social media platforms.

SWA has a "social care" team on Twitter, Instagram, and YouTube that responds to customers' concerns, according to the *Dallas Business Journal* (Hoopfer, 2019). Often with highly visual posts such as videos with customers and representatives, the airline dramatizes how it values personal service.

Similarly, SWA harnesses social media influencers to post "Southwest Stories" where popular influencers post highly scenic and exciting images and are rewarded with free trips and passes to desirable locations. When we're attuned to these cultural clues, we're able to diagnose and decide if this is an organization we might want to work with or work for.

BECOMING A CULTURE DETECTIVE

LO2 Assess organizations through analysis of visuals.

When researchers and consultants go about their work, they gather data from many sources. They use ethnography, participant observation, and immersion in a culture to get deeper understanding of the values, attitudes, and beliefs that shape and drive individual and organizational behaviors, success, or failure. In marketing, researchers also use ethnographic approaches to understand people's shopping behaviors and their relationships with brands. **Ethnography** usually involves participant observation where researchers embed themselves in an organizational setting to learn more about culture from the inside.

Many organizations hire experts to conduct **communication audits**, assessing the channels of communication internal and external to an organization and evaluating their effectiveness. Often, they will gather stories of successes and failures, finding who are the heroes and villains in a narrative. For the purposes of this chapter, we'll touch on these various sources but will emphasize the visual aspects of organizational culture diagnosis.

Retail shops and restaurants put considerable thought into decor, layout, and size of each part of the store. Consider two coffee shops, Dunkin' (formerly Dunkin' Donuts) and Starbucks. Dunkin' features bright pink door handles, many colorful photos of food, and has a sugary, confectionary vibe. Starbucks offers a more muted interior with artsy prints, soft lighting, and an upscale feel. Different retail specialties also call for different decoration. Whereas SWA deployed visuals communicating a warm, fun working environment, banks generally provide an environment that suggests solidity, stability, and trustworthiness.

Values and Visuals

If you decide to become a culture detective – and it can be fun to do – following are some important things to look for as you gather clues:

- *Workspaces of people at different levels of the organization.* Different settings can reveal how employees of all classes are valued. Premiere workspaces of executives may contrast with poor or spartan working conditions for other employee categories.

- *Layouts of the workplace.* An ongoing trend for office design has been in creating open plans following the belief that such plans foster communication and collaboration. But some workers object saying that open plans are distracting, often loud, and don't allow needed privacy for certain tasks such as personnel reviews or other confidential activities. In addition, if just a few top employees have what some consider to be premium private spaces, it may send a message of unfairness and secrecy.

- *Signage.* Many office environments will feature signage and safety reminders along with company logos. For certain industries, prominent signs feature the number of days a facility has gone without an accident.

- *Wall decor.* Some companies feature videos, photos, and portraits of founders, early facilities, and timelines of growth. They may have prominent employee awards. Many offices have inspirational or positive thinking messages or reminders of the importance of customer service.

- *Artifacts of the brand's saga and history.* Some organizations feature timelines that show their history and growth. The Louisville, Kentucky, headquarters of KFC offers a museum with many artifacts from founder Colonel Sanders, photos, and even an animatronic Colonel Sanders that moves and speaks when there's movement in the room.

- *Employees' clothing and accessories.* Sometimes there's an unspoken dress code that constitutes a uniform of sorts. If some staff members violate or breach those codes, they may be seen as not fitting in with the culture. Employees in different functions may have different uniforms. For instance, in the advertising business, the account supervisors are actually called "the suits" whereas the creative employees dress in hipster or more casual garb.

- *Cleanliness and clutter.* Some offices are set up with almost military precision with clean desks and orderly filing systems. Others are more casual with stacks of paper, many projects in the works, and even piles of work on the floor.

- *Individual offices.* If you look carefully at someone's office or cubicle, you'll get an indication of what the employee values. Are there family photos? Cartoons? Sports memorabilia or trophies? All of the clues and cues have an impact on both employees and visitors. As you go for job interviews or simply visit an organization as a customer, you can gain insights. It can be fun to consider the visual cues in other people's homes as well as your own. And you may ask yourself, what messages am I sending to people who come to my house?

FOCUS: User-Generated Videos in the Workplace

With video shot entirely on iPads, Lowes store managers recorded employees who inspired them. On the recording, the managers explained to the employees why they were selected and what aspects of their performance and personality made them stand out. Managers had the outline of a script to guide them and were encouraged to record a diverse group of employees.

Then, at Lowe's annual national sales meeting, more than 3,000 leaders from across the organization watched a video compilation featuring outstanding employees recorded at stores around the country. For leaders at Lowes, the compilation dramatized the outcomes of a culture that "serves its people" and acknowledges their importance.

The employees displayed a wide range of emotions from surprise, happiness, and gratitude. The goal of the video was to encourage and inspire managers to recognize their employees and to see the benefits of building an inclusive culture.

PR Daily (2017) awarded Lowes, the home improvement retail company, a first-place video award for user-generated content.

Visual Cues in Marketing and Promotion

As you saw in the SWA example, many visual elements can contribute or detract from a company's culture and how it's perceived. Increasingly, organizations seek to dramatize their values through highly visual and social expressions. They do this in marketing and product promotions as well as in efforts to showcase and promote their corporate cultures. Audiences for these efforts are both internal and external and lines are blurring between an organization's physical and virtual spaces. On Instagram, Hootsuite, a social media management company, gives its followers a look behind the curtain at its company culture with #HootsuiteLife. The postings are upbeat and exciting showing employees working out, having fun at events, and bringing their dogs to work.

Marriott Careers showcases people enjoying their jobs as well as highlighting support for veterans and Marriott's commitment to improving communities with the hashtag #WeMakeMarriott (Burgess, 2017).

As visuals become increasingly crucial for brands, planners focus on ensuring that the social media and other marketing comport with the brand ethos it wants to promote. Famous for its luxurious jewelry and its iconic blue boxes, Tiffany & Co. features the exact shade of blue in almost every Instagram post. The visuals are elegant and cool and echo the design on its website. A much different organization is the dating app Bumble. It has a colorful and fun website and Instagram account. It partnered with tennis star Serena Williams in a television and Instagram promotion called "Make the first move" encouraging women to move forward in many aspects of their lives (Izea, 2019).

IMAGES GONE WRONG

LO3 Recognize and critique when visuals misfire.

While powerful visuals can be great tools, they can quickly go wrong if they hit the wrong tone or if the creators don't consider unintended effects on some audiences or different perspectives. Particularly on social media platforms, visual elements are expanders and accelerants depending on how they're deployed and interpreted. And it's easy to go wrong spectacularly and publicly.

Controversies and Crises

Reformation, a popular fashion line, posted a picture of a model sitting provocatively on a table wearing a featured dress as workers labored in the background (Figure 11.4). The social media marketing platform Falcon praises Instagram as a great platform for visual storytelling (Gollin, 2019) but cautions it can also be a minefield of mistakes. While the Reformation fashion image was striking, many people found it offensive and tone-deaf.

In addition, when companies are embroiled in crises or controversy, their image management needs to be in sync with the issues. Following problems or crises, social media and especially visuals can be toxic if not handled correctly or if an organization continues with business as usual. After a deadly engine explosion aboard a SWA flight, the company moved instantly to change all images to a plain, blue icon.

However, it was a different story in December 2018 when a Hilton Hotel security guard called the police to complain about a black hotel guest "loitering" in the hotel lobby. It sparked significant controversy and was widely reported in national media. But in the wake of the incident, the hotel posted a cheery holiday message on Twitter, ignoring what had happened (see Figure 11.5). Even worse, they didn't respond to the issue until three days later. In a crisis situation, it's crucial to understand that a business as usual attitude won't work. As Hootsuite bloggers Christina Newberry and Sarah Dawley (2019) suggest, "humble and informative posts will help you . . . put your crisis communication plan in action."

♥ **445 likes**

reformation Hot out the factory. The Guava Dress is back.

View all 25 comments

hlyhwrd @yasminmoonmoon yeah it does

olivia.agostino @sarahgeo

loveannax Good work social media manager !

Figure 11.4 Reformation's image on Instagram struck an offensive tone with many people. *Source:* Sunny Co Clothing.

Figure 11.5 One response to Hilton's failure to address an issue: "For Christmas this year, I'll be telling all my friends to avoid your hotel, and to tell their families not to stay there when they visit. Instead of wasting time trying to ignore what happened, why don't you fire the security guard in question and make some real changes?" *Source:* Aleksandr Yakovlev/Getty Images.

THE POWER OF VISUALS IN ORGANIZATIONAL COMMUNICATION

LO4 Apply visuals for influence.

Most of us communicate with others without giving it too much thought; we're generally on autopilot. In this section we'll go over three areas where you can become more effective as a communicator armed with more effective use of visuals and visual cues: communicating interpersonally, communicating using digital media and virtual technologies, and communicating to groups through speeches and presentations.

Communicating Interpersonally: You're the Visual

When you're speaking to someone, you may use intentional and unintentional physical and behavioral cues that transmit meaning (McCornack and Morrison, 2019). Your body language is a highly important "visual" and can either enhance or undermine the content of the discussion. Your stance, hand movements, facial expressions, and eye contact all matter. If your demeanor makes it appear that you're bored, distracted, or not listening, the quality of the conversation will suffer. Proximity to others matters too. Some cultures tend to be more comfortable with greater interpersonal distance and "close talking" makes people feel as if the other person is a space invader.

While smiles are more welcoming than frowns, it's important that expressions comport with the goals and content of the discussion. If the verbal and nonverbal elements aren't in agreement, the nonverbals will dominate. Beyond body language, your clothing and accessories say something about you that will be interpreted by others. Whether you wear designer clothing, a logo sweatshirt, a formal dress, or any combination, you'll be communicating. In fact, you can't *not* communicate: you're the message.

FOCUS: Hey, You!

Cisco is a global company that produces high-tech products and services. To attract new employees, it needed to change perception of the company as a stodgy tech dinosaur into one of an organization with the vibe of a cool new startup. The vcompany retooled its website and in 2018 launched an innovative and award-winning talent branding initiative (PR Daily, 2018).

Job seekers were getting their first impressions of Cisco on its website careers page. The company conducted research and identified unnecessarily complex navigation and a design that didn't represent the talent it was appealing to. After navigation problems were solved, Cisco focused on a new design that was consistent with themes already perfected and successful on social media: "Be you, with us. #WeAreCisco."

The talent branding program showcases real employees talking about their jobs and what it's like to work at Cisco. The team carefully selected and

---

trained employees and trusted them to livestream on Facebook Live and Instagram. Cisco promoted the streams with paid and organic content and the results were outstanding: eight Facebook streams generated 12,300 views, 39,000 minutes watched, and Instagram videos had an average of 114 views and hundreds of replays.

Source: Cisco.

Communicating Using Digital Media

Many of us communicate in organizations mainly through texting, social media, email, or sometimes through proprietary networks. Given how often we use technology to interpersonally communicate, building online competence becomes extremely important. We often deduce more meaning from people's nonverbal rather than verbal communication (McCornack and Morrison, 2019). However when online, we just don't have the context that these cues provide in face-to-face conversations. Emails and texts can lead to hostile reactions because people have less information on which to assess the sender's goals, intentions, and attitudes. With every communication, we human beings are trying to figure out others' actions and predict how it might affect us.

If a certain emoji is fun for us and potentially offensive to others, we need to back off. While visuals are becoming increasingly important for effective communication, many common technologies often omit visual elements and thus don't communicate effectively (Morgan, 2019). In face-to-face interactions, we are able to contextualize what's said with nonverbal indicators such as a shrug, smile, raised eyebrow, relaxed or tense postures. For instance, emojis are generally associated with informal texting among friends.

How to Use GIFs in the Workplace

The **GIF** (graphics interchange format) is a bitmap image that allows communicators to create simple images that can be animated. Many free animated GIF makers are available online. Daniel Foster of TechSmith (Foster n.d.) shares tips on why and how to use GIFs at work:

The benefits of using GIFs:

- Quick to create
- Easy to distribute
- Attention-grabbing

In the workplace, digital communication via email social platforms, and an internal Intranet (private Internet only accessible within an organization) allow communicators to create and include animated GIFs that serve multiple purposes.

For example, GIFs can show:

- *Steps in a process*. Skip the details and visually guide viewers through a series of maneuvers.
- *Cause and effect*. Make it easy to see impact of an action by illustrating how one thing changes another.
- *Before and after*. When space is tight, create a two-for-one in the same area.
- *Comparisons*. Butt-up two animations together for an immediate delivery of opposites and similarities.
- *Walkthroughs*. Make introductory tutorials easy to grasp.
- *Mini demonstrations*. Show off a new process.
- *Concept illustrations*. Enliven topics by introducing new features.
- *Quick tips*. Help solve employees' problems faster.

How To Put the Visual Edge in Presentations

The picture superiority effect reveals that people remember pictures better than words (Defeyter et al., 2009). Experts say that when people view or hear text or audio information, they retain only 10% of the material while if they view text and related visuals, they'll retain up to 65% of the information. The best explanation for the picture superiority effect appears to be that our brains are able to perceive and process images more quickly and with more impact than spoken words or textual materials.

We've all suffered through PowerPoints and keynotes that have loads of text, complicated diagrams, and way too many slides. To add clarity, excitement, and interest, here are some quick guidelines:

Most important:

1. **More visuals, less text**. The slides should enhance your presentation, not take its place.

2. **Use images that tell the story**. We process visuals 60,000 times faster than written words. Create your presentation around a story or narrative and let your visuals build on the story.

3. **Don't read what's written on the slide verbatim unless it's really simple**. You audience reads faster than you do.

4. **Limit yourself to one major idea per slide.**

5. **Use visuals and animations to support a data point**. Don't just make pretty slides. And be very cautious about animations and tricky slide transitions as they can be distracting.

6. **Practice your stagecraft**. Your body language should include eye contact. Find some friendly faces in the audience – maybe four or five – and look them in the eyes. If you feel comfortable moving about the stage, fine, but don't overdo pacing or striding around.

7. **Use visual language and action verbs.**

8. **Make meaning immediately clear**. For charts presenting data such as sales results or changes in customer behavior, make sure that the meaning is immediately clear.

9. **Use contrast**. Figure 11.6 shows how effective this can be.

Many resources are available to help with presentation visuals.

- An excellent one is Nancy Duarte: www.duarte.com
- Grove Tools: https://grovetools-inc.com
- How to become a great presenter: https://visme.co/blog/tips-on-how-to-become-a-great-presenter
- The art of concise presentations: www.pechakucha.com

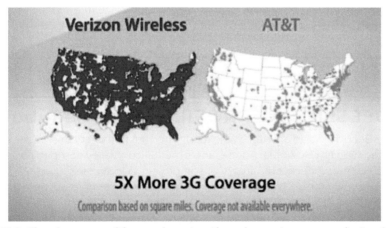

Figure 11.6 Simple composition and contrasting elements communicate clearly in slide presentations. *Source:* YouTube.

FOCUS: Using Visual Systems to Drive Business Results

Gagen MacDonald (GM) is a strategy execution consulting firm in Chicago that helps companies with the human struggle of change. Its work centers around three specific areas: culture change, employee engagement, and leadership.

The firm's primary role is helping clients execute their business strategy. One way is by using visual models and systems, which it did for Astellas Pharma, a Japanese pharmaceutical company with US headquarters in the Chicago suburbs. Astellas has a truly unique culture but found itself in a war to attract and retain top talent, especially in the pharmaceutical industry. Astellas recognized its culture was key to building interest and loyalty, but it needed to define it, activate it, and showcase it internally and externally.

GM identified and articulated the Astellas culture and created a visual system that brought the culture to life throughout the organization (Gagen MacDonald, 2017). It was simple, memorable, emotional, and actionable, serving as the foundation for the campaign. It featured the values that are tenants of the Astellas culture, tied together with the mantra "We Live It." The visual system used color coding for recall and communicated that when employees live the Astellas culture, "The Astellas Way," they are moving forward, progressing.

Posters communicated the five behaviors GM wanted to drive, some containing employee photos along with their voices and perspectives on the most valued aspect of their work: helping patients. Hanging banners and floor graphics also brought the campaign to life throughout the organization. On a commitment wall, which traveled throughout North America to each Astellas location, employees hand wrote their pledges of how they would live the culture by each of the values.

Each employee was also given a poster for their workspace, calendars with reminders of how to live the culture, and laptop clings. GM also did extensive leader training, equipping Astellas leaders to talk about the culture and to model the behaviors they wanted to see from employees. *Source:* Gagen MacDonald (2017)

PROFESSIONAL PROFILE: Terry Beaubois

Terry Beaubois is an architect who focuses on sustainability design. He's consulted with NASA, Apple, Adobe, and other Silicon Valley companies, and is currently working on a smart village project in India. He's also CEO of Building Knowledge Systems, a web-based resource to help builders go green, and he teaches smart communities at Stanford University.

In 7th grade, my art teacher said to me, "you are good in art, math, and science, you should consider a being an architect." That 10 seconds sentence changed my life. Because we take classes that separate what we are learning into silos of knowledge and specialties, they can seem separate and different. At that time, I didn't have the vision to see how each of those separate subjects could be important parts of a very rewarding career.

The silo thinking continues today. I had a student tell me she was interested in biology and architecture but was told that she would have to choose between the two, because she couldn't do both. I don't see things that way. I am encouraging us all to consider the various silos that our interests span.

Students should identify what excites them about any subject and find how each topic interconnects.

Source: Building Knowledge Systems.

As you progress in your career, there will be government and business involvement, as well as application of knowledge you've gained from academia. I suggest we look at all those areas as an iterative process. This means as you move forward, you also look back and make sure everything you've done until now considers the additional information you've gotten talking to more people.

And as we all become competent, knowledgeable, and experienced, we want to be on teams where we're recognized for our contribution, as well as teams benefiting us in the long run, so you're learning and growing and implementing things. If you're looking to be a good leader in your company or community, people love someone who knows something they don't know. Power doesn't come from being quiet and secretive, it's about sharing knowledge and elevating the whole group so all can go to the next level.

For the last couple of years, I've been working within a team in Andhra Pradesh, India, on the issues and elements of smart villages. It's not like buying some real estate and getting rid of the people living there and improving the economy by gentrification. We go in and look at the village and the elements that make it up.

The first village we studied had weavers doing gorgeous fabrics for saris and different Indian clothing, people hand processing cashews, people shrimp farming in ponds, rice paddy operators, and coconut farmers. How

(*Continued*)

can we help the village be more successful doing what they're doing? Well, local potters have a clay from the riverbank they call black clay, and it's well known for that characteristic.

The Tata lab at MIT helped us analyze the clay so we could come up with a lower flame, less polluting brick kiln. Now materials from the village could be used to make bricks instead of bringing them in from elsewhere. We created a local economy, something with meaning: Muri black clay brick, not just any old brick.

There are elements of reaching out. I'm sure you, in your own work and in the classroom, use resources. A really important part of not only finding resources and using them is leaving a trail of breadcrumbs so other people can find out what you've done and where you've been and where you got your information.

CHAPTER SUMMARY

By engaging with this chapter, you've become aware of the many visual elements that can contribute or detract from a company's culture and how it's perceived. You've become immersed in interpreting the visual culture of organizations. You've explored how they create brand stories and both physical and virtual environments and how they engage (or alienate) publics with images and nonverbals. You've discovered the power of visual symbols in organizations as diverse as criminal motorcycle clubs and popular airlines. And you've reviewed how social media visuals can amplify both positive and negative public reception. Finally, you've reflected on personal performance: from using GIFs in workplace emails to visual design of slide presentations and the speaker's visual body language.

KEY TERMS

Organizational culture   A group or social unit that has a shared history, patterns, behavioral norms, and assumptions; organizations socialize newcomers so they understand the expected behaviors.

Graphic design   Utilizing design elements to create a desired effect or convey information.

Data visualization   Representation of data and information using visual elements such as statistical graphs, charts, and maps with the goal of showing the relationships and trends in clear and accessible ways.

Visual facilitation   An extension of strategic planning where facilitators work with a group creating visuals that spur creativity, increase processing time, and provides clarity among group members. It is frequently used as a decision-making tool.

Ethnography   Systematic analysis of an organization or group based on multiple observations and interactions. It seeks to understand the worldviews and perceptions of group members.

Communication audit   Systematic analysis of an organization's communication practices and tools; evaluates communication effectiveness of communication to both internal and external stakeholders.

PRACTICE ACTIVITIES

1. **Website analysis**. Analyze a website for an organization such as SWA and evaluate what it communicates visually, or compare two sites. Consider these factors:

    *   *Balance*. How are the elements placed on the page? Is the design balanced and formal or more relaxed and informal? Is there a lot of "white space" or area not occupied by images or words?

    *   *Dynamism*. Does the design give a feeling of movement or stability?

    *   *Fonts/typefaces*. Does the typeface "personality" resonate with the overall design of the ad? Is it light and airy or heavy?

    *   *Colors*. How is color used? Is it a major element in the persuasive message? Are the colors bright or muted?

    *   *Perspectives*. Are objects or people large or small? Shot from above or head on?

    *   *Subject*. If there are people or animals on the site, what are their characteristics? Are they celebrities? Old or young? What emotions can you infer from their expressions? Nonverbals and body language? What's the scene? What are the people doing and wearing? Are they sophisticated or down-home?

    *   What emotions do the visuals seem to elicit or try to elicit from viewers? (Berger, 1998)

2. **Ethnography**. Identify a setting. Find a work, school, or recreational setting where people are interacting with each other. It could be a place you already frequent such as your workplace, a club, or a classroom. It could be a business such as a hair salon, a gym, or a restaurant. It might be a volunteer setting. In any case, clear it with your professors before starting.

    *   *Length of observations*. You'll want to plan for three to five hours total. For instance, if you're observing a meeting of a club or a class, you'll perhaps spend an hour at a time over several days. If you're looking at a workplace or a volunteer effort such as the Food Bank, you might spend half an hour at about the same time every day. Similarly, at a breakfast place you might want to go in for half an hour each morning.

- *Consider the ethical elements of your work.* In a more public setting, you'd likely not need to inform others that they're being observed. Think about strategies for remaining incognito. Be careful that your observations don't draw undue attention. If someone asks, tell them that you're working on a research project about communication in various settings.

- *Don't let your expectations about what you'll find unduly shape your observations.* Keep an open mind and make notes and even drawings about what you're seeing. Remember, you're trying to put yourself into the experience that other people in the environment are having. Look for patterns, similarities, and themes. How do people interact with the physical environment? Do people sit in the same place every time? Are there regulars and cliques? For instance, in many small communities, McDonald's and other fast food restaurants have become gathering places for retirees. Are some people outliers?

3. **Report your findings**. Keep your field notes with dates, locations, times, and hours as you'll hand them in as the appendix as evidence of your observations. Your report should be two to three pages (about 2000 words). Cover the following issues:

   - Describe the setting and why you selected it. In addition, tell us about your expectations about what you might find as you began your observations.

   - Tell us the major findings from your observations. You'll want to answer questions like this:

     o Who were the main people you saw? What were their characteristics? Did any individuals stand out as leaders or more dominant? Others less so? Who were the insiders or outsiders?

     o You probably saw unwritten rules manifested such as where people sat, what people wore, what kind of speech and speech patterns were preferred. What rituals or repeated patterns of behavior did you see? What physical characteristics did you see in the work or meeting space? Was it neat? Messy? Formal or informal?

     o Think of how best to describe and label the culture you saw. What surprised you or was unexpected?

     o Reflect on your own reactions to what you saw and heard. Did you find yourself approving or disapproving of behaviors and communication?

     o Conclusion. Sum up your findings in a paragraph or two.

REFERENCES

Berger, A.A. (1998). *Media Research Techniques*. Thousand Oaks, CA: Sage.

Burgess, C. (2017). 8 examples of brands using Instagram to showcase company culture. https://www.toprankblog.com/2017/05/company-culture-instagram (accessed June 14, 2020).

Defeyter, M.A., Russo, R., and Graham, P.L. (2009). The picture superiority effect in recognition memory: A developmental study using the response signal procedure. *Cognitive Development* 24 (3): 265–273.

Eisenberg, E.M. and Goodall, H.L. (1997). *Organizational Culture: Balancing Creativity and Constraint*. New York: St. Martin's Press.

Fairhurst, G.T. (2011). *The Power of Framing: Creating the Language of Leadership*. San Francisco, CA: Wiley.

Foster, D. (n.d.). 11 ways to use GIFs in workplace communication. https://www.techsmith.com/blog/11-ways-to-use-gifs-at-work-right-now-today (accessed October 16, 2020).

Gagen MacDonald. (2017).Astellas Americas and Gagen MacDonald win 2017 North America In2 SABRE Awards. https://www.gagenmacdonald.com/news-events/astellas-americas-and-gagen-macdonald-win-2017-north-america-in2-sabre-awards/ (accessed October 16, 2019).

Gollin, M. (2019). 15 of the Worst Instagram Marketing Mistakes by Companies. Retrieved June 16, 2019 from https://www.falcon.io/insights-hub/topics/social-media-strategy/15-brands-most-embarrassing-instagram-marketing-mistakes (accessed January 9, 2021).

Hoopfer, E. (2019). Social media LUV: how Southwest Airlines connects with customers online. https://www.bizjournals.com/dallas/news/2019/03/03/southwest-airlines-social-media.html (accessed October 6, 2019).

Izea. (2019). Best influencer marketing campaigns of 2018. https://izea.com/2019/03/08/best-influencer-marketing-campaigns (accessed June 17, 2019).

Kovaleski, S. (2018). How to crush an outlaw biker club: Seize its . . . logo? https://www.nytimes.com/2018/11/21/us/mongols-motorcycle-club-government.html (accessed October 16, 2019).

McCornack, S. and Morrison, K. (2019). *Reflect & Relate*, 5the. Boston: Bedford/St. Martin's Press.

Meyer, R., Hollere, M., Jancsary, D., and van Leeuwen, T. (2013 [2009]). The visual dimension in organizing, organization, and organization research: Core ideas, current developments, and promising avenues. *The Academy of Management Annals* 7 (1): 489–555.

Newberry, C. and Dawley, S. (2019). How to manage a social media crisis. https://blog.hootsuite.com/social-media-crisis-management (accessed June 14, 2019).

PR Daily. (2017). Videos by Lowe's store managers create powerful sales meeting content. https://www.prdaily.com/awards/video-visual-awards/2017/winners/user-generated-video (accessed June 14, 2019).

PR Daily. (2018). Cisco Systems scores with live streaming video. https://www.prdaily.com/awards/video-visual-awards/2018/winners/live-video (accessed June 14, 2019).

Rubin, J. (2019). Judge refuses to strip Mongols biker club of trademarked logo. *LA Times*, Jan. 21. https://www.latimes.com/local/lanow/la-me-mongols-trademark-ruling-20190228-story.html (accessed October 6, 2019).

Schein, E.H. (2017). *Organizational Culture and Leadership*. Hoboken, NJ: Wiley.

Sibbet, D. (2012). *Visual Leaders:* New Tools for Visioning, Management, and Organization change. Hoboken, NJ: Wiley.

Southwest Airlines (n.d.) https://careers.southwestair.com/culturetemplate (accessed January 9, 2021).

Chapter 12
Intercultural Communication

Welcome to Middle Earth

Source: RoBenatti/Shutterstock.com.

Visitors to New Zealand can experience "Middle Earth" on a *Lord of the Rings* (**LOTR**) tour offered by one of the country's many private tour companies. The monumental LOTR

Visual Communication: Insights and Strategies, First Edition. Janis Teruggi Page and Margaret Duffy.
© 2022 John Wiley & Sons, Inc. Published 2022 by John Wiley & Sons, Inc.

movie trilogy, filmed in New Zealand, resulted in a 50% increase in visitors since the first film was released in 2001 with many tourists visiting places featured in the films (Pinchefsky, 2012). In fact, the country's ad slogan "100% Pure New Zealand" became "100% Middle-earth" (Pannett, 2018).

Countries use nation-branding efforts to manage their reputations and influence foreign publics. Among the many strategies, popular books, TV series, and movies are powerful cultural exports that can influence perceptions. Well before the LOTR tourism, the Transylvanian region of Romania has benefited from the Gothic horror novel Dracula, and more recently the HBO series Game of Thrones has been a boon for Northern Ireland tourism.

Realizing the advantage of movies to promote tourism, countries will offer incentives and subsidies to attract international moviemakers. However, one outcome is the creation of virtual and real scenic elements. LOTR used special effects to add buildings and mountains, creating a mediated and digitized takeover of a natural environment where both guests and residents adopt identities in relation to it. Long after the filming ended, parts of the Hobbiton movie set remain in a time capsule of mediated culture (Couldry, 2003). Global visitors wanting to experience both the filmed and mythical environments for a simulated intercultural experience can book vacations in a "real" Hobbit Hole and wander around a fully functioning Middle Earth resort. In fact, the crushing swarm of visitors has given rise to a "Lord of the Rings" effect similar to other global "overtouristed" spots like Venice, Barcelona, and Thailand (Pannett, 2018).

Not all genres or stories are welcomed by tourist destinations and some countries establish guidelines to restrict or encourage visitors. Violent movies, in particular, are often seen as problematic in having an adverse influence on a country's image. Such movies threaten or use physical force to cause harm, are often concerned with crime, and provoke anxiety and fearful excitement with an audience, among other negative outcomes (Yang and Vanden Bergh, 2017).

Will viewers of violent movies be more interested or less interested in visiting its location? Surprisingly, researchers found that when a violent movie transports a viewer into its story, that answer is "more" (Yang and Vanden Bergh, 2017). You've no doubt experienced this transportation when you become immersed in a movie and lose yourself in the storyline. This immersion makes people feel as if they're part of the story and can affect beliefs about issues and reality (Green and Brock, 2000). The state is one of complete focus on the story, in which viewers "may lose track of time . . . and experience vivid mental images of settings and characters," (Green et al., 2008, p. 513).

As you've been transported into a film's story, you may have felt strong emotional connections to its exotic foreign locations or heroic characters. Depending on the authenticity of the narrative and representations – for example, as in some documentaries – you may have developed understanding and empathy for the characters shown in the film. You also may have traveled internationally, drawing some understanding of the culture from obvious visual signs like people's physical appearances, posters, and architecture as you explored new terrain. Yet, as we turn to intercultural communication in professional practices, you'll find that we can understand this communication in systematic and scientific ways.

Key Learning Objectives

After engaging in this chapter, you'll be able to:
1. Recognize the breadth of intercultural imagery across mass communication fields.
2. Assess ethical and practical issues in intercultural imagery in mass communication.
3. Identify and critique the use of visual rhetoric in intercultural imagery in mass communication.

Chapter Overview

This chapter covers an important consideration applicable to all past chapters; it builds your intercultural literacy. Acknowledging, understanding, and respecting different cultures is an obligation of communication professionals and is something you will practice almost every day. You'll first get an overview of the field, drawing from Native American, British, Honduran, Indian, African American, and Czech perspectives. You'll then consider ethical implications such as the fair treatment of LGBTQ+ populations worldwide and the misuse of sacred Chinese symbols. Finally, you'll venture into the popular technologies of virtual reality (VR) and 360° video.

WAYS OF LOOKING AT INTERCULTURAL COMMUNICATION AND ITS PLACE IN MASS COMMUNICATION

LO1 Recognize the breadth of intercultural imagery across mass communication fields.

Boundaries between "foreign" and "domestic" are disappearing with advancements in technology, information distribution, and the proliferation of media entertainment. Most public communication today is global communication carrying a dynamic flow of visual images across cultures.

Yet while transmission ranges far and wide, it's crucial to remember that audiences are diverse and rooted in local cultures and political realities. Intercultural communication is challenging and there are no clear guidelines about how to do it sensitively and effectively. For producers and users of visual communication, these differences require acknowledgment, understanding, care, and tailored approaches. Ultimately, the more knowledge you have about another culture, the better you can communicate.

Intercultural Visual Communication

Culture is "the collective programming of the mind that distinguishes the members of one group or category of people from others" according to Geert Hofstede, a dominant intercultural researcher of social and organizational cultures (2011, p. 3). Thus, culture manifests not only in words, but in feelings, actions, and visual representations.

Cultural values can affect the meaning of visual images. Hofstede (2011) identified six clusters of values within cultures. They include power distance, uncertainty avoidance, individualism versus collectivism, masculinity versus femininity, short-term versus long-term life orientation, and indulgence versus restraint (see Hofstede's Six Cultural Dimensions elsewhere in this chapter).

Hofstede's broadly accepted classical view, drawn from his research spanning five decades beginning in the late 1960s, sees culture as widely predictable. Yet Hofstede and other researchers caution that finer cultural nuances and changes in political landscapes should be taken into consideration (Eringa et al., 2015).

Visual images in the diverse field of intercultural mass communication may appear very different but share the common goal of communicating with culturally diverse publics. Questioning these images calls us to examine their cultural relevance, design, and implementation. Most important, communicators must evaluate how ignorance and poor choices risk miscommunication in intercultural contexts.

FOCUS: The Founders: Hall and Hofstede

In the 1960s and 1970s, two researchers, social psychologist Geert Hofstede and anthropologist Edward Hall, independently developed theories for the organization and identification of cultures. They produced dimensions or values applicable to cultures all over the world. In her 2014 research, Brumberger reviewed 17 intercultural studies on advertising, design, marketing, psychology, technical, and computer-mediated communication, finding the visual characteristics of materials from different cultures appear to reflect the values outlined by Hofstede and Hall.

Hall's Theory of High- and Low-Context Cultures

High-context cultures tend to rely more heavily on implied or implicit communication and nonverbal cues. Generally speaking, Latin American, Central European, Arab, and Asian cultures are thought to be high-context cultures. *Low-context cultures* expect more concrete and detailed communication: visuals that incorporate textual explanations. Countries in the Western tradition such as the United States, the United Kingdom, Western Europe, and Australia tend to be low-context cultures. What does this mean for successful intercultural communication? Carol Gorman (2011) argues that people in most industrialized nations tend to favor written messages over spoken and face-to-face

(Continued)

interactions. Japan is a notable exception in that it is highly industrialized and yet most people prefer in-person communication. In low-context cultures, people rely on personal relationships in business dealings while high-context cultures insist on carefully worded documents and agreements. Gorman warns that successful communication often depends on creating and sustaining personal relationships, not only on legal documentation.

Hofstede's Six Cultural Dimensions

1. *Power distance* is the extent to which the less powerful members of organizations and institutions (like the family) accept and expect that power is distributed unequally. In a low power distance culture like the United States, people have a greater tendency to question authority. In a high power distance culture, people tend to be more deferential to authority.
2. *Uncertainty avoidance* relates to the level of stress, anxiety, and distrust in a society in the face of an unknown future: the wish to have fixed habits and rituals.
3. *Individualism* versus *collectivism* relates to the integration of individuals into primary groups, or not. Individualism is the feeling of independence; making one's choices and decisions. Collectivism means being interdependent on a larger whole where life is socially determined.
4. *Masculinity* versus *femininity* is not about individuals but about expected emotional gender roles. A masculine society's traits are, for example, winning and toughness. Traits such as sympathy and care characterize a feminine society.
5. *Long-term* versus *short-term orientation* are related to the choice of focus for people's efforts: the future or the present/past. Future-oriented (long-term) means the world is always in flux and preparing for the future is always necessary. Short-term means accepting the world "as is" and relying on the past for guidance.
6. *Indulgence* versus *restraint* relates to gratification versus control of basic human desires related to enjoying life. Indulgence means following impulses is good; restraint means life is hard and duty, not freedom, is the norm.

Hofstede's cultural dimensions have been criticized but they are generally accepted as guidelines and not hard-and-fast rules. You can compare countries at https://www.hofstede-insights.com/country-comparison.

Let's consider how McDonald's designs websites keep power distance in mind. Advertising and website design can use insights such as power distance scores to guide visuals strategies based on Hofstede's dimensions. For example, Norway is a low power distance country. The McDonald's website features photos of employees, fresh vegetables, and considerable information including locating restaurants, learning more about the company, and sustainability issues. The rich trove of information invites the viewer to take charge of their experience.

Source: Used with permission from McDonald's Corporation.

Hong Kong, however, is a region of China, a high-power distance country, and the website has a different look and feel from that of Norway's. The site is clear about its offerings and gives users a sense that they can easily make decisions based on authoritative recommendations. While more detailed information is available on the website, the focus is primarily on products.

Source: Used with permission from McDonald's Corporation.

Sources Brumberger (2014) and Hofstede (n.d., 2011).

Corporate Intercultural Communication

A *PR Daily* video series award recognized efforts to protect and promote the image of the Cherokee Nation, the largest tribal government in the United States. The ambitious series was sponsored by Cherokee Nation Businesses, a for-profit corporation. It contains 30-minute profiles of Cherokee Nation citizens, highlights events and figures from

Figure 12.1 Cartoons explaining Cherokee culture is just one of many art forms practiced by artist Roy Boney Jr. *Source:* Youtube.

history, and passes on the Cherokee language. The main goal of the series is to correct misperceptions about Cherokees through documentary-style stories, language and history segments, news shorts, and profiles of interesting people (Figure 12.1). The series is broadcast widely across Oklahoma and carried on the organization's website and YouTube channel. Nationally it airs on FNX (First Nations Experience), the only broadcast television network in the United States devoted exclusively to Native American and World Indigenous content.

Outside the United States, the world economy continues to integrate with global brands using **glocal** strategies, that is, customizing communications (among other things) to local consumer tastes (Holt et al., 2004). However, they don't ignore their global characteristics which have grown in appeal along with the growth of cross-border tourism, popular culture, and rapid expansion of the Internet. Global consumers may not share the same preferences and values, but they do respect powerful brands, seeing them as desirable global symbols of quality and innovation (Holt et al., 2004).

The image economy is also globalizing, making the role of pictures increasingly important in corporate communication. There are approximately 150 international marketing awards and global advertising awards cataloged by Boost Awards, an awards entry consultancy (International Awards List n.d.). One of them, the Cannes Lions International Festival of Creativity, in 2018 awarded its Grand Prix for Creative Data to the Irish agency Rothco for "JFK Unsilenced" (Figure 12.2). Its client, the news company *The Times*/News UK and Ireland, as part of its "Find Your Voice" campaign, had decided to let US President John F. Kennedy deliver to the world the final speech he never gave at the Dallas Trade Mart – 55 years after his assassination on November 22, 1963 – and on the 100th anniversary of his birth.

The agency reviewed 831 of JFK's speeches to make a database of more than 100 000 phonetic sounds that required extensive editing due to a wide range of audio quality. Rothco told the story of this engineering feat in a two-minute video with images of computer screens showing digitized data interspersed with video roll of JFK during his presidency. Through innovative artificial intelligence (AI) and virtual reality (VR) technology,

Figure 12.2 Artificial intelligence and virtual reality techniques allowed JFK to deliver his final speech to a large global audience 55 years after his death. *Source:* Youtube.

the final product, a 22-minute video hosted on *The Times*'s website, presented him finally delivering the speech, and generating more than one billion media impressions and coverage in 59 countries (Figure 12.2). Locally, the video aligned with the historically close relationship between JFK and the United Kingdom. Globally, JFK, as US president, is generally viewed as a great, if not the greatest, president. The two-minute video's inclusion of historical footage combined with images of cutting-edge digital processes also acknowledges its broad audience and its respect for a meaningful historical moment while embracing new technology.

Intercultural Communication and the News

The "JFK Unsilenced" video, while sponsored and carried by an international news outlet, was the award-winning product of an advertising agency. Photojournalists' coverage of contemporary global news also may merit awards. Among them are the Pulitzer Prize in Breaking News and Feature Photography, the World Press Photo Awards, Reuters Pictures of the Year, the International Photography Awards, and the Pictures of the Year International (POY) – the oldest photojournalism competition.

The POY archive contains great news photographs from around the world and dates back seven decades, totaling nearly 40,000 images in categories such as spot news, features, portraits, sports, science, and more. In 2019, two of the four winning photographers of the World Understanding Award were freelancers (POY, 2019). Antonio Faccilongo of Getty Images won the top award for his series "Habibi" (Arabic for "love") about the struggle of Palestinian prisoners' wives to conceive children. Finalists featured reportage on the genocide of the Ixil Community in Guatemala, mental asylums in Russia, and autism in Italy.

The Newseum was first located in Washington, DC, in an interactive museum devoted to increasing public understanding of the importance of a free press and other First Amendment rights. It continues to offer an online database of more than 800 newspapers' front pages (Newseum n.d.). Nearly 15% of them are from countries beyond the United States. A search conducted on November 26, 2019, found that two countries provided far more newspaper front covers than the rest of the foreign press: Brazil delivered the covers of 27 newspapers and India delivered 16. Of them, two of the newspapers, India's *Dainik Bhaskar* (Figure 12.3) and Brazil's *Folha de San Paulo* (Figure 12.4), feature covers that differ substantially in their use of visual imagery.

The density of text in *Dainik Bhaskar* may be explained by the cultural significance that Indians are the most avid readers in the world (McCarthy, 2016). The high number of visual images suggest the rich environment of news values on this front cover. The dominant emotive imagery in *Folha de San Paulo,* on the contrary, emphasizes a child. Understanding local cultural and political situations would contribute to a deeper analysis. Another way to use the Newseum newspaper archive is to select a common news story and observe how papers from various cultures cover it.

Figures 12.3 and 12.4 Two popular newspapers, one from India and the other from Brazil, convey vastly different cover designs reflecting their cultural, political, and economic difference. *Source:* DB Corp Ltd. and Folha de S. Paulo.

FOCUS: La Peña: Intercultural Understanding and Social Justice

La Peña Cultural Center, an internationally known nonprofit, opened its doors in the San Francisco Bay Area in 1975 to welcome Chilean political exiles. Thousands were fleeing the repressive military regime that had overthrown Chile's democratically elected government of Salvador Allende a few years earlier. The center soon became a "home" not only for Chilean exiles, but for exiles from other troubled Latin American countries, intercultural and international performers touring the United States, and members of marginalized ethnic groups in the Bay Area. Equally at home were sympathetic area residents who volunteered to help run its restaurant, manage its cultural events, tend its bar, and wash its restaurant's dishes, as well as help communicate the center's social justice story to its broad community and to the media.

In its 44-year history, La Peña has hosted multicultural musical, theatrical, and dance performances, poetry readings, film screenings, benefits for political prisoners, art and photo exhibits, public speeches, testimonial panels, and "roots" classes in indigenous music. The center also celebrated two symbols of Chile's former government; its kitchen served empanadas (humble meat and onion turnovers) and its stage frequently featured music from "La *Nueva Canción*" movement (folkloric instruments combined with social justice lyrics). Prominent personalities have shared its stage, including Cesar Chavez, cofounder of the United Farm Workers labor union, folksinger, and social activist Pete Seeger, and Alice Walker, African American novelist and author of *The Color Purple*.

La Peña brought the idea of "other cultures and other languages" to the national level in the United States through its arts advocacy work: it was a founding member of the National Network of Cultural Centers of Color. Still operating in 2019, the center researches and plans how to respond to changing needs and expectations of its publics. Its leadership evaluates its progress, social

Source: La Peña.

(Continued)

impact, and goals through strategic planning sessions, focus group research, audience polling, and conversations with volunteers and partners. It regularly revisits its mission at annual board and staff retreats. Results from its research and conversations guide content on the La Peña website and on its Instagram and Facebook pages.

Intercultural Communication in Nonprofit Organizations

Cultural museums and cultural centers that deal with intercultural communities typically are guided by mission statements that establish their visual identities and communications. African- and African American-centric organizations communicate Black and organizational identities on site and on their digital platforms. One way to understand this communication is through the lens of **cultural projection**, a concept developed by Richard Merelman, a cultural political scientist at the University of Wisconsin. He described cultural projection as "the conscious effort of a politically, economically and socially subordinated group to place new, more positive images of itself before dominates, for the purposes of increasing its own cultural capital" (1995, p. 3).

Looking closely at 46 websites of museums in the United States, researchers Johnson and Pettiway (2017) described their images, sound, and visual dynamism. The museums featured elements to build "cultural capital:" positive photographs of Africans, African Americans, and Black culture: professionals, historic persons, contemporary leaders, soldiers, and notable creatives (Figure 12.5). They also used selective logo emblems (such as

Figure 12.5 "Watching Oprah," a special exhibition at the National Museum of African American History and Culture uses the story of Oprah Winfrey and her successful TV talk show as a lens through which to explore contemporary American history and culture. *Source:* The Orange Country Register.

Figure 12.6 This sweeping vignette is part of the online virtual 3D experience offered by the Museum of Romani Culture in Brno, Czech Republic. *Source:* Museum of Roma Culture.

architectural elements and trees) and warm color palettes that were culturally relevant and positive, contradicting any historically negative portrayals.

The Museum of Romani Culture in Brno, Czech Republic, is the world's only museum dedicated to communicating the history and culture of the Roma, from their origins in ancient India and their migration through Europe to present-day life in Czechia. Its goal is to break the society-wide aversion to the Roma – sometimes referred to as "gypsies" due to a mythical notion that their origins were in Egypt. The museum promotes Romani culture through its physical space in a former Roma ghetto and an immersive digital presence online via vivid still and moving imagery on its website and social media. On display are selections from approximately 25,000 items documenting the Romani culture and history. Visitors can see and experience interior furnishings, clothing and jewelry, fine arts and crafts, written materials, posters, audio, photo and video documentation, as well as faithful replicas and audiovisual elements. Life-size dioramas are viewable online in virtual 3D (Figure 12.6).

CULTURAL IMAGERY AND ITS ETHICAL IMPLICATIONS

LO2 Assess ethical and practical issues in intercultural imagery in mass communication.

The complexities of different cultures are evident in mass media photography. Photographs that capture scenes from across the world can communicate forceful emotions and claim authenticity. However, they may be simplistic, they may omit context, they may represent the ideology of the photographer. Captions aid our interpretation, but we also draw on our own social and cultural frameworks. Developing intercultural visual literacy can help us interpret images, and create and use images, that communicate intended meanings and avoid cultural stereotypes.

Figure 12.7 Screenshot from Reuters' Openly: the first global digital platform with the mission to fairly report LGTB+ news. *Source:* Mariana Bazo/Reuters.

Fair LGBTQ+ Reporting

"Openly" is a global digital platform that consciously avoids cultural stereotypes. Launched in fall 2018 by the Reuters Foundation, its mission is to deliver "fair, accurate, and impartial LGBT+ news to a world that isn't" (Openly n.d.). "The role of the media is essential in shaping perceptions and attitudes towards LGBT+ people," said Antonio Zappulla, Reuters Foundation CEO (Qweerist 2018, para 4). A visit to the website finds English language content supported by still and video photojournalism, and regional news coverage from Africa, Asia Pacific, Europe, Latin American, the Middle East, and North America. One story, reporting on the attempt to legalize gay marriage in Peru, featured citizens lying prone on a public street holding signs in support of pro-gay unions with statements such as, "my life has value" and "hate crimes never again" (Figure 12.7). The platform launched with an outdoor campaign in London and New York City, supported by social media.

FOCUS: First Impartial LGBTQ+ Global News Service Confronts Stereotypes

"Openly" is a Thomson Reuters Foundation service that launched in fall 2018 to bring impartial LGBTQ+ news to the world.

Its launch campaign used bold and captivating imagery shot by London-based photographer Leonora Saunders to represent the diversity, dynamism, and openness of the LGBTQ+ community. Displayed in Times Square, New York, and on 300 screens across London, the Openly campaign featured real derogatory words previously used in headlines and news stories by media around the world in reporting on LGBTQ+ people. The campaign was based on the idea of denouncing the misrepresentation against LGBTQ+ people and expressing the urgent need for fair and impartial reporting. The second phase of the campaign featured portraits of LGBTQ+ people who are openly being themselves, empowered, and standing up to prejudice.

The campaign received pro bono support from Omnicom agencies Fleishman Hillard and TBWA\London in developing the Openly brand identity and launch campaign. Openly's social media campaign was built upon the outdoor messaging, with participants of the Openly photoshoot sharing offensive language used against them by the general public and countering such language with words they feel truly represent them.

Businessweek ✓
@BW

Follow ⌄

In 2013, Barilla's chairman publicly rebuked gay families and set off an international boycott of its pasta products. His CEO worked to reprogram the company into an inclusive, accepting workplace

Barilla Pasta's Turnaround From Homophobia to National Pride
After chairman Guido Barilla rebuked gay families on national radio, his CEO spent five years cleaning up the company's reputation.
bloomberg.com

3:43 PM - 7 May 2019

Source: https://www.bloomberg.com/news/features/2019-05-07/barilla-pasta-s-turnaround-from-homophobia-to-national-pride?utm_source=pocket-newtab. Reuters.

One major supporter, the prominent Italian pasta company, Barilla, practiced the change that Openly hopes to generate. Barilla's support of the LGBTQ+ start-up is part of the company's five-year reputation recovery strategy after its chairman disparaged homosexuals in a radio interview. When complaints poured in, he stated gay customers should just buy another brand of pasta. Amid calls for a global boycott, Barilla's CEO appointed a chief diversity and inclusion officer who led a company transformation. Since 2014, it has earned the highest possible score on the Human Rights Campaign's corporate equality index.

Honored and Misused Cultural Symbols

Localized messaging can be successful if done right, or it can fail miserably due to cultural missteps. Looking at 10 multinational companies' advertising campaigns in China, Ha and Zang (2010) provided examples of both types to illustrate the not so fine line between approval and outrage. The winners and the losers?

First, the winners: over the years, Coca-Cola has celebrated Chinese New Year with specially designed Chinese cans and commercials with the popular Chinese mascot Afu (meaning fortune in Chinese). It also respected the holiday's customs with the use of red color, lanterns, images of fireworks, banging drums, and the suggestion of family gatherings. Historically, multinational advertising in China has respected cultural differences, for example, Marlboro changed its hero image from a rugged American cowboy to a localized Chinese masculine hero. Crest portrayed smiles of diverse Chinese people in its ads – those hailing from different regions with differing ethnic lifestyles – while also communicating the Chinese values of charity and goodwill.

A loser (one that offended): Nike's "Chamber of Fear" ad, which was forced off the air because many accused the ad of insulting Chinese culture. In the ad, NBA star LeBron James fights his way up a five-story building to victory. It attempts to communicate courage and winning (as do other Nike ads in the United States) by associating the Chinese symbols of Kung Fu, traditional female dancers, and dragons with the Nike brand spirit (Figure 12.8). However, these are sacred symbols and their use was perceived as disrespectful, causing the ad to be banned by the Chinese government as an insult to the country's dignity.

Figure 12.8 A Nike ad featuring LeBron James fighting respected Chinese symbols was banned from the country. *Source:* http://kungfugripzine.blogspot.com/2013/07/retrospective-nikes-chamber-of-fear-ads.html.

More losers: Toyota offended Chinese viewers by combining car ads with sensitive historic events; Coca-Cola offended viewers with uneasy references to Chinese politics; Nippon Paint misused Chinese history and cultural symbols in a "Dragon" ad for its products. To explain the negative receptions, one must know that Chinese culture is collectivist, appreciating an indirect approach, and has a long-term orientation with deeply ingrained beliefs and ideals. Thus, localization by international advertisers can be successful in appropriate settings with appropriate use of Chinese traditional symbols and customs. Doing otherwise by disrespecting religious beliefs, associating a brand with sensitive historic events, and misusing cultural symbols all can lead to offending and public outrage (Ha and Zang, 2010).

Ads Lost in Translation

No ad is local anymore with the Internet, so clashing cultures can intrude on a global brand. *Ad Age* provides reports on ads made for consumers overseas that offended Americans (Hall, 2008). For example, American brand Snickers was pulled off the air in the United Kingdom after US pressure groups spoke up. "The Snickers spot shows Mr. T – the star of 1980s TV show 'The A-Team' – disparaging a speed walker for being 'a disgrace to the man-race.' He forces the guy to 'run like a real man' by firing Snickers bars at him," writes Hall (para 5). While UK LGBTQ+ rights groups didn't complain, it did attract the attention of the US Human Rights Campaign that identified it as antigay and lobbied Snickers' owner Mars to kill it. The cultural difference was underscored by a spokesman for Stonewall, the UK LBGTQ+ rights group, who stated the ad seemed harmless and without any implication that the speed walker was gay. It's clear that when ads break out of their national borders, they can carry new and sometimes disturbing meanings to viewers in other countries.

DECONSTRUCTING INTERCULTURAL IMAGERY

LO3 Identify and critique the use of **visual rhetoric** in intercultural imagery in mass communication.

In today's intercultural communication, the medium is part of the message. It crosses borders and languages as part of the global communication flow. The visual may not always dominate the verbal, but it captures attention, facilitates understanding, clarifies facts with visual evidence, and illustrates complicated processes often through infographics. Yet visual overload can confuse. And how do we determine when a national versus a local message is best? Take the use of colors: are they culture-bound? Consider the orange color branding of easyJet and the sacred association of the color orange in Hinduism. Symbols are not universally shared, and humor doesn't always successfully cross borders.

Culture-Specific Public Relations

Catalan! Arts is part of the Ministry of Culture for the Government of Catalonia, Spain. Its mission is to create and use a unified brand to promote Catalan cultural and creative businesses to organizations outside the region. To deliver this brand identity to European and broader audiences, the organization uses digital and traditional public relations strategies. On its website are two downloadable e-magazines that are visually powerful. Sometimes 90+ pages, the publications are produced multiple times a year. One focuses on film and the other on music, with both featuring large, vibrant photographs and links to YouTube and Spotify (Figure 12.9).

Figure 12.9 Part of Catalan! Arts unified brand to promote Catalan cultural and creative businesses. *Source:* http://www.catalanarts.cat/web/sites/default/files/CatalanMusic_Jazzahead_2019.pdf.

The organization's social platforms are equally visually rich with images of music album covers, event flyers, and photos of performers and performing arts venues. In their study of Catalan! Arts, Johnson and Cester (2015) found its digital and mobile communications use dramatic visuals accompanied by effective sound techniques. They noted that "vibrant colors, large photos wherever possible, and bold mostly sans serif typefaces characterize the visuals" (p. 812). Judging the organization's branding successful, they note it "fits with Catalonia's branding, because the brand emphasizes cultural values, such as expressiveness and innovativeness, for which the autonomous region and its residents are known" (p. 813).

FOCUS: Using Photography to Build Intercultural Literacy

Source: Author.

The more you know about a culture, the better you can communicate within it. Capturing and analyzing images will help you build literacy in intercultural communication. It will allow you to define "cultural difference" and recognize media stereotypes. Photography has a powerful emotional force and can present itself as authentic when it's not quite so. In our lives overpopulated with imagery, we're forced to make shortcut judgments on what we see. Working to build your visual literacy helps you to critically behold images, analyze them, and separate the

(Continued)

myths from the truths. Alvaray (2014) offers this exercise in using photography for intercultural awareness and understanding.

If you're traveling or studying abroad, this is an ideal exercise. However, it can be done right at home. Identify a geographic area – a neighborhood or nearby town – where people with a unique cultural heritage live and go about their daily lives. Identify the cultural group and do some preliminary research on their history and social structures. This will require online library searches for published research. Identify the cultural stereotypes assigned to this group and how they may, or may not, be performed in daily living.

Traditions provide great opportunities to capture culture in photographs. For example, each year, crèche makers gather in the Market Square in Kraków, Poland, on the first Thursday of December to parade and exhibit their work.

Next, take a field trip to the chosen site, bring a camera or cell phone with camera, and a notebook. Take pictures of things and people you find unique or different from your own reality. Perhaps physical spaces, architectural elements, signage, murals, window displays, street scenes, and foods. Also, of course, people in action: events, rituals, casual activities, random acts, and so forth. Look beyond what you immediately recognize as traditionally beautiful or any simplistic visual signs. See differently. A close-up may be more meaningful than a wide shot. If there's an event, what's happening on the edges may be more interesting that the focal point. Remember to be courteous and respectful when photographing people. If taking close-ups, first ask for permission.

After two or three hours, return to your classroom or home and download the images. Select 20 to 30 that are most significant. Then, share your images with your classmates and instructor to collectively look for themes and brainstorm a narrative. Listening to other students' comment on your images helps you locate what's not so obvious to you. Possible themes include the following: identity through portraiture, public versus private spaces, appreciation of history and culture, family experiences, community cohesion, and perhaps just the vibrancy of color, graffiti, or nature in everyday life.

Finally, put together your visual essay and use one of the rhetorical theories to write an analytical essay about this cultural experience.

The Transcultural Greenspeak of Greenpeace

The visual images in the global environmentalist campaigns of Greenpeace offer guidelines for environmental communications. Greenpeace's outputs show their cultural adeptness at localizing, or regionalizing, globally orchestrated campaigns.

Catellani (2018) analyzed and found six types of visuals including both moving and still images. This typology may assist other international environmentalist associations, such as the World Wildlife Fund (WWF) and Friends of the Earth as well as help critics in identifying and categorizing the visual rhetoric:

Figure 12.10 Greenpeace uses "pictograms" to dramatize the destruction of forests. Greenpeace images libraryGreenpeace images library

1. **Pictograms**. Small, simplified images accompanying verbal text (Figure 12.10).

2. **Anonymous and specific illustrations; proof images**. A large category, it includes fixed and moving images that offer the visual equivalent of accompanying verbal text. The subtype, "proof images," are images supporting the logic of a claim, showing visual proof of a phenomenon (e.g. photo with caption or videos illustrating a claim).

3. **Referential narrative images**. Typically, videos that present a situation, telling a story.

4. **"Ethical" images (in the sense of Aristotelian "ethos")**. Images that expose an archetypal character, for example, a hero in action.

5. **Knowledge images**. A diverse category including maps, diagrams, abstract elements like arrows, and so on, making a connection to reality.

6. **Spectacular images**. Visual parodies.

For example, the Greenpeace campaign on behalf of tigers demands companies stop buying palm oil from producers who are destroying forests. It uses simple "pictograms" to reference the destruction of forests and a guilty corporation (Figure 12.10). In another campaign to save bees, an example of the "spectacular image" is the self-parody video in which bees take action to defend their survival against pesticides and industrial agriculture.

PROFESSIONAL PROFILE:
Cynthia M. Frisby

Cynthia M. Frisby, PhD, is Professor of Strategic Communication at the University of Oklahoma.

The saying, "a picture is worth a thousand words," refers to the idea that complex ideas such as challenging stereotypes can be conveyed with an image, and that images may effectively convey meaning and the essence of ideas more than words will do.

This concept led me to study nonverbal communication, the impact of visuals on cognitive processing, and media effects of exposure to images in media, and specifically depictions of minorities. Diversity and difference are concepts that we cannot avoid as

Source: Curators of the University of Missouri.

they are present in every part of our lives. This includes our religion, hometown, gender, sexual orientation, political affiliation, music preferences and, yes, the ethnic/racial group to which we belong.

What people think is "representative" imagery in media is not, in fact, representative of the groups they purport to include. This is my passion and the lack of realistic portrayals needs to change. For example, the interracial relationships audiences see in ads, in movies, and on primetime TV are often skewed and inaccurate. Many people think that the most common interracial relationships are those of Black men and White women. However, research shows that more than 45% of Asian American women in the United States are married to White men (Frisby, 2015) whereas a mere 24% of all Black men and slightly more than 11% of all Black women are actually married to others from different racial background (Livingston and Brown, 2017). Yet these realities are not reflected in our media today.

As another example, people of color account for nearly 40% of the US population, but women of color appear in less than 4% of major Hollywood movies (Medvedeva et al., 2017). The gap in diversity in visual images of minorities is also found in mainstream media. Our study "Always A Bridesmaid, Never a Bride: Portrayals of Women of Color in Bridal Magazines" (Frisby and Engstrom, 2006) revealed that Caucasian brides were found to dominate the covers of bridal magazines, with none of the 50 issues studied featuring a woman of color on the cover. The consequence of the absence of this visual communication is an "annihilation" of certain visual images, relegating women of color to second-class citizenship.

The theory of "symbolic annihilation" describes, predicts, and helps us understand the effects of underrepresented visuals of minorities. For example, when consumers never see women of color on bridal magazines, they may conclude that Black women just do not participate in weddings or get married, which again is not an accurate conclusion. My research (Frisby, 2004) has also found similar effects of symbolic annihilation in health messages about breast cancer and other life-threatening illnesses. The absence of people of color in advertisements and public relations campaigns for breast cancer screening and sunscreen leads many at-risk people to believe that those issues simply do not affect them.

As you can tell, there is still much more work to be done in terms of using visual communication to provide representative imagery. Media images must extend beyond increasing the number of visuals that feature minorities; rather, images should challenge inaccurate stereotypes.

CHAPTER SUMMARY

Your sensitivity should now be heightened after this chapter's journey across the globe bringing you examples of both successful and damaging intercultural visual communication. Hall and Hofstede provided significant lessons in how to identify and evaluate cultural differences. You were challenged to take your own intercultural journey, either abroad or nearby, to document the everyday lives of a cohesive culture and then analyze the narrative found in your photos. You may have even heard the guitar chords of the New Chilean Song as you read about cultural activism and how culture centers can welcome and integrate peoples of different cultures, with visual imagery a strong component. And you inspected an award-winning advertising campaign that bridged cultures. Now, the exercises below should challenge you to use this new knowledge to further expand your visual cultural competencies.

KEY TERMS

Culture   Shared patterns of beliefs, behaviors, and norms that define group identity, both large and small.

Glocal   Often used in management and marketing, the term generally refers to practices and messages that have global reach but are customized for local cultures and preferences.

Cultural projection   Purposeful efforts of culturally subordinated groups to place new, more positive images in order to increase their own cultural capital.

Visual rhetoric   Use of images, typography, and other visuals in efforts to persuade others.

PRACTICE ACTIVITIES

1. Visit Hofstede's country cultural dimensions site at https://www.hofstede-insights. com/country-comparison/. Compare several countries that have differing dimensions.

Then, seek out the countries' official tourism websites and analyze how each visually expresses these qualities.

2. You and a group of your classmates are on a creative team with the Ad Council (https://www.adcouncil.org/), tasked by your client, Voice of America, with strategizing a campaign to communicate the US values of freedom of speech and assembly to a developing nation. Choose the country, research its cultural dimensions, and outline a visual strategy guided by one of the visual theories.

3. Explore the national symbols of selected countries and conduct a semiotic analysis to evaluate how they represent distinctive themes and ideologies.

4. Compare the cultural features of corporate websites in two countries (for example, KFC China and KFC US). Use one of the visual analysis methods to explore more deeply.

REFERENCES

Alvaray, L. (2014). Snap Shots: Using Photography for Intercultural Awareness and Understanding. *Communication Teacher* 28 (2): 109–116.

Brumberger, E. (2014). Toward a framework for intercultural visual communication: a critical review and call for research. *Connexions, International Professional Communication Journal* 2 (1): 91–116.

Catellani, A. (2018). Environmental multi-modal communication: semiotic observations on recent campaigns. In: Visual Public Relations: Strategic Communication Beyond Text (eds. S. Collister and Roberts-Bowman), 161–175. New York: Routledge.

Couldry, N. (2003). Media Rituals: A Critical Approach. Oxford: Berg.

Eringa, K., Caudron, L.N., Rieck, K. et al. (2015). How relevant are Hofstede's dimensions for inter-cultural studies? A replication of Hofstede's research among current international business students. *Research in Hospitality Management* 5 (2): 187–198. https://doi.org/10.1080/22243534.2015.11828344.

Frisby, C.M. (2004). The changing faces of advertising: minority images and the media. In: Journalism Across Cultures (eds. F. Cropp, C.M. Frisby and D. Mills), 187–201. Ames, IA: Iowa State Press.

Frisby, C.M. (2015). Dating inside the color line: Racial preferences of college students on online dating sites. In: How You See Me, How You Don't, 95–124. Mustang, OK: Tate Publishing & Enterprises, LLC.

Frisby, C.M. and Engstrom, E. (2006). Always a bridesmaid and never a bride: portrayals of women of color as brides in bridal magazines. *Media Report to Women* 34 (4): 10.

Gorman, C. K. (2011). How culture controls communication. *Forbes*, Nov. 28. https://www.forbes.com/sites/carolkinseygoman/2011/11/28/how-culture-controls-communication/#763e6ee2263b (accessed October 17, 2020).

Green, G.J. and Brock, T.C. (2000). The role of transportation in the persuasiveness of public narratives. *Journal of Personality and Social Psychology* 79 (5): 701–721.

Green, G.J., Kass, S., Carrey, J. et al. (2008). Transportation across media: repeated exposure to print and film. *Media Psychology* 11 (4): 512–539.

Ha, L. and Zang, L. (2010). Multinational advertising campaigns as intercultural communications: successes and blunders in mainland China. International Communication Association
Annual Conference. Singapore. June 24–26. https://scholarworks.bgsu.edu/smc_pub/29

Hall, E. (2008). In YouTube world, humor can get lost in translation. *Ad Age*. https://adage.
com/article/news/youtube-world-humor-lost-translation/130260 (accessed October
17, 2020).

Hofstede, G. (n.d.). The dimensions explained. https://geerthofstede.com/culture-
geert-hofstede-gert-jan-hofstede/6d-model-of-national-culture (accessed October
19, 2020).

Hofstede, G. (2011). Dimensionalizing Cultures: The Hofstede model in context. *Online
Readings in Psychology and Culture* 2 (1): 8. https://doi.org/10.9707/2307-0919.1014.

Holt, D., Quelch, J., and Taylor, E. (2004). How global brands compete. *Harvard Business
Review*. https://hbr.org/2004/09/how-global-brands-compete (accessed October
17, 2020).

International Awards List. (n.d.). World's largest FREE list of Business Awards. https://
awards-list.com (accessed October 17, 2020).

Johnson, M.A. and Cester, X. (2015). Communicating Catalan culture in a global society.
Public Relations Review 41 (5): 809–815.

Johnson, M.A. and Pettiway, K.M. (2017). Visual expressions of black identity: African
American and African museum websites. *Journal of Communication* 67: 350–377.

Livingston, G. and Brown, A. (2017). Trends and Patterns in Intermarriage. https://www.
pewsocialtrends.org/2017/05/18/1-trends-and-patterns-in-intermarriage/ (accessed
January 9, 2021).

McCarthy, N. (2016). Which Countries Read the Most? https://www.statista.com/
chart/6125/which-countries-read-the-most/ (accessed October 17, 2020).

Medvedeva, Y., Frisby, C.M., and Moore, J. (2017). Celebrity capital of actresses of color: a
mixed methods study. *Advances in Journalism and Communication* 5 (3): 183–203.

Merelman, R. (1995). Representing Black Culture: Race and Cultural Politics in the United
States. New York: Routledge.

Newseum. (n.d.) Today's Front Pages. https://www.newseum.org/todaysfrontpages
(accessed October 17, 2020).

Openly. (n.d.) Welcome to Openly. https://www.openlynews.com/about-us (accessed
October 17, 2020).

Pannett, R. (2018). Anger over tourists swarming vacation hot spots sparks global backlash. Dow Jones International News, May 22, 2018. https://www.wsj.com/articles/
anger-over-tourists-swarming-vacation-hot-spots-sparks-global-backlash-1527000130
(accessed May 18, 2019).

Pinchefsky, C. (2012). The impact (economic and otherwise) of Lord of the
Rings/The Hobbit on New Zealand. *Forbes*. https://www.forbes.com/sites/
carolpinchefsky/2012/12/14/the-impact-economic-and-otherwise-of-lord-of-the-
ringsthe-hobbit-on-new-zealand/#3fc1995d31b6 (accessed October 17, 2020).

POY. (2019). World Understanding Award. Pictures of the Year International. https://poy.
org/76/37 (accessed October 17, 2020).

Qweerist. (2018). Thomson Reuters Foundation's Antonio Zappulla named top LGBTQ+ public sector executive in OUTstanding list. https://www.qweerist.com/news/thomson-reuters-antonio-zappulla-top-lgbtq-executive (accessed October 17, 2020).

Yang, F. and Vanden Bergh, B. (2017). Movies' influence on country concept. In: Shaping International Public Opinion: A Model for Nation Branding and Public Diplomacy (eds. J. Fullerton and A. Kendrick), 113–131. New York: Peter Lang.

Index

Visual Communication: Insights and Strategies, First Edition. Janis Teruggi Page and Margaret Duffy.
© 2022 John Wiley & Sons, Inc. Published 2022 by John Wiley & Sons, Inc.

Printed and bound by CPI Group (UK) Ltd, Croydon, CR0 4YY

16/04/2025

14658468-0003